Praise for Richard M. Rosenfield's *African American Core Values: A Guide for Everyone*

"In what has obviously been a labor of love, Richard Rosenfield compiles a useful compendium of folk wisdom which, while coming out of the African American community, is of profound relevance to all Americans. Reaching across the generations and spanning the range from academic to popular discourses, Rosenfield reproduces here one nugget of insight after the other. All of our young people need to read and reflect upon this invaluable book."
—**GLENN C. LOURY**, Merton P. Stoltz Professor of the Social Sciences in the Department of Economics at Brown University, Distinguished Fellow of the American Economic Association

"I was struck by the academic possibilities of this compilation. Educators, counselors and scholars would find it very useful. Having these ideas collected in one place and accessible would be very convenient for those who are speaking to, or working with, young people."
—**JOHNNETTA B. COLE**, Director of the Smithsonian National Museum of African Art, President Emerita of Spelman and Bennett Colleges

"It was a great idea to edit such a book, and a major contribution."
—**JAMES P. COMER**, Founder and Chairman of the School Development Program at the Yale University Child Study Center

"*African American Core Values: A Guide for Everyone* serves as a poignant collection of hard-fought, common-sense values that every American—no matter their color—can benefit from. The values of self-reliance, hard work, education, and the willingness to endure to overcome obstacles were once common in the black community. It is books such as this one that can help bring these values back."
—**REVEREND JESSE LEE PETERSON**, Founder and President of Brotherhood Organization of a New Destiny

"A great piece of work. Every student, of every color, should read this. It should be part of the social studies curriculum."
—**ANDREW D. WASHTON**, author of *What Happens Next? Stories to Finish for Intermediate Writers,* Teachers College Press, Columbia University

Shared Values

Shared Values

African Americans and Republicans

Richard M. Rosenfield

Core Values Publishing
New York

Shared Values

African Americans and Republicans

Copyright © 2016 Richard M. Rosenfield

All rights reserved. No part of this book may be reproduced, stored in a retrieval system, or transmitted, in any form or by any means, electronic, mechanical, photocopying, rlecording, or otherwise, without the prior written permission of the publisher.

For information: Contact Core Values Publishing at sharedvalues2016@gmail.com. Manufactured in the United States of America.

ISBN 13: 9781535308014
ISBN 10: 153530801X
Library of Congress Control Number: 2016912110
CreateSpace Independent Publishing Platform
North Charleston, South Carolina

Rosa Parks, from *Dear Mrs. Parks*:

I am proud to be an American. America is a wonderful country.

Table of Contents

Acknowledgments ································ xi
On Senator Obama's Cover Quotation ············ xiii
Preface ······································· xvii
Introduction ···································· xxv

Part I Background ······························· 1
Chapter 1 Oppression ······························ 3
Chapter 2 Progress and Opportunity ··············· 18
Chapter 3 Self-Reliance ·························· 38

Part II Core Values ····························· 51
Chapter 4 Marriage ······························· 53
Chapter 5 Education ······························ 78
Chapter 6 Work ·································· 100

Part III Obstacles to Progress ················ 125
Chapter 7 Crime ································· 127
Chapter 8 Conformity ···························· 156

Biographical Notes ····························· 165
Notes ·· 173

Acknowledgments

I thank Amazon for giving everyone the opportunity to publish. A big thanks to all the CreateSpace workers who helped me.

I appreciate the supportive words and helpful criticism that I received from Bernie, Chris, Paul, Andrea, Asher, Sharon, Felix, Andrew, Ellen, Mary, John, Sam, and Yael.

Beginning in the 1800s, African Americans encouraged others to speak about racial issues. Most recently, Attorney General Eric Holder said, "And yet, if we are to make progress in this area, we must feel comfortable enough with one another, and tolerant enough of each other, to have frank conversations about the racial matters that continue to divide us."[1] I thank all of those speakers for helping me feel welcome in the conversation.

On Senator Obama's Cover Quotation

The statements in this book suggest that African Americans and Republicans share conservative values. If this premise is correct, then African Americans have good reason to give some of their votes to Republican political candidates. By doing so, they would be voting for their own values and interests. But taken as a group, African Americans today give almost complete loyalty to the Democrat Party. In the past, from the time they began to vote until the era of Martin Luther King Jr., they often voted for Republicans.

Frederick Douglass
I am a Republican—a Black Republican dyed in the wool—and I never intend to belong to any other party than the party of freedom and progress.[2]

Taylor Branch, Martin Luther King Jr. biographer:
Dr. King lived at a time, believe it or not, when his Dad and all the black folk that he knew were Republicans.[3]

Aside from the sharing of values, there's another reason for African Americans to return to voting for Republicans: doing so would increase their influence over both political parties.

US senator Barack Obama
> Moreover, I am not somebody who subscribes to the view that because somebody is a member of a minority group they somehow have to subscribe to a particular ideology or a particular political party. I think it is wonderful that Asian Americans, Latinos, African Americans, and others are represented in all parties and across the political spectrum. When such representation exists, then those groups are less likely to be taken for granted by any political party.[4]

Carter G. Woodson, from *The Mis-Education of the Negro*:
> It is unfortunate, too, that such a large number of Negroes do not know any better than to stake their whole fortune on politics. History does not show that any race, especially a minority group, has ever solved an important problem by relying altogether on one thing, certainly not by parking its political strength on one side of the fence because of empty promises.[5]

Reverend Ralph David Abernathy
> It seemed increasingly obvious to me that because our voting patterns were so predictable, blacks were being neglected by both parties.[6]

Herman Cain
> Black people are being played. They have been taken for granted by Democrats for decades.[7]

Stephen A. Smith
> Black folks in America are telling one party, "We don't give a damn about you." They're telling the other party, "You've got our vote." Therefore, you have labeled yourself "disenfranchised" because one party knows they've got you under their thumb, the other party knows they'll never get you and nobody comes to address your interest.

I hate the fact that anybody is allowed to believe that they have a bloc of people in the palm of their hands.[8]

Tavis Smiley
I'm disappointed because the Democratic party continues to take its Black voting base for granted.[9]

Milton Coleman
If blacks really are self-interest voters whose politics are defined primarily by race, the most potent way to show it is through genuine two-party swing voting. That would require some serious political independence—like voting Republican in a few elections. In droves. Soon.[10]

Senior Pastor Kevin R. Johnson
[W]hy are we loyal to a Democratic Party that often ignores us and takes our votes for granted?[11]

John Henrik Clarke
Many influential Harlem residents criticized the shift to the Democratic Party.[12]

Robert L. Woodson Sr.
It is in the black community's interest to have more political competition for its votes.[13]

Ben Carson
If politicians have to compete for support, they will have to show results, which will be a big win for the black community.[14]

Stanley Crouch
As hard-nosed, astute black Americans have also been pointing out, less predictable political allegiances should make it more likely that both major political parties would compete

energetically for the black vote and, I might add, given the burgeoning number of black millionaires, eventually, financial support.[15]

Malcolm X
We will not encourage Negroes to become registered Democrats or Republicans. We feel that the Negro should be an independent, so that he can throw his weight either way.[16]

Jackie Robinson
But I have always felt that blacks must be represented in both parties.[17]

Arthur Ashe
[I]s it inscribed in stone somewhere that every black must vote Democratic?[18]

Louisiana State Senator Elbert Lee Guillory recently switched political parties. He explains the change in his video, "Why I Am a Republican."[19]

These statements suggest that if more African Americans voted for Republicans, everyone would win. African Americans would gain greater political influence. Republicans would have more candidates elected. And even the Democrats would gain, because they don't want African Americans to be taken for granted or ignored by the parties.

Preface

During my thirty-year career as a school psychologist, I always faced students' learning and behavior problems that perplexed me. Psychology books and journals provided some help, but with a caseload full of troubled kids, I constantly searched for answers. One day, browsing in a bookstore, I saw a collection of writings by W. E. B. Du Bois. All I knew about him was that he had been an eminent African American leader. I usually worked in schools with lots of African American students, so I was curious.

Within the first few pages, I found statements that seemed to have the potential to help my students avoid problems in school and in life. I went on to read other books by Du Bois, then books and articles by other black writers. I felt that the information I found could be useful to people of all groups. I compiled those statements in my *African American Core Values: A Guide for Everyone.*

While working on that book, I realized that the values in black literature have a political aspect. They are conservative.

Roger Wilkins
>Those of us who have been black people all our lives, know that blacks are more conservative than the media paint us.[20]

Farai Chideya
Conservatives are realizing what liberals have sometimes not: that blacks hold many "conservative" values.[21]

President Barack Obama
In private—around kitchen tables, in barbershops, and after church—black folks can often be heard bemoaning the eroding work ethic, inadequate parenting, and declining sexual mores with a fervor that would make the Heritage Foundation proud.

In that sense, black attitudes regarding the sources of chronic poverty are far more conservative than black politics would care to admit.[22]

Despite their conservatism, black Americans give most of their votes to liberals in the Democrat Party.

Farai Chideya
African Americans are a bit of a paradox: arguably socially conservative on the issues, but loyal to the Democratic Party.[23]

Frank Newport at Gallup, from his article "Blacks as Conservative as Republicans on Some Moral Issues":
In this particular aggregate of data, 65% of blacks identify themselves as Democrats (and another 16% say they lean toward the Democratic Party). Only 5% identify as Republicans. Yet, as seen in the accompanying table, there are major gulfs between the attitudes of black Democrats and the attitudes of nonblack Democrats on a number of moral issues, and in most instances, blacks come much closer to the positions of Republicans than to those of Democrats.

Despite the liberal orientation of the Democratic Party toward moral issues, blacks, perhaps because of their high degree of religiosity, are pulled in the other, more conservative direction that is typical of Republicans.[24]

Compared to Republicans and African Americans, both of whom tend to be religious,[25] it's not unusual for Democrats to be hostile to religion and to people of faith.

President Obama
At worst, there are some liberals who dismiss religion in the public square as inherently irrational or intolerant, insisting on a caricature of religious Americans that paints them as fanatical, or thinking that the very word "Christian" describes one's political opponents, not people of faith.[26]

Wayne Allyn Root, on the 2012 Democrat National Convention:
Their radical platform committee had removed all reference to God in the Democratic platform. Yes, I said ALL references to God. As in "all." As in "God is not welcome in the Democratic Party."[27]

African Americans have suggested that they have moved away from their values and from ways of living that would be consistent with those beliefs.

W. E. B. Du Bois
We have lost our ideals. We have come to a generation which seeks advance without ideals—discovery without stars. It cannot be done.[28]

Willie W. Herenton
But we've lost a lot in terms of core values.[29]

Shared Values

Marva Nettles Collins
[F]or almost every ill in our society, we can realistically point back to a loss of values...[30]

US representative John Lewis
Having values and holding on to our beliefs is what got us through, and it's what will get you through.[31]

Kevin Jackson
Our forefathers pictured an America where faith in God, family, love of country, education and work-ethic were the core of what represented the black community.[32]

Reverend Floyd H. Flake and **Reverend M. Elaine McCollins Flake**:
The time has come to discover our moral strength, to reclaim those attitudes and beliefs we seem to have lost along the way as our own again.[33]

This book espouses conservative values that Americans of all groups have strayed from, so that they might be reconsidered and reclaimed. It sees those values as a basis for a closer alliance between African Americans and Republicans.

Producing a book with statements from African Americans, Republicans, and Democrats raises issues of who's who. Considering that an NAACP chapter elected a white woman to be its president, apparently seeing her as black, how can I know who is black? If a person identifies himself as black, or if websites do, or if his Internet images show African American features, then for the purposes of this book, he's considered to be black. In cases of multiple authors and people in a conversation, when at least one is black, I place the statements in sections with African Americans.

How do I know who is a Republican or a Democrat? When someone talks like a Republican, I place his words in a Republican section, regardless of his political affiliation. Democrat-sounding statements are placed in Democrat sections. This keeps similar ideas together.

For the purposes of this book, "liberal," "progressive," "left wing," and "blue state" all refer to Democrats. "Conservative," "right wing," "libertarian," and "red state" are terms meaning Republican. I accept that an individual can be a liberal Republican or a conservative Democrat. But my understanding is that today most Democrats are liberals who lean left; most Republicans are conservatives who lean right.

President Obama speaks as a Democrat politician and as a conservative African American. His statements are placed in both Democrat and African American sections.

I feel that some classic statements in this book express truths that are valid for all time periods. Consequently, statements including "today" or "at this time" may have been written years or even decades ago. The Notes contain the statements' dates.

Many of the people who speak in this book have degrees such as Dr., MD, PhD, EdD, and JD. Listing them all would clutter the text and impede the reading process, so I left them out. There are a few exceptions, such as Dr. J and Dr. Dre.

I usually identify speakers by their highest position achieved. For instance, "President Barack Obama." But there are exceptions. When Mr. Obama spoke the words on the cover, he was a US senator, and he's identified as such. Simply put, to avoid the messiness of listing individuals with multiple titles and designations such as "former," I typically identify them by their highest title.

Some readers may be displeased to see the inclusion of statements by individuals they dislike, considering them to be too radical in some way. The statements were chosen because decades of reading black and political literature taught me that they are constructive. To me, they tell truths that many of us don't understand well or have forgotten. This is a book about ideas, not people.

Most of the speakers are African Americans, many of whom are probably Democrats who have conservative values. Nonblack Republicans, such as President Ronald Reagan, speak for conservatism.

Shared Values

Democrats, such as Secretary of State Hillary Clinton and Senator Bernie Sanders, speak for liberalism and socialism.

Did I select statements to make it look like African Americans are speaking in favor of values that are actually mine? They are my values now because people from Frederick Douglass to W. E. B. Du Bois to Thomas Sowell to ordinary African Americans convinced me of their merit. An early title for this book was *Black Literature Made Me a Republican.* That's what happened. In my opinion, anyone who attributes these ideas to me is playing that old trick of giving a white man credit for something black people accomplished. The ideas, which are often expressed eloquently, are theirs. They deserve the credit.

Statements were not chosen to represent anyone's body of writing. If someone often wrote against marriage, for instance, and then had an insight and wrote persuasively *for* marriage, I included the latter statement. My goal was to highlight the values that black and political literature taught me are wholesome, not to represent anyone's total viewpoint.

I have no authority to speak for any group. As a novice Republican, I do not represent them. As an ex-Democrat, I'm not their spokesperson. As a white person, I don't speak for black people. This book represents my reading and understanding of black and political literature.

Some readers may find that the information in this book contradicts their beliefs about race and politics. Many have been misinformed by the liberal bias of our schools, colleges, news media, search engines, social media news reports, movies, and television programs. Open-minded individuals can correct that misinformation by accessing black literature and sources such as *Fox News, Drudge Report, Independent Journal Review, National Review, Breitbart, The Blaze, World News Daily, Commentary Magazine,* and the opinion pages in the *Wall Street Journal* and the *New York Post.*

Readers might find statements reflecting their own values there. Perhaps some would have an insight similar to that of Susana Martinez. Planning to run for district attorney in New Mexico as a

Democrat, she and her husband accepted a lunch invitation from two Republicans. They wanted her to switch parties. When they described their positions on a number of issues, she realized that she agreed with them.

Susana Martinez
> And when we left that lunch, we got in the car and I looked over at Chuck and said, "I'll be damned, we're Republicans."[34]

Martinez is now the Republican governor of New Mexico.

Introduction

This book affirms conservative values that are held by African Americans and Republicans. It focuses on the core values of marriage, education, and work, taking these core values as a basis for a closer alliance between the two conservative groups.

Each of these three values can improve one's life; together, they provide a powerful guide to well-being and progress.

Juan Williams

The good news is that there is a formula for getting out of poverty today. The magical steps begin with finishing high school, but finishing college is much better. Step number two is taking a job and holding it. Step number three is marrying after finishing school and while you have a job. And the final step to give yourself the best chance to avoid poverty is to have children only after you are twenty-one and married. This formula applies to black people and white people alike.

The poverty rate for any black man or woman who follows that formula is 6.4 percent.[35]

Ron Haskins

Brookings Institution calculations of census data for 2009, a deep recession year, show that adults who graduated from at least high school, had a job, and were both at least age 21 and married before having children had about a 2 percent chance of living in poverty and a better than 70 percent chance of making the middle class—defined as $65,000 or more in household income.[36]

Arguably, the most important value is marriage. Compared to singles, people in married couples tend to be healthier, wealthier, and happier.[37] They typically bring greater resources to the task of raising children: more money, more time, two heads, four arms, and two hearts. Married couples enable their children to learn well in school, which fosters their success in the workplace. Those individuals, the second generation, having moved up the economic ladder, are in position to give their children, the third generation, even greater advantages.

Maya Angelou
The result is a widening gap in the African-American community between the dual-headed families and the single-headed families and their progeny. This is critical, because more often than not, people who come from homes where two parents are present will be supported by the family, will receive more education, will earn their degrees, will more than likely go on to become a part of the middle and upper-middle class. And more than likely, those who come from the single-parent homes will not make it as far.[38]

George Will
Family structure is a primary predictor of an individual's life chances, and family disintegration is the principal cause of the intergenerational transmission of poverty.[39]

People in all groups have used these common-sense, conservative values to improve their lives.

Shelby Steele
> The middle-class values by which we were raised—the work ethic, the importance of education, the value of property ownership, of respectability, of "getting ahead," of stable family life, of initiative, of self-reliance, et cetera—are, in themselves, raceless and even assimilationist.
>
> These values are almost rules for how to prosper in a democratic, free-enterprise society that admires and rewards individual effort.[40]

Part I, Background, provides context for this discussion of race and politics. In Chapter 1, Oppression, black and white speakers from the political left and right assert that Democrats were the slaveholders, the major segregators, and the Ku Klux Klan. These speakers recognize the crucial role that Republicans played in emancipation, reconstruction, and establishing civil rights.

In Chapter 2, Progress and Opportunity, African Americans say that our nation has decreased discrimination to the point that it is not the primary factor impeding their advancement. They say that they have made impressive progress and that their optimal path to further gains is making more effective use of opportunity.

In Chapter 3, Self-Reliance, African Americans speak of dependence derisively. They assert that they are the ones who can best move their race forward.

In Part II, Core Values, African Americans and Republicans speak more positively than Democrats about marriage. Both conservative groups favor giving students the opportunities offered by charter schools and voucher programs. They both want to foster business success to increase jobs and prosperity.

Part III, Obstacles to Advancement, begins with Chapter 7, Crime. African Americans and Republicans take a tough anti-crime stance to protect citizens. They both recognize that African Americans are disproportionately victimized by criminals, typically from within their own group. Both African Americans and Republicans see crime as impeding African American advancement. By contrast, Democrats take a softer approach to crime.

Chapter 8, Conformity, discusses the pressure some African Americans feel to adhere to counterproductive concepts of "blackness." In this chapter, African Americans advocate rejecting conformity and accepting the freedom of individuality as a means of achieving personal and group fulfillment.

Part I
Background

One

Oppression

Democrats believe that the oppression of the past persists as a major cause of African American problems today.

President Barack Obama
> For too long, we've been blind to the way past injustices continue to shape the present.[41]

President Obama said that among African Americans, a "legacy of defeat was passed on to future generations":
> As William Faulkner once wrote, "The past isn't dead and buried. In fact, it isn't even past." We do not need to recite here the history of racial injustice in this country. But we do need to remind ourselves that so many of the disparities that exist in the African-American community today can be directly traced to inequalities passed on from an earlier generation that suffered under the brutal legacy of slavery and Jim Crow.[42]

University of California at Santa Barbara, Conference:
> The legacy of slavery continues to shape the nation's politics in ways that are not fully appreciated by a citizenry who would

Shared Values

rather ignore its history in the vain hope that they might escape it.[43]

Deborah Foster, of *PoliticusUSA: Real Liberal Politics*, asserted that the legacy of slavery:
…plays a significant role in the instability of male-female relationships to this day. We have no precedent for the recovery time required to overcome this type of assault on a fundamental societal institution.[44]

To the extent that this pessimistic viewpoint is valid, those who bear the major responsibility for past oppression deserve to be recognized. Who were they? Which political party was for slavery and discrimination? Which party was for freedom and opportunity?

Robert Oliver
All of the slave masters were Democrats.[45]

Dinesh D'Souza
The Democrats want us to believe they're the party of equal rights and human rights and civil rights. The truth is the Democrats are the party of slavery and Indian removal, of broken treaties and the Trail of Tears, they're the party of segregation and Jim Crow and lynching and the Ku Klux Klan, they're the party of Japanese internment, and opposition to the Civil Rights Act of 1964 and the Voting Rights Act of 1965 and the Fair Housing Bill of 1968. This is their actual history, so what they do is they try to cover it up.[46]

Angela McGlowan
The long arm of slavery and Jim Crow oppression, Democrats tell us, explain all that plagues our community. Wisely, they leave out that unfortunate part about their party being the primary cause of the plague.[47]

Frances Rice, Chairman, National Black Republican Association:
Etched in history is the fact that the Democratic Party, through its racist agenda and "States' Rights" claim to own slaves, sought to protect and preserve the institution of slavery from 1792 to 1865, thus keeping enslaved millions of blacks.

The Democratic Party enacted fugitive slave laws to keep blacks from escaping from plantations; instigated the 1856 "Dred Scott v. Standford" decision which legally classified blacks as property; passed the Missouri Compromise to spread slavery into 50% of the new Northern states; and passed the Kansas-Nebraska Act designed to spread slavery into all of the new states.[48]

Michael Steele
When women and men were bound in chains, it was the Republican Party that took action to end slavery.[49]

The Economist
During its 160-year history, the Republican Party has abolished slavery, provided the votes in Congress to pass the Civil Rights Act and helped bring the cold war to a close.[50]

Governor Rick Perry has stated that his Republican Party was founded "on the principle of freedom for African-Americans."[51]

Louisiana State Senator Elbert Guillory
The first Republican president was Abraham Lincoln, the author of the Emancipation Proclamation. It was Republicans in Congress who authored the 13th, 14th, and 15th Amendments, giving former slaves citizenship, voting rights, and due process of the law. The Democrats on the other hand were the party of Jim Crow. It was Democrats who defended the rights of slave owners.[52]

Shared Values

Michelle Alexander
Following the Civil War, party alignment was almost entirely regional. The South was solidly Democratic, embittered by the war, firmly committed to the maintenance of a racial caste system, and extremely hostile to federal intervention on behalf of African Americans. The North was overwhelmingly Republican and, while Republicans were ambivalent about equality for African Americans, they were far more inclined to adopt and implement racial justice reforms than their Democratic counterparts below the Mason-Dixon line.[53]

After the war, Republicans began Reconstruction to transform the South and provide full freedom for the former slaves.

Eric Foner wrote that modern historians view Reconstruction as "the first attempt to introduce a genuine interracial democracy in the United States."[54]

Democrats opposed Reconstruction.

Eric Foner, referring to Democrat president Andrew Johnson:
The vast majority of white southerners, supported vociferously by the Democratic Party of the North, were deeply opposed to any recognition of legal and political equality for the former slaves. Johnson encouraged them to resist the implementation of congressional measures, helping to set the stage for the wave of terror by the Ku Klux Klan and kindred groups that did much to undermine Reconstruction.[55]

David Catron, referring to Democrat president Woodrow Wilson:
Wilson was an unabashed racist who reintroduced segregation to the federal civil service when he took office. And, when a group of African-American professionals came to the White House to protest this outrage, Wilson threw them out after

pompously declaring: "Segregation is not a humiliation but a benefit, and ought to be so regarded by you gentlemen."[56]

Walter E. Williams
President Wilson was a progressive and an avowed racist who racially segregated the civil service and delighted in showing D. W. Griffith's racist "The Birth of a Nation" to his White House guests.[57]

Republican president Dwight Eisenhower signed civil rights bills into law in 1957 and 1960, sent federal troops to Little Rock, Arkansas to integrate schools, created the US Civil Rights Commission, desegregated the military, and appointed Earl Warren as Chief Justice of the Supreme Court. Warren voted on the side of desegregation in the instrumental *Brown v. Board of Education* case, which overturned the Democrat, pro-segregation *Plessy* decision.[58]

Bruce Bartlett
We have come to call the latter half of the nineteenth century in the South as the era of "Jim Crow," during which the oppression of blacks throughout the region became institutionalized. It is seldom pointed out that *all* of the Jim Crow laws were enacted by Democratic legislatures and signed into law by Democratic governors. It could not have been otherwise, since there were virtually no Republicans in positions of authority in state governments in the South after the end of Reconstruction in 1877.[59]

Ben Carson
The Democrat Party, of course, is the party of the KKK.[60]

Eric Foner
In effect, the Klan was a military force serving the interests of the Democratic party, the planter class, and all those who desired restoration of white supremacy.[61]

Shared Values

Frances Rice
> Georgia-born Democrat Nathan Bedford Forrest, a Grand Dragon of the Ku Klux Klan wrote on page 21 of the September 1928 edition of the Klan's *The Kourier Magazine*. "I have never voted for any man who was not a regular Democrat. My father… never voted for any man who was not a Democrat. My grandfather was…the head of the Ku Klux Klan in reconstruction days…. My great-grandfather was a life-long Democrat….. My great-great-grandfather was…one of the founders of the Democratic party."[62]

Walter E. Williams, on Democrat president Franklin D. Roosevelt's National Recover Act:
> Black spokesmen and the black press were fully aware of the effects of the act. They referred to it variously as the "Negro Run Around," "Negroes Rarely Allowed," "Negroes Ruined Again," "Negroes Robbed Again," "No Roosevelt Again," and the "Negro Removal Act."
>
> In 1935, the US Supreme Court ruled the NRA unconstitutional. New Dealers mourned, but the black community celebrated.[63]

Ta-Nehisi Coates spoke of "the racism implicit in New Deal policies."[64]

Bruce Bartlett, on Robert Byrd, Democrat US senator until 2010:
> Byrd, for example, was elected Senate Democratic Whip in 1971 and Majority Leader in 1977 even though he was known to have once been a member of the Ku Klux Klan and had personally filibustered the Civil Rights Act of 1964.[65]

Jeffrey Lord, in an open letter to the Democrat National Committee:
> Time and time and time again your party selected Klan members to represent it in the U.S. Senate and the U.S. House as well as state governorships and all manner of local officials.

Oppression

One troubling sign of just how close was your party's relationship with the Klan was President Franklin Roosevelt's appointment [1937] of Alabama's liberal New Deal Senator Hugo Black to the Supreme Court. Black held a "golden passport"—aka a lifetime membership in the Klan.

The notorious Eugene "Bull" Connor, the Birmingham, Alabama Public Safety Commissioner who unleashed both police dogs and fire hoses on civil rights protesters in 1963, was both a Klan member and a member of your Democratic National Committee.[66]

The most virulent racists included Democrats James Eastland, Allen Ellender, Orval Faubus, J. William Fulbright, Ernest Hollings, Russell Long, Lester Maddox, Richard Russell, and John Stennis. **George Wallace** blocked Alabama school doors, saying, "Segregation now, segregation tomorrow, segregation forever."[67]

Malcolm X, 1964:
> You, today, have—are in the hands of—a government of segregationists, racists, white supremacists who belong to the Democratic party, but disguise themselves as Dixiecrats. A Dixiecrat is nothing but a Democrat.[68]

Progressive Democrats approved of Margaret Sanger's eugenics policies that prevented women from having babies. Those policies often focused on aborting African American babies.

Irin Carmon, on the North Carolina Eugenics Board's involuntary sterilizations:
> The targets of that board's 45-year reign, from 1929 to 1974, were disproportionately black and female, and almost universally poor.

Shared Values

"These people were dehumanized," said Latoya Adams, whose aunt, Deborah Blackmon, was sterilized under the state's eugenics law. "They treated them like animals."[69]

Thomas Sowell
In America, among those to whom pioneer birth-control advocate Margaret Sanger took her message was the Ku Klux Klan.[70]

Bishop E. W. Jackson
No wonder the KKK loved her. She began her career by trying to reduce the population for black and other minorities through eugenics.[71]

Margaret Sanger started the organizations that became Planned Parenthood, which conducts hundreds of thousands of abortions annually. Considering that Planned Parenthood facilities are disproportionately located in African American communities, it is likely that the abortions are disproportionately performed on African Americans.

Margaret Sanger
Birth Control does not mean contraception indiscriminately practised. It means the release and cultivation of the better elements in our society, and the gradual suppression, elimination and eventual extinction, of defective stocks—those human weeds which threaten the blooming of the finest flowers of American civilization.[72]

Secretary of State Hillary Clinton
I admire Margaret Sanger enormously.[73]

Jason L. Riley, on abortions:
[T]he rate for black women is nearly five times higher than the white rate and well above the national average.

10

In New York City, home to the largest black population of any U.S. urban area, more black babies are aborted than born.

But if liberal activists and their media allies are going to lecture America about the value of black lives, the staggering disparity in abortion rates ought to be part of the discussion.[74]

Democrat politicians give Planned Parenthood hundreds of millions of taxpayer dollars. Planned Parenthood donates millions back to Democrat politicians.[75]

European countries, which Democrats see as enlightened, typically limit on-demand abortions to twelve weeks after conception.[76]

African Americans and Republicans have been exceptionally patriotic in serving in the defense of our nation.[77] On the other hand, **Melissa Harris-Perry** said that the US military is "despised as an engine of war by many progressives."[78]

It is likely that African Americans and Republicans are disproportionately represented among our wounded veterans. Under the current Democrat leadership, the Veterans Health Administration has not been fulfilling its obligation to care for our service men and women. For example, African American cancer patient Gilford Anderson died while futilely trying to make an appointment at the VA.[79]

Dan Merica and **Ashley Killough**, 2015:
> A more recent CNN investigation found the problem is actually getting worse—veterans continue to wait months for care at some VA facilities, and a September federally funded report concluded the agency remains "plagued" by problems including growing bureaucracy, staffing challenges and unsustainable costs.[80]

Scott Davis, Veterans Administration program specialist, Atlanta, 2015: The VA, again, intentionally has artificial barriers to reduce the number of people who can use the system.[81]

Pete Kasperowicz, 2015, referring to the Office of Inspector General: The OIG report confirms the worst fears of members of Congress, who said in July that they would investigate unsubstantiated claims that thousands of veterans died before they ever became eligible for VA benefits.

The government watchdog for the Department of Veterans Affairs reported Monday that it was able to substantiate claims that the VA's Los Angeles office was sending mail from veterans to the shredder.[82]

Roger L. Simon
It should be remembered that many of the veterans who have been mistreated, possibly killed, are members of minorities that traditionally, indeed reflexively, vote Democratic. The Democratic Party's exploitation of black people has been one of the great, virtually unconscionable, tragedies of our time.[83]

Peggy Noonan
If they cared, they'd oversee. They'd make sure it works when the rubber hits the road. They'd make sure the thing they supposedly want to happen (first-rate treatment for vets, for instance) happens.[84]

Sarah Palin
And if you love your freedom, thank a vet.[85]

D espite their callousness, Democrats say that they are the party that cares.

Garrison Keillor
I am a liberal and liberalism is the politics of kindness.

This is Democratic bedrock: we don't let people lie in the ditch and drive past and pretend not to see them dying.[86]

Paul Krugman wrote that right-wing politicians "are always arguing that we can't afford to help the poor and unlucky."[87]

But Republicans give more to help people in need.

Arthur C. Brooks
As I found in my 2006 book *Who Really Cares*, the average conservative household contributes significantly more to charity than does the average liberal household despite earning less income.[88]

Nicholas D. Kristof
Arthur Brooks, the author of a book on donors to charity, "Who Really Cares," cites data that households headed by conservatives give 30 percent more to charity than households headed by liberals. A study by Google found an even greater disproportion: average annual contributions reported by conservatives were almost double those of liberals.

People in red states are considerably more likely to volunteer for good causes, and conservatives give blood more often.

We liberals are personally stingy.[89]

Shared Values

Democrats depict Republicans and Americans in general as racists. MSNBC's **Chris Mathews** referred to Republicans as the "Grand Wizard crowd."[90] **Keith Olbermann** called the Tea Party the "Tea Klux Klan."[91] College professor **Brent Terry** told his students that Republicans are "racist people" who "want things to go back—not to 1955, but to 1855."[92] **Vice President Joe Biden** told a predominantly black audience that if elected, Mitt Romney would "put you all back in chains."[93] Presidential candidate **Barack Obama** said that Americans in small towns feel "antipathy toward people who aren't like them."[94]

In contrast with Democrat accusations of Republican racism, African Americans have criticized liberals and Democrats harshly.

Robert Oliver
Based on a correct interpretation of history based on documented facts, does the Democrat Party owe Black America an apology for past support of slavery, Jim Crow, the Ku Klux Klan, and violent acts of racism such as lynching?[95]

Shelby Steele
We can mark up the black underclass, the near disintegration of the black family, and the general decline of public education—among many other things—to liberal social policies.[96]

David Webb
Pay attention and you'll notice a trend in America's big cities under Democrats.[97]

Walter E. Williams
There is the greatest black poverty, poorest education, highest crime and greatest family instability in cities such as: Detroit; St. Louis; Oakland, California; Memphis, Tennessee; Birmingham, Alabama; Atlanta; Baltimore; Cleveland; Philadelphia; and

Buffalo, New York. The most common characteristic of these predominantly black cities is that, for decades, all of them have been run by Democratic and presumably liberal administrations.[98]

Robert L. Woodson Sr.
To me the example of the failure of liberal Democratic politics of blacks is Detroit, Michigan.[99]

Joseph Watkins, Chicago:
We're always talking about what the Republicans ain't done for us, but my life has been hurt by Democrats.[100]

Paul McKinley, Chicago:
The Democratic Party is abusin' us.

The only thing they offerin' the black community is abortion on demand.

They're not pushin' a black agenda, they're not pushin' a family agenda, they're pushin' a neo-liberal agenda.[101]

Harold "Noonie" Ward, Chicago:
And we got it in our mind, that we always gotta keep votin' Democrat.

They only come around when it's time for elections. When they see they can give you a toy or a turkey or something and everything is good.

And we got a most important thing that we got that we can stop all this. Everybody gotta vote. And if you use your vote wisely, you could stop a lot of this stuff.[102]

Shared Values

Milwaukee County **Sheriff David A. Clarke**, speaking to Sean Hannity on *Fox News*:
> The failed liberal Democrat policies have kept people mired in misery in the American ghetto.

> By the way, I continue to hear the president talk about the economic recovery. Tell that to the people of Baltimore. Tell that to the people in American ghettos who can't find work, whose kids have to attend failing schools, who are living in poverty. Tell that to them, that there's been this wonderful economic recovery, because they've been left behind, Sean.[103]

James Golden, a.k.a. **Snerdley**, referring to Detroit, Chicago, Harlem, Los Angeles, Atlanta, and Ferguson:
> Are any of these places any better from Democrats ruling them for the last 60, 70, 80, 100 years? Where's the progress?[104]

> What liberalism has done to black communities is horrific.[105]

Malcolm X
> [T]he liberal is more deceitful than the conservative. The liberal is more hypocritical than the conservative. Both want power, but the white liberal is the one who has perfected the art of posing as the Negro's friend and benefactor; and by winning the friendship, allegiance, and support of the Negro, the white liberal is able to use the Negro as a pawn or tool in this political "football game" that is constantly raging between the white liberals and white conservatives.[106]

Man
> This idea that liberalism is sort of our liberator is ridiculous.[107]

Patricia L. Dickson
The negative effects that liberal policies have had on black Americans should be enough to convince anyone that the Democratic Party does not, as it claims, care about black Americans.[108]

Two

Progress and Opportunity

Compared with Democrats who discuss the possibility of equality for African Americans by emphasizing past and current obstacles, Republicans recognize the progress that has been made and the opportunity that exists for further advancement. To Republicans, the brave, brilliant work of Dr. King, Rosa Parks, and countless others brought about very positive change. Those freedom fighters appealed to the better nature of Americans and the nation responded. Millions of black Americans have been taking advantage of the increased opportunity.

The most persuasive voices of progress and opportunity are those of African Americans.

Secretary of State Condoleezza Rice
> We are not race blind. Of course we still have racial tensions in this country. But the United States of America has made enormous progress in race relations and it is still the best place on Earth to be a minority.[109]

Orlando Patterson
> The sociological truths are that America, while still flawed in its race relations and its stubborn refusal to institute a rational,

universal welfare system, is now the least racist white-majority society in the world; has a better record of legal protection of minorities than any other society, white or black; offers more opportunities to a greater number of black persons than any other society, including all those of Africa; and has gone through a dramatic change in its attitude toward miscegenation over the past 25 years.[110]

US representative John Lewis

No one, but no one, who was born in America forty or fifty or sixty years ago and who grew up and came through what I came through, who witnessed the changes I witnessed, can possibly say that America is not a far better place than it was. We live in a different country than the one I grew up in.[111]

Marian Wright Edelman

My life is one of the countless lives that attest to the vibrancy of the American Dream under circumstances much harder than today's. The segregated world of my childhood in the 1940s and early 1950s seemed impenetrable. Never could I have envisaged the positive changes I have seen since my youth.[112]

Quincy Jones

But I think we've got plenty of reason to feel good about what we've managed to accomplish so far. Because we've taken enormous strides. I think people get a misleading impression of what's really going on, because negativity is what makes news. They don't hear about all the folks who are getting along fine together. They don't see the everyday progress that's going on all over the country, North and South. I speak at a lot of universities, and I see all these brothers and sisters out there getting it together and doing their thing, competing in the marketplace, building careers, living in nice homes, raising kids who go to good schools—building their own proud version of the American dream.[113]

William Julius Wilson

On the other hand, the state, instead of reinforcing the racial barriers that were created during the previous periods, has, in recent years, promoted racial equality.[114]

It is clearly evident in this connection that many talented and educated blacks are now entering positions of prestige and influence at a rate comparable to or, in some situations, exceeding that of whites with equivalent qualifications.[115]

Walter E. Williams

If black Americans were thought of as a nation with their own gross domestic product, they'd rank among the 20 wealthiest nations.

A few black Americans are among the world's wealthiest. Many black Americans are among the world's most famous personalities.

The significance of all this is that in 1865, neither an ex-slave nor an ex–slave owner would have believed that such progress would be possible in less than a century and a half. As such, it speaks to the intestinal fortitude of a people. Just as importantly, it speaks to the greatness of a nation within which such progress was possible. That progress would have been impossible anywhere except in the United States of America.[116]

Thomas Sowell

How far have we come in reducing or eliminating discriminatory pay differences among individuals with the same qualifications and different racial or ethnic backgrounds? Among the younger generation, we have come just about all the way. By the late 1960's, young blacks and whites from families with similar reading (or non-reading) habits, and with the same individual levels of education, had the same income.[117]

Black college-educated couples with husband and wife working had by 1980 achieved incomes higher than white couples of the same description.[118]

Perhaps the most striking pattern among American ethnic groups is their general rise in economic conditions with the passage of time. Progress is so generally taken for granted in the United States that it is necessary to realize that it is not automatic. In many parts of the world, people still live at an economic level not much above that of their ancestors.[119]

James P. Comer and **Alvin F. Poussaint**:
There are efforts to recruit blacks in almost every professional and technical area and business. Blacks are excelling in the arts and in athletics in ways that were only dreamed of thirty years ago.[120]

Charles Johnson
We have been mayors, police chiefs, best-selling authors, MacArthur fellows, Nobel laureates, Ivy League professors, billionaires, scientists, stockbrokers, engineers, theoretical physicists, toymakers, inventors, astronauts, chess grandmasters, dot-com millionaires, actors, Hollywood film directors, and talk show hosts (the most prominent among them being Oprah Winfrey, who recently signed a deal to acquire her own network); we are Protestants, Catholics, Muslims, Jews, and Buddhists (as I am).[121]

Jerald Wolff, Atlanta:
> I believe Dr. King would have loved to see a black neighborhood like the one we live in, because he would have observed the prosperity and the progress and would have been very proud.[122]

Secretary of State Colin L. Powell
> When I was coming up, the opportunities were limited. But now they are there. You can be anything you want to be.[123]

Randall Kennedy
> One of the great achievements of the Civil Rights Revolution was its delegitimization of racial prejudice. It placed a moral as well as a legal cloud over racial discrimination. It made racial bigotry not only unfashionable but contemptible. It made racism an object of scorn and a target for ostracism. A result is that the prevalence of racial discrimination has been diminished.[124]

Richard Thompson Ford
> Today racism is socially, as well as legally, unacceptable.... This means that a lot of people sincerely abhor racism, and presumably those people would also seek to avoid it for their own part—not just because they're afraid of getting sued, but because they sincerely believe that racism is wrong. This reflects a profound change in social values.[125]

Hank Thomas, Freedom Rider:
> Good news about racial relations is all over the place.[126]

Bebe Moore Campbell
> That's the story that never gets told: how many of us really like each other, respect each other.[127]

Progress and Opportunity

Lloyd Marcus

Interracial random acts of kindness happen every day in America.[128]

US senator Tim Scott

When I was growing up, my now 93-year-old grandfather would hold the paper—just right, in plain view—at the breakfast table every day. He looked like an executive, or a doctor, or an attorney, hoping an impressionable young man would see the benefit of education.

But my grandfather could not read. The circumstances of life forced him out of a segregated classroom in the third grade to a cotton field so he could help support his family.

He has now lived long enough to see a grandson elected to Congress, and a great-grandson graduate from Georgia Tech and start graduate school at Duke.

That is the power of opportunity in America.[129]

Maya Angelou, speaking to Tavis Smiley, on the candidacy of Barack Obama for president:

I think this is an extraordinary moment, Tavis. We have a chance to do something that, in my lifetime, I could never have imagined.[130]

Henry Louis Gates Jr.

We figured that a black man could be king of England before he'd be elected president of the United States![131]

Cora Daniels

I never expected to see a black president in my lifetime.

I must admit that occasionally I am a bit embarrassed by my racial cynicism, considering how far we have come. It almost feels disrespectful to the shoulders I stand on and the benefits I am allowed because of those who came before.[132]

Randall Kennedy

When people exclaimed that they never thought that they would live to see the day a black man was elected president, they were indicating how little they expected of their fellow Americans. They were saying that they didn't anticipate that within their lifetimes a predominantly white electorate would be willing under any circumstances to entrust to a black, any black, the highest office in the land. For many, the joyful tears of November 4, 2008, reflected surprise that a sufficient number of whites would be willing to vote for an African American to enable him to become president.[133]

Ta-Nehisi Coates

Whole sections of America that we had assumed to be negrophobic turned out in support of him in 2008.[134]

Harry Belafonte

[A]mazingly enough, we have a black president. Few if any of us in the early civil rights days would have imagined that would come to pass in our lifetimes—or ever. It's an astonishing show of progress in American attitudes about race....[135]

Deroy Murdock

Indeed, Obama's breakthrough stirred Americans of all backgrounds. His first inauguration moved even his opponents. Obama back then enjoyed 69 percent approval.[136]

Tavis Smiley

But I still believe, having traveled all around the world, that I live in the world's greatest country, and for that I am grateful.[137]

R. Donahue Peebles

I would say to any American, this is the greatest country in the world. There's no limitation to your dreams. There's no limitation to what you can achieve if you're willing to prepare yourself, work hard, and do everything you can to be successful. You can.[138]

Shawn Carter, a.k.a. Jay Z:

I've been to shantytowns in Angola that taught me that what we consider to be crushing poverty in the United States has nothing to do with what we have materially—even in the projects, we're rich compared to some people in other parts of the world.[139]

Ben Carson

I have been privileged to travel to more than fifty countries and each time I return I am more thankful that I was born in the United States.[140]

Julius Erving, a.k.a. Dr. J:

Still, after a month of traveling, when we finally land back in New York, at JFK, I actually kneel and kiss the American tarmac. The USA, with all its problems, still seems like the place to be. Here I've been to three very different countries, including the great Cold War rival Russia, and none of them compare to America.[141]

I love America.[142]

Lloyd Marcus

The truth is America is the greatest land of opportunity on the planet for all who choose to go for it.[143]

I am extremely grateful and proud to be born an American.[144]

Shared Values

Robin Roberts
This is my country, the land that I love.[145]

Capt. Norman Alexander McDaniel, US Air Force:
America is the black man's best hope.[146]

Voletta Wallace, mother of the late Christopher Wallace, a.k.a. Notorious B.I.G., Biggie:
We don't know how fortunate we are here in America.[147]

US representative John Lewis
I love this country.

This is unquestionably the greatest nation on earth, a land of limitless opportunity and possibility, not just in material terms but in moral, ethical and spiritual terms.[148]

Eldridge Cleaver, after having lived in Cuba and other communist countries:
When I look back at my own life experience, I have to bow my head and thank God Almighty for preserving my life through many perilous situations that I've been involved in. But most of all, far beyond just having my life preserved, I'm thankful that I've had an experience that has enlightened me to the beauty and the greatness of the United States of America and its people.[149]

Rosa Parks
I am proud to be an American. America is a wonderful country.[150]

Ray Charles sings "America the Beautiful," with lots of love, here.[151]

Does discrimination block African American advancement?

W. E. B. Du Bois, Philadelphia, 1899:
As a matter of fact, color prejudice in this city is something between these two extreme views: it is not to-day responsible for all, or perhaps the greater part of the Negro problems, or of the disabilities under which the race labors; on the other hand, it is a far more powerful social force than most Philadelphians realize.[152]

John McWhorter
Of course there is racism. The question is whether there is enough to matter. All evidence shows that there is not.[153]

Lloyd Marcus
Is racism alive and well in America? Absolutely, on both sides.[154]

Racism along with every other sin will exist until Jesus comes to take us home. However, the undeniable truth is there is not enough racism to stop anyone from achieving his or her American dream.[155]

Jason L. Riley
Racism still exists, alas, and no one reading this is likely to see the day when it doesn't. But anti-black animus doesn't explain racial gaps in employment, crime, income, learning and single-parent homes.[156]

Bayard Rustin
What is not often remembered, however, is that were we to eliminate racism today, we would have solved only part of the problem, and perhaps not even the major part.[157]

Orlando Patterson
Black youth in particular have insisted that their habits, attitudes, beliefs, and values are what mainly explain their plight,

even after fully taking account of racism and their disadvantaged neighborhood conditions.[158]

James Golden, a.k.a. **Snerdley**:
The progress for black people is not gonna be found in politics, it's gonna be found inside.[159]

Minister Louis Farrakhan
The white man is not a problem for us.[160]

Those who claim that discrimination blocks African Americans from moving forward may have the sequence reversed. Others say that it is advancement that lessens discrimination.

W. E. B. Du Bois
It seems to me almost inevitable that in the long run the result of greater political and economic equality would be the fading away of racial discrimination.[161]

Robert L. Woodson Sr.
Although racism still taints the American character, the contention of most civil rights leaders that its eradication is the precondition to black advancement is, at best, a confession of impotence and, at worst, a retreat from responsibility. Historically, substantive gains have been achieved in spite of racial barriers—and by a black community that had to rely on its own resources to survive and prosper.[162]

Jason L. Riley
The notion that racism is holding back blacks as a group, or that better black outcomes cannot be expected until racism has been vanquished, is a dodge.[163]

Progress and Opportunity

Walter E. Williams
Surely one doesn't want to sit around waiting for the end to discrimination.[164]

Marcus Garvey
Be assured of this, that in the Negro's rise to wealth will come the adjustment of most of the wrongs inflicted upon him.[165]

Ida B. Wells Barnett
When he has a dollar in his pocket and many more in the bank, he can move from injustice and oppression and no one to say him nay.[166]

John Hope Bryant
Dr. King said, "The only way to social justice in a capitalist country is economic parity…."[167]

~

Exaggerating the potency of racism adds to the difficulties of black Americans.

John H. Johnson
The last thing I need is someone telling me that I can't make it.[168]

Booker T. Washington, advised his daughter Portia:
I think you will make a mistake if you will let your mind dwell too much upon American prejudice, or any other racial prejudice. The thing is for one to get above such things. If one gets in the habit of continually thinking and talking about race prejudice, he soon gets to the point where he is fit for little that is worth doing. In the northern part of the United States, there are a number of colored people who

29

make their lives miserable, because all their talk is about race prejudice.[169]

Reverend Martin Luther King Jr.
But just as we must avoid a superficial optimism, we must also avoid a crippling pessimism.[170]

Itabari Njeri
[A] discouraged soul is of use to no one....[171]

Thomas Sowell
How are you going to tell a young black man to work hard, or study hard, in order to get ahead, when both the media and many so-called "leaders" are constantly telling him that everything is rigged against him? Why knock yourself out on the job, or miss the Saturday-night party in order to study, if whitey is just waiting in ambush to pull the rug out from under you anyway?[172]

Among the insidious dangers are the undermining of minority and female self-confidence by incessant reiteration of the themes of pervasive discrimination, hypocritical standards, and shadowy but malign enemies relentlessly opposing their progress.[173]

Louis W. Sullivan
The tragic truth is that the language of "victimization" is the true victimizer—a great crippler of young minds and spirits. To teach young people that their lives are governed—not by their own actions, but by socio-economic forces or government budgets or other mysterious and fiendish sources beyond their control—is to teach our children negativism, resignation, passivity and despair.[174]

Progress and Opportunity

Walter E. Williams
As a black person, born in 1936, who's witnessed and experienced gross discrimination and seen the personal sacrifices made by both blacks and whites to create today's opportunities, I find the victimization vision not only offensive and racially demeaning but a gross betrayal of the monumental bravery and sacrifice of those who came before us.[175]

Malcolm X, in Mecca, on so-called racial segregation in America: I saw that people who looked alike drew together and most of the time stayed together. This was entirely voluntary; there being no other reason for it. But Africans were with Africans. Pakistanis were with Pakistanis. And so on. I tucked it into my mind that when I returned home I would tell Americans this observation; that where true brotherhood existed among all colors, where no one felt segregated, where there was no "superiority" complex, no "inferiority" complex—then voluntarily, naturally, people of the same kind felt drawn together by that which they had in common.[176]

Jo-Issa Rae Diop, a.k.a. **Issa Rae**:
I've decided to focus only on the positivity of being black, and especially of being a black woman. Am I supposed to feel oppressed? Because I don't.[177]

Pharrell Lanscilo Williams, a.k.a. **Pharrell**:
The New Black doesn't blame other races for our issues.[178]

Randall Kennedy
Hope is a vital nutrient for effort; without it, there is no prospect for achievement. The belief that we can overcome makes more realistic the possibility that we shall overcome.[179]

Shared Values

Robert L. Woodson Sr.
Development for any people begins with the belief that development is possible.[180]

Hyping allegations of racism and blaming them on one's political rivals is playing the race card.

Mary Frances Berry
Tainting the tea party movement with the charge of racism is proving to be an effective strategy for Democrats. There is no evidence that tea party adherents are any more racist than other Republicans, and indeed many other Americans. But getting them to spend their time purging their ranks and having candidates distance themselves should help Democrats win in November. Having one's opponent rebut charges of racism is far better than discussing joblessness.[181]

US senator Tim Scott
I've been to dozens of Tea Party rallies. I've given at least a half a dozen or more speeches. I have yet to find the first racist comment or the first person who approaches me from a racist perspective.[182]

Thomas Sowell
Any fool can say the word "racism." In fact, quite a few fools do say it. But clever people can also say "racism" in order to get fools to vote their way.[183]

Richard Thompson Ford
Playing the race card places all claims of racism—valid and phony—under a cloud of suspicion.[184]

People who "play the race card" opportunistically and with intentional deceit are the enemies of truth, social harmony, and social justice.[185]

Secretary of State Condoleezza Rice
The idea that you would play such a card and try fearmongering among minorities just because you disagree with Republicans, that they are somehow all racists, I find it appalling. I find it insulting.[186]

Larry Elder
To earn their near-monolithic 95 percent black vote, the Democratic Party repeatedly tells blacks of their continued oppression.[187]

Booker T. Washington
There is another class of coloured people who make a business of keeping the troubles, the wrongs, and the hardships of the Negro race before the public. Having learned that they are able to make a living out of their troubles, they have grown into the settled habit of advertising their wrongs—partly because they want sympathy and partly because it pays. Some of these people do not want the Negro to lose his grievances, because they do not want to lose their jobs.[188]

Shelby Steele, on black leaders who overstate racism:
All of them will do one thing and one thing only: they run to the church of racism. They love racism. They roll around in racism as though it were money and it very often is money. They love it. If white people stopped being racists they wouldn't know what to do and they wouldn't know who they are. And they just absolutely adore it and cannot get enough

of it. If there's a racist event somewhere they rent a jet plane and fly to it. Because they smell the power in it. They smell the money in it. These people love racism.[189]

Ron Christie
I wish many who decry racism at the drop of the hat would be honest enough to admit the amazing strides we have made and continue to make as American citizens bound by our love for this great country.[190]

B lack Americans have urged one another to take greater advantage of opportunities.

Booker T. Washington
We have a right in a conservative and sensible manner to enter our complaints, but we shall make a fatal error if we yield to the temptation of believing that mere opposition to our wrongs… will take the place of progressive, constructive action…An inch of progress is worth more than a yard of complaint.[191]

Nor should we permit our grievances to overshadow our opportunities.[192]

John McWhorter
The civil rights era ended a long time ago, victorious.[193]

Russell Simmons
I'm not saying that racism is completely gone and people should forget about it and not fight to make whatever civil rights issues that are still there go away. I'm saying that you have to recognize what opportunity you do have.[194]

Progress and Opportunity

Glenn C. Loury
But the nature of problems facing the black community today, the significant recent expansion of opportunities for blacks in American society, and the changing political environment in which black leaders now operate, all dictate that greater stress should be placed upon strategies which might appropriately be called "self-help."[195]

Ron Christie
The marches for equality during the civil rights era have resulted in an America where people are free to learn, live, and work as equals with their fellow citizens. The barriers that once blocked blacks from entry into America's finest public and private institutions of higher learning have been removed, but the new opportunities will remain useless unless children are prepared to learn and compete at an early age.[196]

Willie Anthony Jones, award-winning school principal, to his son Van:
I think that's what is wrong with your program, son. You are just blaming the system, fighting the system, but you are creating no opportunities for that individual kid who wants to excel. If you want to stop the violence, focus on jobs. That's harder than suing someone, but you might make more of a difference, in the long run.[197]

You want to stop the violence? Well, like they say, nothing stops a bullet like a job.[198]

Van Jones
What I'm doing these days goes beyond reacting against racism and oppression. That only gets you so far.[199]

Michael Steele
For African-Americans, we must recognize that the battle for civil rights in the twentieth century has become a struggle for economic prosperity in the twenty-first.[200]

John Hope Bryant
So much of the intellectual firepower in the black community today is about fighting oppression.

We have enough civil rights lawyers.

We need our kids to be getting their degree in business economics. We need them to become entrepreneurs, and to create some jobs.[201]

Shelby Steele
Our leaders must take a risk. They must tell us the truth, tell us of the freedom and opportunity they have discovered in their own lives.[202]

Debra J. Dickerson
It is time to chart black life after the movement.[203]

Reverend Ralph David Abernathy, referring to Dr. King:
He envisioned a time when black people would have an opportunity to move into the mainstream of American life, when, as he put it, the bottom rung would become the top. That time has arrived, but as a people we have not yet taken full advantage of the opportunity.[204]

Michele Wallace
Can you imagine what the newly emancipated slaves would have done with the opportunities that are now available to blacks in this country?[205]

Supreme Court Justice Clarence Thomas
My grandparents always said there would be more opportunities for us. I can still hear my grandfather, "Y'all goin' have mo' of a chance than me," and he was right. He felt that if others sacrificed and created opportunities for us, we had an obligation to work hard, to be decent citizens, to be fair and good people, and he was right.[206]

Three

Self-Reliance

The leading Democrats see self-reliance as a conservative value. **President Obama** said that "self-help" is "quintessentially American—and yes, conservative."[207] **Secretary Hillary Clinton** spoke of "individual responsibility" as one of the "conservative beliefs" she was raised with.[208]

In the United States, the typical alternative to relying on yourself is to rely on the government. Democrats think very highly of the government.

US senator Chuck Schumer
Together, Democrats must embrace government. It's what we believe in; it's what unites our party; and, most importantly, it's the only thing that's going to get the middle class going again.[209]

US senator Harry Reid
[T]he American government is the greatest force for good in the history of mankind.[210]

Vice President Joseph Biden
> Every single great idea that has marked the 21st century, the 20th century and the 19th century has required government vision and government incentive.[211]

Believing in government, they increase its size and its influence over citizens' lives. This decreases people's freedom.

Justice Louis D. Brandeis
> Experience should teach us to be most on our guard to protect liberty when the Government's purposes are beneficent. Men born to freedom are naturally alert to repel invasion of their liberty by evil-minded rulers. The greatest dangers to liberty lurk in insidious encroachment by men of zeal, well-meaning but without understanding.[212]

Democrats' values are reflected in their 2012 presidential campaign ad "The Life of Julia." It depicted a woman who is dependent on government services from the time she is born until her death.[213]

Mary Kate Cary
> Because she's a woman, the message becomes one of a benign, paternal state taking care of vulnerable women.[214]

Jessica Gavora
> One milestone is pointedly missing: marriage.
>
> But, then again, why should Julia get married? She doesn't need to. Like a growing number of single women with children, Julia is married to the state.[215]

Shared Values

Gov. Jerry Brown
We need more welfare and fewer jobs.[216]

Republicans are more impressed with the American people than with the American government. They believe that the government will not take care of you as well as you will take care of yourself. They are in favor of a safety net for those in need, but their goal is to have more people move up the economic ladder and not need government assistance. They don't want to give the kind of "help" that traps people on the bottom. To them, increasing dependency is the opposite of caring.

President Ronald Reagan
We're a humane and a generous people and we accept without reservation our obligation to help the disabled, the aged and those unfortunates who, through no fault of their own, must depend on their fellow man. But we are not going to perpetuate poverty by substituting a permanent dole for a paycheck.[217]

The nine most terrifying words in the English language are "I'm from the government, and I'm here to help."[218]

A government can't control the economy without controlling people.[219]

Speaker of the US House of Representatives, Paul Ryan
We believe a renewed commitment to limited government will unshackle our economy and create millions of new jobs and opportunities for all people, of every background, to succeed and prosper.[220]

First Lady Barbara Bush
Your success as a family...our success as a nation...depends not on what happens inside the White House, but on what happens inside your house.[221]

African Americans have responded with scorn to those who said that the government or anyone else would take care of them.

Frederick Douglass, on the man who held him in slavery:
He said, if I behaved myself properly, he would take care of me. Indeed, he advised me to complete thoughtlessness of the future, and taught me to depend solely upon him for happiness. He seemed to see fully the pressing necessity of setting aside my intellectual nature, in order to contentment in slavery.[222]

W. E. B. Du Bois
He has his tempters and temptations. There are ever those about him whispering: "You are nobody; why strive to be somebody? The odds are over-whelming against you—wealth, tradition, learning and guns. Be reasonable. Accept the dole of charity and the cant of missionaries and sink contentedly to your place...."[223]

Carter G. Woodson Sr.
History shows that it does not matter who is in power or what revolutionary forces take over the government, those who have not learned to do for themselves and have to depend solely on others never obtain any more rights or privileges in the end than they had in the beginning.[224]

Shared Values

Zora Neale Hurston, on New Deal programs:
> But under relief, dependent upon the Government for their daily bread, men gradually relaxed their watchfulness and submitted to the will of the "Little White Father," more or less. Once they had weakened that far, it was easy to go on an' on voting for more relief, and leaving Government affairs in the hands of a few. The change from a republic to a dictatorship was imperceptibly pushed ahead.[225]

Louisiana State Senator Elbert Guillory
> Programs such as welfare, food stamps, these programs aren't designed to lift black Americans out of poverty. They were always intended as a mechanism for politicians to control the black community. The idea that blacks, or anyone for that matter, needs the government to get ahead in life, is despicable.
>
> Our self-initiative and our self-reliance have been sacrificed in exchange for allegiance to our overseers who control us by making us dependent on them.[226]

US representative Mia Love, spoke of:
> …the slavery that comes from being dependent on people in power.[227]

Bishop E. W. Jackson
> We must limit the scope of government in order to maximize our freedom. It is up to each able bodied American to take personal responsibility for our own lives and the well being of our families. The support of family, church, friends and faith in God are the answers to the trials we all face in life. We must cease to cultivate dependence on government, for such dependence only serves to rob us of our autonomy and freedom.[228]

Jason L. Riley

Democrats tend to consider greater government dependence an achievement and use handouts to increase voter support.[229]

Alfonzo Rachel

Well, let's be fair, Democrats. If you want to accuse Republicans of being for the rich, while Democrats are for the poor, then that must mean Democrats need the poor. If Democrats want to stay in power, then they need to make sure poor people stay in poverty. Also, if the Democrats want more power, then they need more poor people.[230]

Michael Steele

It's in the liberals' political interest to create dependency, because it creates a need for more and more government.[231]

Thomas Sowell

Leading people into the blind alley of dependency and grievances may be counterproductive for them but it can produce votes, money, power, fame and a sense of exaltation to others who portray themselves as friends of the downtrodden.[232]

Shelby Steele

If you are a liberal, then you must see black people as victims. You must see them as people who are oppressed and who have no ability to help themselves and can't, really. You have to see them as people whose fate is contingent on your goodwill.

Liberalism is this fundamental insult to us as human beings.[233]

Patricia L. Dickson
> As a black American, it is infuriating for me to listen to white Democrats' claims of helping blacks when all they are doing is making sure that blacks remain dependent upon government handouts. That stance reveals what they really think about black Americans.[234]

Tom Joyner
> We've got to stop going to other people to get what we need.[235]

Shawn Carter, a.k.a. **Jay Z**:
> The highest level of giving…is giving in a way that makes the receiver self-sufficient.[236]

African Americans on self-reliance:

Marian Wright Edelman
> No one is more aware of the folly of relying solely on government to solve black community problems than the black community. The black American journey is one of making a way out of no way because we often had no one, save God, to lend us a hand.[237]

Frances Ellen Watkins Harper, 1875:
> The most important question before us colored people is not simply what the Democratic party may do against us or the Republican party do for us; but what are we going to do for ourselves? What shall we do towards developing our character, adding our quota to the civilization and strength of the country, diversifying our industry, and practising those lordly

virtues that conquer success, and turn the world's dread laugh into admiring recognition? [238]

Frederick Douglass

We must improve our condition, and here the work is ours. It cannot be done by our friends. They can pity as they can sympathize with us. But we need more than sympathy—something more than pity. We must be respected. And we cannot be respected unless we are either independent or aiming to be.[239]

We have errors of our own to abandon, habits to reform, manners to improve, ignorance to dispel, and character to build up. This is something which no power on earth can do for us, and which no power on earth can prevent our doing for ourselves, if we will.[240]

Others may clear the road, but we must go forward, or be left behind in the race of life.[241]

W. E. B. Du Bois

[T]he bulk of the work of raising the Negro must be done by the Negro himself, and the greatest help for him will be not to hinder and curtail and discourage his efforts. Against prejudice, injustice and wrong the Negro ought to protest energetically and continuously, but he must never forget that he protests because those things hinder his own efforts, and that those efforts are the key to his future.[242]

James Brown

The record I put out in March of 1969 explains where I've always been. It's called, "I Don't Want Nobody to Give Me Nothing." "Just open the door," it says, "and I'll get it myself."[243]

Shared Values

I said we had a lot of problems in the black community that we had to solve ourselves—wasn't anybody could do it for us.[244]

Malcolm X

The black man never can become independent and recognized as a human being who is truly equal with other human beings until he has what they have, and until he is doing for himself what others are doing for themselves.[245]

Spike Lee

Malcolm always talked about, do for self. The Black man has to learn to stand on his own two feet. Do for self.[246]

Robert L. Woodson Sr.

We can't believe that for every problem that exists, white folks are somehow responsible and therefore if they're responsible, the solution is for white folks to do something.[247]

Susan L. Taylor

All that our race needs begins with us.[248]

Glenn C. Loury

But it is now virtually beyond dispute that many of the problems of contemporary Afro-American life lie beyond the reach of effective government action, and require for their successful resolution actions which can only be undertaken by the black community itself.[249]

Jason L. Riley

[T]here are limits to government benevolence, however well-intentioned and expertly executed. A group's culture—its habits, behaviors and attitudes toward work, marriage and parenting—is likely to play the bigger role in reducing dependency long-term.[250]

Sarah L. Delany
A big part of self-respect is self-reliance—knowing you can take care of yourself.[251]

Orlando Patterson
There can be no moral equality when there is a dependency relationship among men....[252]

Jelani Cobb
But if you think that the problem is within us, then at least it gives you the idea that you have the capacity to change it.[253]

James Todd Smith, a.k.a. LL Cool J:
When you blame others, you give up your power to effect change. When you point the finger at others instead of looking in the mirror, you're letting yourself off the hook. If every failure or disappointment in your life is someone else's fault, there is no need for you to improve, right?[254]

Shelby Steele
After all, it was our assumption of responsibility that made the civil rights movement successful.[255]

Others joined our struggle, but clearly we did not allow the movement to be contingent on what others did. We also have never allowed our performance in sports, music, literature, or entertainment to be contingent on whether or not others helped us.[256]

The problem we have now is development and that's where our energies have to go into. It's not something that can be reached by legislation, it has to be reached by a cultural transformation in black America.[257]

Shared Values

We're not gonna go anywhere we don't take ourselves.[258]

Self-reliance requires having a degree of financial independence.

Sojourner Truth, 1867:
What we want is a little money.[259]

Reverend Martin Luther King Jr.
It's alright to talk about "long white robes over yonder," in all its symbolism. But ultimately people want some suits and dresses and shoes to wear down here.[260]

C. Eric Lincoln and **Lawrence H. Mamiya**:
The liberation strategy in the black community, on the other hand, focused on gaining both upward mobility from poverty and eventual economic independence.[261]

Alice Walker
Without money, one becomes dependent on other people, who are likely to be—even in their kindness—erratic in their support and despotic in their expectations of return. Zora was forced to rely, like Tennessee Williams's Blanche, "on the kindness of strangers."[262]

Dennis Kimbro and **Napoleon Hill**:
Money is a warm home and healthy children; it's birthday presents and a college education; it's a family vacation and the means to help the less fortunate.[263]

Susan L. Taylor
You can't give from an empty cup.[264]

George Clinton
Broke don't travel.[265]

Bernie Mac
It's good to be upper middle class. We are that now, would you know; and we still got our roots.[266]

Oprah Winfrey
I don't think of myself as a poor, deprived ghetto girl who made good. I think of myself as somebody who from an early age knew she was responsible for herself—and I had to make good.[267]

Reverend Frederick J. Eikerenkoetter II, a.k.a. **Reverend Ike**:
The only thing I have to say about poor people is don't be one of them.[268]

But money has limitations.

Massachusetts **governor Deval Patrick**, as a student at a New England prep school:
They opened up and allowed me to see how universal the human condition really is. Despite their venerable names and magnificent homes and important art collections, the men and women of privilege bore struggles hardly different from those I had seen at home. They told me about their bad marriages, their estranged children, their family traumas. There was alcoholism, addiction, infidelity, suicide, ruin, and loss. One student got pregnant during her senior year and decided to keep the baby. The father of another could not keep a job and spent most of his days in his pajamas, staring out his

bedroom window at the garden. Money may have helped some of these people cope with calamity, but it did not immunize anyone from it.[269]

Serena Williams
Even though you might think that becoming rich can solve all your problems, it can't. Venus and I know that no amount of our cash can buy the most important things in life: love, family, friendship, good health, and happiness.[270]

Part II
Core Values

Four

Marriage

Republican View

The Republican Party is the party of family values. Republicans understand that married people are more likely than singles to be emotionally and financially well-off.[271] They also have more and better sex than singles.[272]

Republicans accept that children who are raised by their married, biological parents tend to be healthier, physically and emotionally, and learn more in school than other children. The children of married couples grow up to enjoy greater work success than the children of singles. That enables them to avoid the temptations of crime and drugs.[273] When they become parents, they pass their advantages on to their children.

Marriage doesn't automatically or quickly lift couples to prosperity, but it gives them a better chance than singles.

David Popenoe

Marriage and the nuclear family—mother, father, and children—are the most universal social institutions in existence. In no society has nonmarital childbirth been the cultural norm.[274]

US senator Jim DeMint

Marriage predates government and is the fundamental building block of all human civilization.[275]

Bill O'Reilly

The traditional American family has always been the foundation for success in America.[276]

Robert Rector

Being married has roughly the same effect in reducing poverty that adding five to six years to a parent's education has. Interestingly, on average, high school dropouts who are married have a far lower poverty rate than do single parents with one or two years of college.[277]

William A. Galston

Cohabitation is not a replacement for marriage. On average, cohabiting couples stay together for only 18 months.

It turns out that the effects of family instability are measurably worse for boys than for girls—and worst of all for African-American boys.

In fact, the researchers conclude, neighborhoods and schools are less important than the "direct effect of family structure itself."[278]

Barbara Dafoe Whitehead

Contrary to popular belief, many children do not "bounce back" after divorce or remarriage. Difficulties that are associated with family breakup often persist into adulthood. Children who grow up in single-parent or stepparent families are less successful as adults, particularly in the two domains of life—love and work—that are most essential to happiness. Needless to say, not all children experience such negative effects. However, research shows that many children from disrupted families have a harder time achieving intimacy in a relationship, forming a stable marriage, or even holding a steady job.[279]

David Popenoe
[T]he evidence is strong: Fathering is different from mothering; involved fathers are indispensable for the good of children and society; and our growing national fatherlessness is a disaster in the making.[280]

Ellen Sauerbrey
Since a father in the house virtually disqualifies a woman from collecting her government check, the welfare system encourages men to abandon their children.[281]

Paul Winfree
For 50 years, welfare has driven fathers from the home. As a consequence, single mothers have become increasingly dependent on government aid. Meanwhile, low-income fathers, deprived of meaningful roles as husbands and breadwinners, have drifted into the margins of society. Their attachment to the labor force has deteriorated, and the tendency toward self-destructive and anti-social behavior has increased.[282]

Elizabeth Gilbert
Married men live longer than single men; married men accumulate more wealth than single men; married men excel at their careers above single men; married men are far less likely to die a violent death than single men; married men report themselves to be much happier than single men; and married

Shared Values

men suffer less from alcoholism, drug addiction, and depression than do single men.[283]

Kay S. Hymowitz
[I]t has become clear that family breakdown lies at the heart of our nation's most obstinate social problems, especially poverty and inequality.[284]

Isabel V. Sawhill
[N]o government program is likely to reduce child poverty as much as bringing back marriage as the preferable way of raising children.[285]

George Gilder, from *Wealth and Poverty*:
[T]he first priority of any serious program against poverty is to strengthen the male role in poor families.[286]

Democrat View

Democrats are less likely to marry than are Republicans.[287] Apparently, they are less fond of marriage.

People who are hostile to the institution of marriage tend to lean to the political left.

Bernardine Dohrn, **Bill Ayers**, **Jeff Jones** and **Celia Sojourn**:
The individual capitalist family structure is a wasteful social form, not healthy for children to grow up in, a trap for women.[288]

Gloria Steinem
A woman needs a man like a fish needs a bicycle.[289]

Robin Morgan
> We can't destroy the inequities between men and women until we destroy marriage.[290]

To leftists, Republicans' support for marriage is part of a "war on women." This Democrat leader claimed that, as part of that "war," Republicans block women's access to birth control pills.

US senator Elizabeth Warren
> Republicans in Washington have decided that the most important thing for them to focus on is how to deny women access to birth control.[291]

But when Republican senators Kelly Ayotte and Corey Gardner tried to make birth control pills available without a prescription, it was Democrats, joining with Planned Parenthood, who opposed the initiative.

S. E. Cupp
> For years, pro-choice groups have been peddling the charge that Republicans are against access to birth control. But it's utterly (and provably) false.
>
> But rather than do the right thing for women, progressives are putting politics before women's health.[292]

US senator Kelly Ayotte
> Our legislation will help increase women's access to safe and effective contraceptives and further empower women to make their own health care decisions.[293]

Do Democrats respect parents' primary role in raising their children? Hillary Clinton wrote an entire book about the community's role in parenting. She implied that the community, including the

Shared Values

government, has responsibilities equal to those of parents in raising children.

Secretary of State Hillary Clinton
Keeping children healthy in body and mind is the family's and the village's first obligation.[294]

One of the family's—and the villages [sic]—most important tasks is to help children develop those habits of self-discipline and empathy that constitute what we call character.[295]

It takes a village to raise a child.[296]

It is likely that most Americans accept that parents are responsible for raising their children.
Democrats' positive view of the village contrasts with the general knowledge that the government has often been less than caring towards children. For example, the state-run Florida School for Boys severely abused its students for more than a century.[297] The United States Environmental Protection Agency recently allowed citizens in Flint Michigan to be harmed by contaminated water.[298]

Black Americans have written and spoken positively of marriage and family. They refer to marriages in which husbands and wives love and respect one another and are devoted to their children.

Alex Haley
But, yes, to me the family has always been the source and heart of every culture.[299]

President Barack Obama

Of all the rocks upon which we build our lives, we are reminded today that family is the most important. And we are called to recognize and honor how critical every father is to that foundation.[300]

William Raspberry

Marriage promotes the economic, social, familial and psychological well-being of black men and women—as it does for men and women generally. Marriage is wonderful for children, who turn out to be less trouble-prone than their peers from single-parent-households.[301]

Restoring fatherhood might do more than the 20 next-best things we could think of to give our children the chance they deserve—the chance they must have if we are to arrest the disastrous slide of recent years.[302]

Thomas Sowell

Married couples have higher incomes, longer lives, better health, less violence, less alcohol and less poverty.

Women who are shacking up are four times as likely as wives to become victims of violence, and their children are 40 times as likely to be abused by live-in boyfriends as by their own parents.[303]

It should also be noted that, despite the prevalence of poverty in many black communities, the poverty rate among black married couples has been in the single digits every year since 1994.[304]

Reverend Jesse Lee Peterson

Men and women both have a natural desire to bond with one another, and form families. That is the way God has constructed us. Deep within each of us is the awareness that we were meant to give ourselves to others, and to contribute to the flourishment of humanity by caring for the next generation. The best way to do this is in the context of the traditional family. This is what is best for children (the support of a mother and a father), and this is what yields the greatest depth of human satisfaction.[305]

Every child has a natural right to a mother and a father, and to the contributions toward his well-being that each parent can uniquely make.[306]

If we as a culture began to embrace the centrality of fatherhood to both the psychological and emotional well-being of children and the stability of our society, we would begin to see massive improvements in our children and the qualities of the families they form as adults.[307]

Geoffrey Canada
The message that babies need mothers *and fathers* has to be delivered more powerfully.[308]

William Raspberry
Children need both parents—not just two breadwinners but two parental roles.[309]

Serena Williams
I was given a lot. I was given two parents.[310]

Judge Lynn Toler
Children done correctly are a great deal of work. They require lots of time, plenty of attention, and massive amounts of patience. You have to come at children fresh every day, just as if they hadn't worked your last nerve the day before. It is not

just about putting food in their mouths and clothes on their backs. It is about keeping them on the straight and narrow while the world is trying to pull them into a ditch.

My husband does one part and I do the other, because they are both full-time jobs.[311]

In a good marriage, we gain a place to set our troubles down.

I believe in marriage.[312]

Don Lemon
The studies show that lack of a male role model is an express train right to prison and the cycle continues.[313]

Earvin "Magic" Johnson Jr.
My dad taught me that if I don't work just a little harder than the other guy, maybe stay a little longer after practice, then my efforts wouldn't pay off. Without hard work, I wouldn't have become what I wanted to be, whether it was an NBA player or a successful businessman. Whatever I wanted out of life, I knew that it was up to me to achieve it.[314]

Byron Hurt, referring to his father, Jackie Hurt:
He lived a great life; he married and stayed committed to his only wife. He loved, honored, and respected his children. He raised his children. He served his church. He served his community.

Thank God for my father. No, he was not a perfect man.[315]

Signatories of the "**Morehouse Conference on African American Fathers**":
Husbands, in general, earn at least ten percent more than similar single men, and in some cases married men earn as

Shared Values

much as 40 percent more. Accordingly, marriage should be promoted as a social institution that not only maximizes emotional benefits, but also one that by itself can have a substantial positive effect on the economic condition of fathers and families.[316]

Richard Williams, on family life and raising Venus and Serena:
We were one family, devoted to each other, with one goal, supporting each other as we went forward.[317]

And we were always there at their side. Oracene and I, working together, teaching together, melding our different styles to bring the best out in both of them.[318]

I was not going to let my girls be swept into a culture of drugs and bad people.[319]

How could any father who loves his children fail to protect them?[320]

Raising my children, fighting for them and protecting them, gave me the utmost love, pride, and satisfaction.[321]

I loved being a father and enjoyed the responsibilities that came with it.[322]

Their appreciation made me super proud to be a dad.[323]

Serena Williams
I really looked up to my dad. I was a daddy's girl.[324]

Oseola McCarty
Family is the greatest blessing in this life.[325]

Ossie Davis
The dinner table was the intellectual, spiritual, and social center of our lives. It was where the day was headed and it was about as close to heavenly satisfaction as a poor man could expect to get.[326]

Eleanor Holmes Norton
Many have overcome deep poverty and discrimination only because of the protection and care of stable traditional and extended families.[327]

James P. Comer and Alvin F. Poussaint:
But, today African Americans are attempting to look beyond the basic struggle for survival and want to participate fully in the dreams and opportunities shared by all citizens. Raising strong children will help these dreams to come true.[328]

Bob Teague
We should concentrate most of our energy and resources on proposing and supporting only those projects that sensibly promise to help the black family to resuscitate itself.[329]

Single parents have raised healthy, happy children. Single mothers, single fathers, grandparents, stepparents, sisters, brothers, aunts, uncles, stepparents, foster parents, and others who try their best to raise children deserve praise for their efforts and sacrifices. But married parents are more successful, more often.

Bob Herbert
Can a woman successfully raise a child on her own? Of course. Examples abound. But a child without a decent father grows

up with a heavy handicap. And the synergistic wonders that can arise from the efforts of two devoted parents are not possible.[330]

Emiel Hamberlin
Single mothers try to do most of it by themselves, and they need a helpmate. They're struggling, and they're doing it; they're doing the best they can with what they have. I'm not bashing them. If the fathers were not there, it was overwhelming for the mothers to do it all by themselves. So when the family structure fell apart, so did order in the schools.[331]

Sylvia Ann Hewlett and **Cornel West:**
It is important to point out that at least some stepfathers do a splendid job by their stepchildren, and these men deserve our admiration and respect. However, the deeper point is that overall, biological dads do a better job. Fatherly love is not something that can be easily replicated.

It does seem that marriage creates safer conditions for children, in that a child is least likely to be abused growing up in a stable family with both biological parents.[332]

President Barack Obama
And the evidence suggests that on average, children with both their biological mother and father do better than those who live in stepfamilies or with cohabiting partners.[333]

Father, whose fifteen-year-old son was murdered by a gang:
But Daddy's gone today. That's why there's so much chaos and deterioration of the family structure. Somehow or other, we've gotta reach back and do what we've done ever since the beginning of time.[334]

Bob Herbert
>The idea that you should care for your children is an idea that is alien to enormous numbers of black men—men who even as they make their babies have one eye on the exit door. There are no excuses for them. They have condemned their children, in so many instances, to lives of poverty and violence, drugs and degradation, ignorance and unhappiness, and bitter, raging failure. They are by far the main reason for the swollen population of blacks in prison and the early termination of so many young black lives.[335]

Jackie Robinson
>To this day I have no idea what became of my father. Later, when I became aware of how much my mother had to endure alone, I could only think of him with bitterness. He, too, may have been a victim of oppression, but he had no right to desert my mother and five children.[336]

John W. Fountain
>But of all the things I experienced and of all the things I saw growing up, the most devastating thing that ever happened to me was growing up without a father.[337]

Alvin Ailey
>The inferiority complex that resulted from being a fatherless child never did go away.[338]

Kevin Powell, to his absentee father:
>She, in turn, took out her bitterness on me—with belts and switches, with extension cords, even with her bare hands. If she couldn't confront you, then I was an easy enough target. What I realize now is that my mother was no child abuser. She was a young woman forced to raise a strong-willed male

child alone after a man—you—had emotionally decimated her.[339]

How many Black boys and Black girls have had their emotional beings decimated by that father void? Certainly Tupac, and certainly me.[340]

Patrice Gaines
At the same time, I have seen girls who miss their fathers try loving their way into a man's heart. These young women are usually considered promiscuous, but I recognize them for what they are: lonely and fatherless.

Fathers are just as important to girls as to boys.[341]

Stephanie Gadlin, as a young girl:
But we had no phone number for Daddy. No address. If the house were to catch fire, we wouldn't know how to reach him, at all. What if something happened to Mama? What if something happened to me? Would he know? Would he come?

And I sometimes wondered if my father had found another daughter and if he loved her more than he loved me.[342]

Lolly Bowean
And everywhere I went I looked for him.

By age nine, I began preparing for the day I would see him again.

Since we didn't know each other, I neatly wrote a list of all my favorite things to help him learn about me. I had to rewrite it four times so there wouldn't be any mistakes. I attached my photo, so he'd know what I looked like and I was sure to tell him that my favorite color was blue.

Marriage

At first I kept the folder, tucked away in my dark blue book bag. I figured I'd offer it up to him, that day we ran into each other. Then I hung it on my bedroom wall, so it would be handy and available for that moment when I'd need it.

After a few weeks I surmised that he probably didn't care about that list. And then, each time I looked at it, I felt as if it were mocking me, reminding me that there was no daddy there to give it to. Eventually, I ripped it from the wall and threw it in the trash.[343]

Welfare continues to harm the black family.

John McWhorter

Welfare became a staple means of living in poor black America because of a deliberate effort to lasso onto the rolls blacks who had previously been under the impression that they were doing the right thing by working for a living.[344]

In other words, after welfare was expanded with poor blacks in mind, poor black fathers rarely helped rear their children, while mothers typically raised the children alone and in poverty, getting by on eagerly anticipated monthly checks from the government instead of working for a living.[345]

The men who created these children felt free to abandon their mates for the exact same reason—welfare ensured that the children would eat in any case, and thus marriage became beside the point.[346]

Welfare culture was the product of a system white leftists created that allowed blacks to realize the worst of human nature, in discouraging individual responsibility, the one thing that pushes most people to make the best of themselves.[347]

Man
I think that not being able to be independent and having to depend on these programs has ruined a lot of American Negroes. It keeps them from bettering their condition if they can halfway make it for nothing.

I don't care who you are, husband, wife, whoever you may be, there is nothing like having your own.

You need something or some way of achieving something for yourself in your lifetime.[348]

Jason L. Riley, on Democrat president Lyndon Johnson's "Great Society":
Marriage was penalized and single parenting was subsidized. In effect, the government paid mothers to keep fathers out of the home—and paid them well.[349]

Don Lemon
We've been giving people incentives to marry the government and allow men to abandon their financial and moral responsibility.[350]

Sylvia Ann Hewlett and **Cornel West:**
One thing we can be sure of: by encouraging out-of-wedlock births and discouraging marriage, welfare has encouraged fatherlessness among poor families.[351]

Marian Wright Edelman
More problematic is the effect of existing welfare rules on good marriages, because we often do not give welfare to two-parent families.

Sadly, the system seems to encourage family breakup as economic strains overwhelm family stability.[352]

Dorothy I. Height wrote of the "anti-family policies of public assistance agencies":
With every single mother struggling alone and in poverty, the Black community becomes weaker.[353]

Reverend Cecil Blye
The paradigm of government as parent has destroyed the black family and made black fatherhood irrelevant. Our welfare policies have incentivized co-habitation, single motherhood, and unemployment.[354]

Star Parker, as a young welfare mother:
"Let me make sure I understand you correctly," I inquired of the welfare caseworker as I presented her with my pregnancy confirmation note from a doctor. "All I have to do for you to send me $465 a month, $176 worth of food stamps, and 100 percent of free medical and dental assistance is keep this baby. As long as I don't have a bank account, find a job, or get married I qualify for aid? Where do I sign up?"[355]

Tammie Cathery
A year passed after I had my baby, and then I got my own apartment. Only if you had a child and you were a certain age could you get an apartment. So most people was like, well, sure, I'm having me a baby to get my own apartment.[356]

Thomas Sowell
America does not raise children. It has never raised children. And it is never going to raise children.[357]

Shelby Steele

No school that we ever create, no social program that we ever devise is ever going to be able to correct for the lack of a sound, solid family structure. So the family is the large problem.[358]

Without marriage and family, then we're consigning ourselves to decades of being at the bottom again.[359]

Until the 1960s, most black people married and raised their children in two-parent families.

Lerone Bennett Jr., in *Ebony*:

Most slaves lived in families headed by a father and a mother and "large numbers of slave couples lived in long marriages," some for 30 years or more.[360]

Farai Chideya

[M]ost current historians believe that the majority of black families during slavery were headed by two parents. Despite the fact that almost all slaves were forbidden to legally marry, and that countless families were broken up by slave trading, many men and women made commitments to each other in legally unrecognized ceremonies ("jumping the broom") and lived out their entire lives as "married" family units.

Until recently, married-couple families were the norm in the black community.[361]

Andrew Young

Slavery didn't break up the black families as much as liberal welfare rules.[362]

Thomas Sowell

The fact that so many black families today consist of women with fatherless children has been said by many to be a legacy of slavery. Yet most black children grew up in two-parent families, even under slavery itself, and for generations thereafter. As recently as 1960, two-thirds of black children were still living in two-parent families.[363]

Blaming social problems today on "a legacy of slavery" is another way of saying, "Don't blame our welfare state policies for things that got worse after those policies took over. Blame what happened in earlier centuries."[364]

Walter E. Williams

From 1890 to 1940, a slightly higher percentage of black adults had married than white adults.[365]

Earl Ofari Hutchinson

If a black man and woman could deal with each other when things were bad, then they can deal with each other now that things are relatively better and they have choices.[366]

Malcolm X's insight applies to a variety of achievements including marriage:

And you know that if you did it, you can do it again; you automatically get the incentive, the inspiration, and the energy necessary to duplicate what our forefathers formerly did.[367]

Secretary of State Colin L. Powell

We need to restore the social model of married parents bringing into the world a desired child, a child to be loved and nurtured, to be taught a sense of right and wrong, to be educated

Shared Values

to his or her maximum potential in a society that provides opportunities for work and a fulfilling life.[368]

Ossie Davis
I certainly hope that we do find a way for men and women to be together.[369]

Johnnetta B. Cole
I also know that when African Americans really want to do something, we are quite capable of figuring out the how.[370]

Joan Morgan
Perhaps one of the most revolutionary acts the hip-hop generation can accomplish is to establish healthy, loving, functional families.[371]

Voices in the popular media contend that black men and women don't like one another, that they can't get along. That idea is belied by the love they have consistently expressed for one another.

Charles Drew wrote to his future wife, Lenore Robbins, while work and college separated them:
Three things there are which are necessary for happiness—someone to love, to be loved by someone, and a job to do.

I love you, I miss you, I want you; the whole place is empty without you.[372]

Daphne Reid described her marriage to Tim Reid:
It's been the twenty-year ride of a lifetime, full of hard work, love, and laughter.[373]

Marriage

Jerald Wolff
I thank God daily for my wonderful wife.[374]

Jackie Robinson
When I was a student at the University of California, a friend introduced me to a pretty brown girl named Rachel Isum. Often now, I wonder where I would be in life and what would have happened to me if I hadn't met Rae—who is now Mrs. Jackie Robinson.

One thing I know for certain. I can't imagine how I would have made it through the bad days or the good if it hadn't been for the understanding, love and devotion she has given me down the years.[375]

There is so much that I owe to Rae that life without her just wouldn't seem to make sense. She has been my critic, my companion, my comforter and inspiration. She was the force behind my drive to make good in the world of sports and she is the force behind my drive today to make good in the world of business. She has been a sweet wife and loving mother to our three children.[376]

Terry English
My wife is simply the best thing to ever happen to me.[377]

Judge Lynn Toler, on being married to Eric Mumford:
We are together, and no one has gotten shot yet. We even have the nerve to be happy these days, more often than not. We talk more often and more effectively. We even smile and laugh fairly frequently. Do we still disagree? Absolutely. Are we certain that our marriage will survive? After Al and Tipper Gore? Are you kidding? No one can say that. But I will say this: the odds have turned in our favor. We are both hopeful, and hell-bent on giving it our best.[378]

Shared Values

Charley Pride, wrote of his wife Rozene as:
My loving, wonderful, understanding, and supportive wife—truly my best friend.[379]

Beth Martin, referring to her husband, John Martin:
We were working at Roy Rogers the year after high school. I saw him and got goose bumps. But it was more about who he was on the inside. He's a deep thinker. He's slow to anger. He wanted to be part of my life. He's got the greatest smile and the cutest butt; calf muscles to die for. He came down the steps recently, had on jeans and an undershirt with no sleeves, and he leaned on the bannister, and I was like, "Ahhhh. Take me. I'm yours."

We can't keep our hands off each other. Our children tell us, "Get a room." The older you get, the better it gets.[380]

Candy Carson, on her marriage to Ben:
Together, we've been through poverty, tragedy, disappointments, joy, successes, and wealth. Even when things have been hard, we've had each other's backs. I can't help but admire and cherish a man who always puts others first. I love this guy.[381]

Mayor David Dinkins, New York City:
I appreciate my family, especially my wife. She has tolerated me all these years. I love to tell the story about when I was mayor and we saw fellows digging a ditch. I said, "Joyce, isn't that the fellow you used to date?"

I'm not knocking ditch-digging. I have a dug ditches, worked in factories, parked cars, washed dishes, waited tables: I've had all kinds of jobs....

She said, "Yeah, as a matter of fact, it is."

I said, "See, if you'd married him, you'd be the wife of a ditch digger."

She said, "No, if I'd married him, *he'd* be mayor."[382]

Susan L. Taylor
Now I have a second chance at marriage. Khephra and I married in 1989. He's compassionate and kind, smart and reliable, the type of beautiful Black man I'd said I was preparing for.[383]

Ruby Dee, interviewed by Susan L. Taylor:
In the beginning of our marriage, Ossie would come home, sit down, kick off his shoes, and read the paper while I struggled with the dinner, the dishes and the babies. I was resentful knowing that he'd get another acting job, be around all these exciting people, and leave me with all the real work. But that resentment faded as we began to work out the details of our marriage. Ossie started pitching in and trying so hard to please me. He became an active husband, and he began to include me more when he got a job. He'd ask if there was a part for me. And when I got a job and he wasn't working, he'd say, "I'll stay here and take care of the children." Sometimes he'd say, "I'll go with you," and we'd take the children along. Ossie was marvelous with the children. He'd get up in the middle of the night to bring the babies to me for feedings, he'd wash diapers and take the children out on Sundays to give me a break.

I threatened to leave him once, and the next day he said to me, "Well, if you ever decide to go and marry somebody else, just tell him to make a space for me, because I'm coming with you."

When I feel like complaining, I remember how blessed I am to have been married to Ossie.

We just loved being together. When I wasn't working, I started going to work with him. I'd visit the set, and it was great being in hotels together. It was like our little honeymoon.

Shared Values

I still have him upstairs; Ossie was cremated. He just wanted an urn big enough for both of us.

Susan L. Taylor
What will you have inscribed on the urn?

Ruby Dee
"We're in this thing together." Ossie made that up.[384]

Couples who feel that marriage requires an expensive wedding ceremony could learn from these role models.

Kierna Mayo described the justice-of-the-peace wedding of Wendy Williams and Kevin Hunter:
After the ceremony, Hunter dropped her off at home and returned to work. She stayed in, had a solo reception with Chinese takeout and was perfectly content. She hadn't wanted a wedding; she wanted a marriage.[385]

Charley Pride married Rozene in 1956. After sixty years and three children, they are still going strong:
Rozene had a new dress and I was in full army uniform. With Hortense as our only witness, we were married in a short civil ceremony. There was not much of a honeymoon. I had only five dollars in my pocket and, besides, I had to be back at Fort Chaffee in a couple of days.[386]

Ruby Dee, on the beginning of her fifty-six-year marriage to Ossie Davis:
There was no big ceremony, no wedding gown, no church service, no pictures.

Marriage

After the "I promises," the "I do's," and the tears, the four of us got on a bus bound from Jersey City back to New York City.[387]

Five

Education

Republican View

Republicans see education as a key to upward mobility for all Americans.

Governor Chris Christie
> Education can be a great equalizer. It can make opportunity possible for you no matter where you're from, no matter where your family is from, no matter where you began economically. It can make a difference in your life, it can open doors.[388]

Republicans support the "school choice" innovations of charter schools and voucher programs. Charter schools are public schools that are free of many bureaucratic restraints. They can extend the instruction day, close underperforming schools, and replace incompetent teachers. Successful charter programs can be replicated. Vouchers are scholarships that enable low-income students to transfer from poor-quality public schools to private schools in which most students learn well.

Critics point out that choice programs yield mixed results for students in general. They neglect to say that charter schools and voucher programs are particularly beneficial to urban, low-income, minority students. They achieve at higher levels and go to college more often than their counterparts in regular public schools.

Martin R. West, professor of education, Harvard University:
[A]ttending a school of choice, whether private or charter, is especially beneficial for minority students living in urban areas.[389]

Mitchell D. Chester, Commissioner of Education, on research results:
They suggest that students in Massachusetts' charter middle and high schools often perform better academically than their peers in traditional public schools. The results are particularly large for students at charter middle schools and at schools located in urban areas, two areas where traditional public schools have found it most challenging to improve student performance.[390]

John Gabrieli, *Harvard Political Review*:
One hundred percent of third-graders at the Harlem Children's Zone Promise Academy I and II tested at or above grade level on the state math exam. One hundred percent of participants in high school after-school programs stayed in school. And 90 percent of the HCZ's high school graduates were accepted into college.[391]

Success Academies
For the seventh consecutive year, Success Academy Charter Schools have scored among the highest-performing schools in New York State. Five of the top ten schools in the state in math, and three of the top 20 schools in English, are Success Academy schools. Among the 3,065 scholars who were

age-eligible to take the tests, 93% were proficient in math and 68% proficient in ELA. In both subjects, students with disabilities and English Language Learners at Success Academy schools not only surpassed their peers statewide, but also outperformed students without disabilities and native English speakers, respectively, across New York.[392]

Knowledge is Power Program
As of spring 2015, 45 percent of KIPP students have earned a four-year college degree after finishing eighth grade at a KIPP middle school ten or more years ago. This is above the national average for all students (34 percent), and five times the rate of the average student from a low-income community (9 percent).[393]

Stephen Ford, on the DC Opportunity Scholarship Program:
Some 17,500 students have applied since 2004, and 6400 have received funds. Last year's graduation rate was 90%, compared to 58% at D.C. public schools in 2014. Of those graduates, 88% enrolled in a two- or four-year college.

The program this year spends up to $8,381 per elementary and middle-school student and $12,572 per high school student, less than half of what the district spends on each public-school student.[394]

The movies *Waiting for Superman*, *The Lottery*, and *Won't Back Down* tell the story of school choice.

Corporate and Wall Street leaders provide generous support to choice programs.[395] In contrast, Occupy Wall Street protesters are not known to have given anything to help minority students.

Republicans have criticized Democrats' opposition to school choice.

William McGurn
> In New York City, Mayor Bill de Blasio does everything he can to keep failing traditional public schools from closing down—while also doing everything he can to block successful charters from opening or expanding. He's been especially vindictive toward the Success Academies run by Eva Moskowitz. Maybe it's because each day her charters prove that black children can achieve if they have schools that set high standards and let the kids know there's nothing they can't accomplish if only they work hard enough.[396]

Carly Fiorina, on Eric Holder's Justice Department:
> In Louisiana, this administration sued to shut down a program that allowed students to leave their failing public school. That's right. They sued to put disadvantaged kids back into schools that they knew were failing.[397]

John Steele Gordon
> One of the first things President Obama tried to do as president was end the school voucher program in Washington, D.C., as a thank you to the teachers' unions, while sending his two daughters to a very expensive, and very good, private school: welcome to modern-day liberalism.[398]

Republicans' enthusiasm for parental choice systems is based, in part, on their knowledge of what doesn't work. They know that beyond a certain point, spending more doesn't significantly enhance learning.

Eric A. Hanushek, Stanford University:
> Differences in student performance are not driven by national levels of school spending.[399]

Naomi Schaefer Riley

From 1970 to 2010, federal spending on education has roughly tripled (adjusted for inflation), while reading, math, and science achievement have stagnated or declined.[400]

CBS News

The United States routinely trails its rival countries in performances on international exams despite being among the heaviest spenders on education.[401]

Wall Street Journal Editorial Board

Teachers are also comparatively well compensated. The Illinois State Board of Education says the average Chicago teacher salary is about $71,000 a year. That compares to Chicago's median salary of $47,270 in 2009-2013, according to the Census Bureau. The average starting pension for a Chicago teacher retiring in 2011 after a public-school career was $77,496, according to the Illinois Policy Institute.[402]

Americans are fair and generous in funding schools that have high percentages of African American students. For example, US Census data show that the three highest ranked states for funding per pupil in 2013 all have substantial African American populations: 1. Washington, DC $29,427; 2. New York $22,587; and 3. New Jersey $20,191. The lowest ranked states all have minimal African American student populations: 49. Arizona $8,599; 50. Utah $7,650; and 51. Idaho $7,408.[403] Baltimore spends more per pupil than schools in wealthy, neighboring Fairfax County and in schools throughout Maryland.[404]

Linda Chavez

A recent General Accountability Office study found no consistent pattern of underfunded city schools. Boston, Chicago, and St. Louis, for example, spend more to educate their mostly black and Latino student populations than do the surrounding suburbs with their largely white student populations.[405]

Naomi Schaefer Riley
As of 2011, Newark, New Jersey spent more than $23,000 per student. What could a mother in Newark do if you handed her $23,000 and asked her to buy the best education she could for her son? Well, the annual tuition at nearby Seton Hall Prep, where 99 percent of the 2011 graduates went to college, is less than $15,000. Seniors there were accepted that year at MIT, Duke, Princeton, Harvard, and the U.S. Naval Military Academy. Mom's only question would be what to do with the extra $8000.[406]

Preschool learning is crucial to child development. But the most effective preschool educators are parents and other family members who talk to, listen to, play with, hug, and kiss their young children. Early childhood education programs such as Head Start do not improve learning.[407]

David J. Armor and **Sonia Sousa**, George Mason University:
The Head Start program has been evaluated using the most sophisticated research designs available to social scientists, and the results have been disappointing. While Head Start appears to produce modest positive effects during the preschool years, these effects do not last even into kindergarten, much less through the early elementary years.[408]

Joe Klein, TIME Magazine:
According to the Head Start Impact Study, which was quite comprehensive, the positive effects of the program were minimal and vanished by the end of first grade.

Head Start simply does not work.[409]

Teachers' unions lead the opposition to charter schools and voucher programs. But criticism of the unions is not criticism of every teacher.

Governor Jeb Bush
> While the nation is blessed with many dedicated and quality teachers whose efforts to educate our children are heroic, the union bosses that represent them are an impediment to the reforms we need to improve our public education system.[410]

An expansion of charter schools and voucher programs would be constructive, but in the face of Democrats' opposition, change is coming far too slowly. Children raised in married-couple families have learned well, regardless of the quality of their schools.

US secretary of education William J. Bennett
> Not all teachers are parents, but all parents are teachers, the all but indispensable teachers. And as teachers, parents always have had the first and largest responsibility for educating their children.[411]

Democrat View

Democrats' concern for American students is compromised by their loyalty to teachers' unions. They support the unions because the unions support them. The American Federation of Teachers endorsed Secretary Clinton's campaign for president, is giving her millions of dollars, and plans to call voters and visit their homes to speak on her behalf.[412] The National Education Association, with three million members, also backs Clinton.[413]

Democrat politicians endorse higher pay for teachers, better pensions, more hires, and tenure laws that keep incompetent instructors

Education

in the classroom. They also protect teachers from the competition of choice programs.

Sam Ford, *WJLA*, on the DC Opportunity Scholarship Program:
>At the Obama administration's urging, Congress agreed in 2009 to phase out the program.[414]

President Barack Obama, speaking to Bill O'Reilly:
>Actually, every study that's been done on school vouchers, Bill, says that it has very limited impact if any.
>
>As a general proposition, vouchers has not significantly improved the performance of kids that are in these poorest communities.[415]

US senator Bernie Sanders described vouchers as he understands them:
>Wealthy parents can use the money to reduce their tuition costs at prep schools.[416]
>
>I think rather than give tax breaks to billionaires, I think we invest in teachers and we invest in public education.[417]

Secretary of State Hillary Clinton apparently opposes charter schools.[418] She said that she would fight voucher systems "with every breath in my body."[419] She explained her objection to giving children scholarships to private schools:
>So what if the next parent comes and says, "I want to send my child to the School of the Jihad?"…I won't stand for it.[420]

Louisiana governor John Bel Edwards, on the state's voucher program:
>We should not divert any resources away from our traditional public schools for unproven gimmicks, especially when we don't have many resources to begin with.[421]

Shared Values

Debbie Meaux, president of the Louisiana teachers' union, referring to Governor Edwards:
> It's not every day that education can say we have a champion in the Governor's Mansion, but today we certainly do.[422]

Left-leaning media organizations join Democrats in rejecting charter schools and vouchers.

Diane Ravitch, in the *New York Review of Books*, reviewing *Waiting for Superman*:
> But contrary to the myth that Guggenheim propounds about "amazing results," even Geoffrey Canada's schools have many students who are not proficient.[423]

Joy Resmovits, in *The Huffington Post*:
> The study reaches the same broad conclusions as the study four years ago: performance of charter school students is extremely varied, but on average, students learn at roughly the same rates as their public school peers.[424]

Democrats believe that the key to better student achievement, from preschool to college, is spending more money. They see the American people as unwilling to spend for the public good.

President Barack Obama
> A free market is perfectly compatible with also us making investment in good public schools, public universities; investments in public parks; investments in a whole bunch—public infrastructure that grows our economy and spreads it around. But that's, in part, what's been under attack for the last 30 years.
>
> And we have not been willing, I think, to make some of those common investments so that everybody can play a part in getting opportunity.

We're going to argue hard for early childhood education because, by the way, if a young kid—three, four years old—is hearing a lot of words, the science tells us that they're going to be more likely to succeed at school. And if they've got trained and decently paid teachers in that preschool, then they're actually going to get—by the time they're in third grade, they'll be reading at grade level.

But it requires some money.

And that's where we, as a society, have the capacity to make a real difference. But it will cost us some money. It will cost us some money. It's not free.[425]

⸻

From the time when learning to read was severely punished, black Americans have valued reading, learning, and knowing.

Frederick Douglass, 1852:
> I have been a slave, and could learn but little, when a slave, of what was going on in this country and world about me. A slave prison is worse than a States prison. In the States prison a man may know something and think something of the past; but the inmates of the slave prison know nothing of the past, present or future.[426]

Carl T. Rowan
> He who would be free must first destroy the basic enemy of liberty—ignorance.[427]

Pam Grier
> We all know that being educated is the only way to be free in this world.[428]

Shared Values

Reverend Claude C. Brown
You cannot free an ignorant, unskilled man because just as soon as you remove the shackles, somebody else will come along and place new shackles on him.[429]

Booker T. Washington
Education is the sole and only hope of the Negro race in America.[430]

US Surgeon General Joycelyn Elders
We cannot keep a person healthy, if she or he is not educated.[431]

Barbara M. Dixon
Education has been the key to progress for all oppressed peoples.[432]

Glenn C. Loury
[B]y far the greater progress has been made among those blacks with the most education.[433]

Ron Christie
I believe education is the civil rights issue of the twenty-first century.[434]

Tavis Smiley
There is no better preparation for life than a quality education.[435]

Malcolm X
Without education, you are not going anywhere in this world.[436]

Education

Rosemary L. Bray, raised in poverty, a Yale University alumna, referring to her parents:
> She and my father reminded us again and again that every book, every test, every page of homework was in fact a ticket out and away from the life we lived.[437]

US representative Shirley Chisholm
> Buying a house had always been my parent's second great goal; an education for their children was the only thing that mattered more to them.[438]

J. L. Chestnut Jr., attorney, civil rights activist:
> When I was going into the second grade, the school ran out of spelling books. My mother borrowed somebody's and copied it all by hand.[439]

Muhammad Ali
> I had a strong foundation growing up; my parents were loving, affectionate people. Ever since I can remember, my father was always hugging and kissing us. He would say "give me those jaws" (his term for kissing our cheeks). Then he kissed us until our cheeks turned red.[440]

Greg Mathis and his mother reacted to receiving his college acceptance letter:
> We knelt in the middle of the living room floor and bowed our heads, giving thanks to God. Mama kept smiling and shaking her head, as if in a state of disbelief. Then the tears started flowing down her cheeks.
>
> "Lord have mercy. Lord have mercy. I don't believe it. I just don't believe it. Thank you, Jesus, thank you, Jesus."[441]

Shared Values

Reverend Eugene Rivers
My wife specializes in math education, and after 20 years of doing community organizing she says the single most important factor shaping the academic achievement of the child is the family and the culture produced by the family. It is not per capita expenditures on public schools; it's about what families do with their children. Stable families produce better, higher-achieving students than families that are broken. [442]

Thomas Sowell, on educational spending:
A ton of evidence suggests the amount of money really doesn't make much difference.[443]

Walter E. Williams
Today, expenditures per pupil in the United States exceed those of nearly every other country in the world.

The most crucial input for a child's education cannot be provided by schools, politicians and government. As such, continued calls for more school resources will produce disappointing results as they have in the past. There are certain minimum requirements that must be met for any child to do well in school. Someone must make the youngster do his homework, ensure that he gets eight to nine hours of sleep, feed him breakfast and make sure that he behaves in school and respects the teachers. If these minimum requirements are not met, and by the way they can be met even if a family is poor, all else is for naught.[444]

Venus Williams, with a message to teens:
Serena and I believe there's nothing more important in life than getting a good education. We want you to become so

determined to learn that you don't allow anyone or anything to come between you and your schoolwork—not your parents' personal problems, not teachers who don't care, or raggedy classrooms and books, not sports practice or big games, not being tempted by your boyfriend or girlfriend, not bullies, not a long bus or train ride, not the snow or wind or rain.[445]

The more you learn, the better your future will be and the more choices you'll have. Education will make such a positive difference in the quality of your life that you shouldn't sacrifice it for anyone.[446]

Serena Williams
When we're off the court, being well educated helps us handle our business dealings.[447]

Venus Williams
But if your acquaintances tell you that the things you're learning in class won't make a difference to your future, or if they tease you for being smart or studying hard, it's time to kick them to the curb. Take it from us: they don't know what they're talking about.[448]

Earvin "Magic" Johnson Jr.
If you're ambitious, if you study hard, if your goals are high, some people may tell you you're "acting white." Stay away from those people! They are not your friends.[449]

In addition to the practical benefits, African Americans have recognized the pleasures of reading and learning.

Shared Values

Frances Jackson Coppin, 1913:
> Our idea of getting an education did not come out of wanting to imitate anyone whatever. It grew out of the uneasiness and the restlessness of the desires we felt within us; the desire to know, not just a little, but a great deal. We wanted to know how to calculate an eclipse, to know what Hesiod and Livy thought; we wished to know the best thoughts of the best minds that lived with us; not merely to gain an honest livelihood, but from a God-given love of all that is beautiful and best, and because we thought we could do it.[450]

Neil DeGrasse Tyson
> I learned that light, traveling at 186,282 miles per second, moves too slowly to escape from the event horizon of a black hole. That was more astonishing to me than a 360-degree slam dunk. I soon became scientifically curious and read everything I could find about the universe.[451]

Malcolm X
> I have often reflected upon the new vistas that reading opened to me. I knew right there in prison that reading had changed forever the course of my life. As I see it today, the ability to read awoke inside me some long dormant craving to be mentally alive.[452]

Oprah Winfrey
> Reading gave me hope.[453]

Richard Wright
> But when no one was looking I would slip into Ella's room and steal a book and take it back of the barn and try to read it. Usually I could not decipher enough words to make the story have meaning. I burned to learn to read novels and I tortured my mother into telling me the meaning of every strange word

Education

I saw, not because the word itself had value, but because it was the gateway to a forbidden and enchanting land.[454]

It had been my accidental reading of fiction and literary criticism that had evoked in me vague glimpses of life's possibilities.[455]

Langston Hughes
I was reading Shopenhauer and Nietzsche, and Edna Ferber and Dreiser, and de Maupassant in French. I never will forget the thrill of first understanding the French of de Maupassant. The soft snow was falling through one of his stories in the little book we used in school, and that I had worked over so long, before I really felt the snow falling there. Then all of a sudden one night the beauty and the meaning of the words in which he made the snow fall, came to me. I think it was de Maupassant who made me really want to be a writer and write stories about Negroes, so true that people in faraway lands would read them—even after I was dead.[456]

Johnnetta Cole, as a college student, discovering anthropology:
I walked into a course that changed my life.

But it was in that extraordinary moment of intellectual excitement that I discovered a field that has become, not just a way that I make a living, but a way that I carry out my life.[457]

Pearl Bailey began and completed college when she was a mature, successful entertainer:
School was my love…[458]

Venus Williams
I just love books.[459]

Shared Values

Young man, recent college graduate:
 I never liked reading growing up. For some reason, I thought it was so difficult to find something that I was interested in reading. But now I do. Reading makes me feel smart.[460]

Talib Kweli
 Education is the key to a wonderful life.[461]

Reading, studying, and learning provide more than just useful information and pleasure, they are also a way to avoid the pain of failure in school.

Woody Strode
 Well, you talk about getting roughed up: they gave me Spanish, Geometry, Physics and Algebra and I flunked them all. I remember sitting in Algebra class thinking I was flunking Spanish.[462]

African Americans join Republicans in wanting all children to have full educational opportunities, including access to private and charter schools.

Secretary of State Condoleezza Rice
 The Republican Party is more the party of education reform and school choice and giving parents a chance to get poor kids out of failing neighborhood public schools, not defending poor teachers, not defending union policies that in California were found actually to be a violation of children's civil rights.

 Poor black kids trapped in failing neighborhoods' schools, that's the biggest race problem of today. That's the biggest civil rights issue of today.[463]

Geoffrey Canada, on students at his Harlem Children's Zone charter school:
> These kids are going to graduate, they are going to college, they are going to have a good life and their children are going to have a good life.[464]

Thomas Sowell, on charter schools:
> These schools have given thousands of low income minority children their only shot at a decent education, which often means their only shot at a decent life. Last year 82 percent of the students at a charter school called Success Academy passed city-wide mathematics exams, compared to 30 percent of the students in the city as a whole.[465]
>
> If anyone wanted to pick a time and place where the political left's avowed concern for minorities was definitively exposed as a fraud, it would be now—and the place would be New York City, where far left Mayor Bill de Blasio has launched an attack on charter schools, cutting their funding, among other things.[466]
>
> So long as public schools are treated as places that exist to provide guaranteed jobs to members of the teachers' unions, do not be surprised to see American students continuing to score lower on international tests than students in countries that spend a lot less per pupil than we do.[467]

Anthony Sanchez, whose son began learning more effectively after he switched to a charter school:
> Right now, my son is growin' up and he's very happy with school, he loves school, he loves his teachers. It's beautiful, it's beautiful for me as a parent.[468]

Jason L. Riley
In fact, study after study using gold-standard, random-assignment methodology has shown that vouchers not only improve student outcomes but have the biggest impact on low-income minorities.[469]

Shawnee Jackson, a DC Opportunity Scholarship Program graduate, high school valedictorian, and now a biology major in college, said that without the scholarship:
I wouldn't be where I am now. It has opened doors for me and can open doors for others.[470]

Denisha Merriweather
By the time I was in the fourth grade, I had been held back twice, disliked school, and honestly believed I'd end up a high-school dropout. Instead, three months ago, I earned a bachelor's degree from the University of West Florida in interdisciplinary social science with a minor in juvenile justice. I am the first member of my family to go to college, let alone graduate. But this didn't happen by chance, or by hard work alone. It happened because I was given an opportunity.

The difference maker was a scholarship that allowed me to go to a secondary school that was the right fit for me. I was lucky to be raised in Florida, home to the nation's largest tax-credit scholarship program, a "voucher" program that helps parents pay for private schools.[471]

Denisha Merriweather said of Florida governor Jeb Bush, Republican:
He was the first candidate for governor in any state with the courage to openly run on a platform of school choice.[472]

Denisha Merriweather speaks here.[473]

Joseph Kelly, on the DC public school that his son Rashawn left, by having a voucher:
> When I walked in the door, outside were two police cars, and that was everyday routine for that school. There was violence. Fighting. Disrespect and drugs. No discipline whatsoever, just chaos.
>
> When I complained to the principal about the chaos, she shook her finger at me and lectured, "Mr. Kelley, don't tell me how to run my school."[474]

Mother of a girl who attends a private school with a voucher:
> I have an 8-year-old in third grade, and she's doing great. It's miraculous the way she has changed.[475]

Anthony Samuels, voucher recipient and college student:
> If more people would get the opportunity I was given, the world would be a better place.[476]

As a girl, Virginia Walden Ford made history by heroically integrating the Little Rock school system. Today, as a parent, she leads the Black Alliance for Educational Options and the DC Parents for School Choice.

Virginia Walden Ford
> When segregationist politicians blocked schoolhouse entrances, they wanted to keep minority children out to deny them a quality education. Today, as anti-voucher politicians block schoolhouse exits, they want to keep minority children in—again denying them a quality education, condemning them to a life of lost opportunities and unfulfilled dreams.
>
> Lack of school choice is a new kind of segregation, one based on economics. Affluent parents have choices about where their kids attend school, while poor parents have none. Vouchers help to address this inequity.[477]

Shared Values

The idea that some people would force kids to stay in failing public schools makes no sense. School choice provides opportunities for children to get a quality education.[478]

President Obama and Secretary Duncan need to face the cameras today and explain to D.C. families why they seek to end one of the most successful federally-funded education programs.[479]

Carlos Battle, DC voucher recipient and college student, on political opposition to the DC program:
> I've come so far from when I was in the sixth grade to now and you're trying to take this all away from us. I don't understand why you would take something away that is legitimately helping.[480]

Kevin P. Chavous
> What is behind the growing dissatisfaction with the national Democratic Party among minorities? One explanation is that Democrats are not offering any new solutions to a problem that many minority voters—particularly in the black community—care deeply about: fixing our failing schools.
>
> Prominent Republicans in the 2016 race already have demonstrated a commitment to discussing these issues and some, such as former Florida Gov. Jeb Bush and Wisconsin Gov. Scott Walker, have built credible education reform records that underscore their positions.[481]

Jonathan Capehart
> Vouchers are anathema to the teachers union and to the Democratic Party pols who depend on the union for support.[482]

The following conversation is from the Fox News program, *The Five*:

Kimberly Guilfoyle

[A]re Democrats hurting our kids by putting unions ahead of education?

Juan Williams

As a lifelong Democrat, a minority, I'm looking into this camera, and I'm challenging President Obama, Hillary Clinton, Elizabeth Warren and the rest of the Democrats to stop favoring unions, start favoring what's best for our kids. Republicans have long supported the idea of school choice.

This is a civil rights issue of this generation. If you deny someone a good education, you can talk about Ferguson. You can talk about whatever you want. You can talk about affirmative action. If the guy can't do the job, if he's not educated, what are you going to stand up and fight for? You've got to fight for education first. Democrats, wake up to it.

Dana Perino

So why don't the Democrats take this issue and run with it?

Juan Williams

You're setting me up because you know that the unions, especially teachers unions, put big money into the party.

Eric Bolling

Service employees at SEIU, $209 million; ACT Blue, $146 million; NEA, $89 million.

Greg Gutfeld

Why are liberals pro-choice when it comes to preventing life but anti-choice when it comes to enhancing it?[483]

Six

WORK

Republican View

Republicans appreciate that businesses create products, services, and jobs. The tax payments of businesses and workers enable the government to provide the military, schools, roads, and a safety net for those in need. Without business success, the money that the government prints would be worthless—otherwise poor countries would print themselves into prosperity.

Contrary to allegations from the left, entrepreneurs who become very rich do not take from the poor. They create wealth for others. The business activities of Magic Johnson, Jeff Bezos, Andre Young (a.k.a. Dr. Dre), Steve Jobs, and Robert L. Johnson improved the lives of countless individuals and families.

Stephen Moore
> It is estimated that Bill Gates alone, whose personal wealth is estimated at $50 billion, is responsible for making over ten thousand people millionaires, including former Microsoft secretaries.[484]

Business people tend to be charitable. Oprah Winfrey gives millions through her Oprah Winfrey Foundation, Angel Network, O Ambassadors, The US Dream Academy, and other initiatives.[485] The Koch brothers give to hospitals and medical research, education including the United Negro College Fund, public television and radio, environmental stewardship, criminal justice reform, and the arts.[486]

Thanks to the success of business men and women, Americans have a higher standard of living than people in most countries. The Wall Street financial industry facilitates that success by bringing people with business proposals and investors together.

Arthur C. Brooks
> A thriving economy creates jobs for all kinds of people at all levels of education and experience.[487]
>
> Only a culture of opportunity, fueled with a policy agenda of education reform, private job creation, and entrepreneurship, can truly set people up to flourish.[488]

Andy Puzder, chief executive officer, CKE Restaurants:
> Jobs, salaries and benefits increase when businesses thrive. If you want to give working-class Americans a path to the middle class, adopt policies that free up the businesses who want to hire them.[489]

John Mackey, cofounder and co-CEO, Whole Foods:
> Profits ultimately create all growth, capital, and prosperity.[490]

Governor Rick Perry, whose one state, Texas, created 30 percent of all American jobs during his fifteen years in office:
> A growing economy will give those at the bottom of the ladder more opportunities to climb, just as it has in Texas.

The only true cure for poverty is a job, and Democratic policies have made it too hard for the poor to find work.[491]

US senator Ted Cruz
We should set an audacious goal of enacting policies to encourage the private sector to create 10 million new jobs. Enough for full recovery. Good, blue-collar jobs with strong wages and work with dignity. High-paying white-collar jobs in expanding technologies. Full-time jobs, not people trapped in endless part-time positions. Multiple, exciting job opportunities for young people coming out of school. Get government out of the way and unleash the creativity of millions of small businesses.[492]

Carly Fiorina
A job unlocks human potential. When young people ask me what it takes to get ahead, I tell them to get a job, any job, because there is dignity in all work. When someone has a job, they not only have a sense of purpose, they learn the habits and skills necessary to get a better job. When politicians fail to emphasize jobs and work, they aren't being compassionate. They are wasting human potential.[493]

Milton Friedman
The great achievements of civilization have not come from government bureaus. Einstein didn't construct his theory under order from a bureaucrat. Henry Ford didn't revolutionize the automobile industry that way. In the only cases in which the masses have escaped from the kind of grinding poverty you're talking about, the only cases in recorded history are where they have had capitalism and largely free trade. If you want to know where the masses are worst off, it's exactly in the kinds of societies that depart from that. So that the record of history is absolutely crystal-clear that there is no alternative way, so far discovered, of improving the lot of the ordinary

people that can hold a candle to the productive activities that are unleashed by a free enterprise system.[494]

Nitin Nohria
The finance industry is essential to the nation's economic health and an integral part of what makes the U.S. economy the envy of the world.[495]

Bret Stephens
Wall Street remains one of America's crowning glories.[496]

Republicans understand that low tax rates foster business creation and expansion. But our current exceptionally high corporate tax rates persuade businesses to move out of the United States.[497] The high rates on individuals also stifle growth.[498]

James Piereson
According to the Congressional Budget Office, the top 1 percent of earners paid 39 percent of the personal income taxes in 2010 (while earning 15 percent of the country's overall before-tax income) compared with just 17 percent in 1980 and 24 percent in 1990. The top 20 percent of earners paid 93 percent of the federal income taxes in 2010 even though they claimed 52 percent of before-tax income.[499]

Grover Norquist
Every time we've cut the capital gains tax, the economy has grown. Whenever we raise the capital gains tax, it's been damaged. It's one of those taxes that most clearly damages economic growth and jobs.[500]

Ira Stoll, author of *JFK, Conservative*:
When Kennedy and Reagan lowered the top marginal tax rates, the economy boomed.[501]

Shared Values

President John F. Kennedy, speaking in an era when Democrats supported business growth:
> The purpose of cutting taxes now is not to incur a budget deficit, but to achieve the more prosperous, expanding economy which can bring a budget surplus.[502]

> It is a paradoxical truth that tax rates are too high today, and tax revenues are too low and the soundest way to raise the revenues in the long run is to cut the tax rates...[A]n economy constrained by high tax rates will never produce enough revenue to balance the budget, just as it will never create enough jobs or enough profits.[503]

Edwin J. Feulner Jr., on President Reagan's tax cuts:
> The Economic Recovery Tax Act of 1981 sparked the longest period of peacetime economic growth in US history, lasting more than two decades.[504]

Governor Haley Barbour, on Reagan's tax cuts:
> Through compromise, he got Congress to pass the Reagan economic plan that tamed high inflation and astronomical interest rates while launching a quarter century of economic growth not just in the United States but across the globe.[505]

Clyde Wayne Crews
> Federal regulation and intervention cost American consumers and businesses an estimated $1.88 trillion in 2014 in lost economic productivity and higher prices.[506]

Walter Russell Mead
> Worse than all this, small business is crushed by high taxes, intrusive and often irrational regulation, which means that new jobs aren't created and new businesses don't start. That reduces demand for workers in the neighborhoods that need

jobs most; it also curtails the ability of inner city residents to develop the entrepreneurial skills and experience that could fuel the rebirth of the Black middle class.[507]

Donald Trump, on his tax plan:
Our current tax code actually discourages business growth and penalizes success. Too many companies, from our biggest brands to innovative startups, are moving their headquarters out of the country, either directly or through corporate inversions.

It makes a lot more sense to create an environment that welcomes business.[508]

In recent decades, pro-business policies in China and India have enabled hundreds of millions of people to rise out of poverty.

The Economist, on China's economic growth:
Between 1981 and 2010 it lifted a stunning 680 million people out of poverty—more than the entire current population of Latin America. This cut its poverty rate from 84% in 1980 to about 10% now.[509]

Dinesh D'Souza
Beyond the economic gain, the ordinary person in China, India, and other emerging countries now has an increased sense of self-worth and possibility. The future no longer looks like a bleak replica of the past. So these are not only material improvements, they are also moral gains.... Technological capitalism has proven to be the greatest anti-poverty scheme ever invented.[510]

John Mackey and **Raj Sisodia**:
In the long arc of history, no human creation has had a greater positive impact on more people more rapidly than free-enterprise capitalism.

> It created a large and prosperous middle class, belying the current inaccurate critique that free-enterprise capitalism necessarily concentrates wealth among a privileged few at the expense of everyone else.[511]
>
> Free-enterprise capitalism has created prosperity not just for a few, but for billions of people everywhere.[512]

Larry Kudlow
> Free market capitalism is the best path to prosperity.[513]

Arthur C. Brooks
> Capitalism has saved a couple of billion people and we have treated this miracle like a state secret.[514]

Republicans are in favor of capitalism, business success, and economic growth. They reject Democrats' acceptance of a "new normal" of economic stagnation and a lower standard of living.[515] They are confident in the American people and our ability to return to prosperity.

Rush Limbaugh
> I reject the notion that America is in a well-deserved decline, that she and her citizens are unexceptional. I do not believe America is the problem in the world. I believe America is the solution to the world's problems.[516]

Democrat View

Democrats sometimes speak positively about businesses, economic growth, profits, jobs, and capitalism, but they often sound like they don't mean it.

Secretary of State Hillary Clinton
Like my father, I support capitalism and the free market system. But I also know that every human endeavor is vulnerable to error, incompetence, corruption, and the abuse of power.[517]

They speak as if they aren't very concerned about poverty–they care more about inequality. Their response to unequal incomes is redistribution: raising taxes on the rich and businesses, then supposedly giving the money to the poor. This taking from one and promising to give to another is similar to the socialist ideal of: "From each according to his ability, to each according to his needs." Unfortunately, their policies have worsened inequality.

Apparently, both senator Bernie Sanders and New York City mayor Bill de Blasio are socialists.[518]

Howard Zinn, historian, 2000:
I still consider myself a socialist.[519]

Garrison Keillor sees Franklin Delano Roosevelt's Democrat policies as "good old American socialism."[520]

Democrats admire Scandinavian socialism. But those nations are neither as successful nor as socialist as claimed.[521] And although socialism is promoted as a system of sharing, which is an appealing idea, it has often brought tyranny and death. Joseph Stalin's socialism killed millions.[522] Chairman Mao starved tens of millions to death.[523] Racism and genocide were central to Hitler's national socialism, called Nazism.[524] The Castro brothers' socialism impoverishes Cubans and oppresses dissenters, blacks, and homosexuals.[525]

In the mid-1970s, pro-business policies had Venezuela thriving while socialism was impoverishing Chile. Then the two countries switched economic policies. Now Chile is prospering and masses of Venezuelans are looting to obtain bags of rice.[526]

Shared Values

Winston Churchill
   The inherent vice of capitalism is the unequal sharing of blessings; the inherent virtue of socialism is the equal sharing of miseries.[527]

Alan Charles Kors
   No cause, ever, in the history of all mankind, has produced more cold-blooded tyrants, more slaughtered innocents, and more orphans than socialism with power. It surpassed, exponentially, all other systems of production in turning out the dead.[528]

Democrats speak as if they dislike Wall Street, corporations, profits, and successful business people.

US senator Bernie Sanders called Wall Street the "most dangerous"[529] entity in our country:
   Let us wage a moral and political war against the billionaires and corporate leaders, on Wall Street and elsewhere, whose policies and greed are destroying the middle class of America.[530]

Secretary of State Hillary Clinton, responding to a question from Dana Bash:
   I spoke out against Wall Street when I was a Senator from New York.[531]

US senator Elizabeth Warren, on the anti-capitalist Occupy Wall Street movement:
   I created much of the intellectual foundation for what they do. I support what they do.[532]

First Lady Michelle Obama, expressing the value that she shares with her husband and many Democrats:
   We left corporate America, which is a lot of what we're asking young people to do. Don't go into corporate America.[533]

Naomi Klein
I think that capitalism increasingly is a discredited system because it is seen as a system that venerates greed above all else.

I don't know why it is so important to save capitalism.[534]

Michael Moore sees capitalism as "evil":
Capitalism is against the things that we say we believe in—democracy, freedom of choice, fairness. It's not about any of those things now. It's about protecting the wealthy and legalizing greed.[535]

I don't think you can reform capitalism at this point because it's become so bastardized to the point where it's only purpose is to protect the wealthy and legalize our greed. We need to come up with a 21st century idea.[536]

Secretary of State Clinton portrays business leaders as exceptionally greedy, claiming they make three hundred times as much as workers.[537] But the Bureau of Labor Statistics reported that the average CEO makes $216,100 per year, only 4.4 times as much as the average worker. Secretary Clinton earned more than most CEOs with each of her $275,000 Wall Street speeches.[538]

US senator Carl Levin and other Democrats refer to profits in general and especially oil company profits as "obscene" and "excessive."[539] Now that the price of oil has decreased, those companies have become less profitable. They are laying off workers. Middle class people who own shares in oil company stocks through retirement plans are losing their savings.[540] Low profits hurt the American people.

Democrat politicians have been hostile to Walmart, for instance, by banning their stores from New York City.[541] Walmart provides jobs for 1.4 million American workers (plus more in ancillary companies) and saves the average household $2300 per year.[542] It is a

Shared Values

strong supporter of the educational reforms that serve minority children. African American Rosalind G. Brewer is president and CEO of Walmart's Sam's Club. But none of that is good enough for Democrats.

New York City Councilman Charles Barron, to Walmart:
>Don't even think about coming into East New York. We're desperate for jobs, but we're not going to take anything.[543]

Secretary of State Hillary Clinton
>[W]e're going to put a lot of coal miners and coal companies out of business.[544]

Democrats perpetually want to raise taxes. They talk about taxing the rich, but they have been raising everyone's taxes.[545]

Vice President Joseph Biden
>Let me tell you something man, the tax code's not fair, it's simply not fair. The wealthy aren't paying their fair share.[546]

Governor Howard Dean
>No matter what people said during the election, you cannot solve this deficit problem without everybody paying more taxes. Not just rich people.[547]

Vice President Al Gore
>But from the very beginning, I preferred a carbon tax.[548]

Presidential candidate Hillary Clinton, who plans to raise taxes by a trillion dollars over ten years:
>We're going to take things away from you on behalf of the common good.[549]

Senator Bernie Sanders
> We will raise taxes, yes, we will.[550]

Sanders is proposing $18 trillion in tax increases.[551]

Alan Cole and **Scott Greenberg**, at the Tax Foundation, on Sanders's tax plan:
> On a static basis, the plan would lead to 10.56 percent lower after-tax income for all taxpayers and 17.91 percent lower after-tax income for the top 1 percent. When accounting for reduced GDP, after-tax incomes of all taxpayers would fall by at least 12.84 percent.[552]

Democrats see the government as deserving much of the credit for the things that business people produce.

US senator Elizabeth Warren
> There is nobody in this country who got rich on his own. Nobody. You built a factory out there—good for you! But I want to be clear. You moved your goods to market on the roads the rest of us paid for. You hired workers the rest of us paid to educate. You were safe in your factory because of police forces and fire forces that the rest of us paid for. You didn't have to worry that marauding bands would come and seize everything at your factory, and hire someone to protect against this, because of the work the rest of us did.[553]

President Barack Obama
> If you were successful, somebody along the line gave you some help. There was a great teacher somewhere in your life. Somebody helped to create this unbelievable American system

Shared Values

that we have that allowed you to thrive. Somebody invested in roads and bridges. If you've got a business, you didn't build that. Somebody else made that happen.[554]

Secretary of State Hillary Clinton
Don't let anybody tell you that it's corporations and businesses that create jobs.[555]

From this perspective, all of these creative business people owe government officials a debt of gratitude: Mark Zuckerberg for Facebook, Harold Schultz for Starbucks, Sara Blakely for Spanx, NBA players for the Alley-Oop shot, and hip hop people for the rhymes, beats, dance moves, art, and clothing.

Democrats acted on their belief in government by passing a $787 billion stimulus bill. It was targeted at improving our infrastructure, but it left some roads and bridges in bad shape. It contributed to increasing our national debt from $10 trillion to $19 trillion. What went wrong? Democrats gave significant amounts of the stimulus money to their political backers. They gave Solyndra, a solar panels company, $535 million of taxpayers' hard-earned dollars. Solyndra gave millions back to Democrat political candidates. Then it went out of business.[556]

Regarding the bloating of our national debt, **Vice President Joe Biden** explained that the way for our country to avoid bankruptcy would be to spend more money:

Now, people when I say that look at me and say, "What are you talking about, Joe? You're telling me we have to go spend money to keep from going bankrupt? The answer is yes, that's what I'm telling you."[557]

Hillary Clinton wants to spend an additional $275 billion on stimulus.[558] Bernie Sanders wants to spend an additional trillion.[559]

Democrats have had more control over the economy than Republicans for almost eight years.

US representative Debbie Wasserman Schultz, chairwoman, Democratic National Committee, 2011:
We own the economy.[560]

Seriously speaking, what have Democrat economic policies produced exactly?

Jim Clifton, Gallup Chairman and CEO, 2015:
The number of full-time jobs, and that's what everybody wants, as a percent of the total population, is the lowest it's ever been.[561]

For the first time in 35 years, American business deaths now outnumber business births.[562]

US senator Phil Gramm, economist:
Compared with the average postwar recovery, the economy in the past six years has created 12.1 million fewer jobs and $6,175 less income on average for every man, woman and child in the country.[563]

Governor Mitt Romney
Under President Obama the rich have gotten richer, income inequality has gotten worse and there are more people in poverty in America than ever before.[564]

Katie Kieffer, on teens and young adults:
We are the first generation of Americans to be financially worse off than our parents.[565]

Adriana Cohen
The sobering facts are after 7 $^{1/2}$ years of Democrats in power, there are 57 million women over the age of 16 out of work while median income and wages have declined.[566]

Paul Krugman, economist, expressed the Democrat concept of the "new normal," 2013:
Again, the evidence suggests that we have become an economy whose normal state is one of mild depression, whose brief episodes of prosperity occur only thanks to bubbles and unsustainable borrowing.[567]

Democrats blame our current financial weakness on the recession of 2008. They were instrumental in causing that downturn. In *Reckless Endangerment*, Gretchen Morgenson and Joshua Rosner identified Democrats as most of the primary players in the housing collapse that precipitated the recession.[568]

William Greider, in *The Nation*:
Candidate Clinton is essentially whitewashing the financial catastrophe. She has produced a clumsy rewrite of what caused the 2008 collapse, one that conveniently leaves her husband out of the story. He was the president who legislated the predicate for Wall Street's meltdown.[569]

Mark Levin
Top congressional Democrats, including Representative Barney Frank (Massachusetts), Senator Christopher Dodd (Connecticut), and Senator Charles Schumer (New York), among others, repeatedly ignored warnings of pending disaster, insisting that they were overstated, and opposed efforts to force Freddie Mac and Fannie Mae to comply with usual business and oversight practices.[570]

US representative Barney Frank
[I]t was a great mistake to push lower-income people into housing they couldn't afford and couldn't really handle once they had it.[571]

African Americans have written positively about business success and economic growth.

Booker T. Washington
More and more thoughtful students of the race problem are beginning to see that business and industry constitute what we may call the strategic point in its solution.[572]

Bayard Rustin
We have now learned that everything which moves and shapes society moves and shapes black people as well. If government policies weaken the economy, stifle economic growth, and contribute to massive unemployment, black people suffer ever more severely than in those days past when they had little connection with the economic mainstream....[573]

William Julius Wilson
That is why the fate of blacks, like that of other disadvantaged groups, is in large measure determined by the structure and functioning of the modern American economy.[574]

Indeed, the significant movement of blacks into higher-paying manufacturing positions from 1940 to the 1960s had much more to do with fairly even and steady economic growth in the manufacturing sector than with equal employment legislation.[575]

Shared Values

Ben Carson
When we have a vigorous and dynamic economy once again, because we have the most powerful economic engine the world has ever known, that's gonna lift all boats. That's gonna provide opportunities for all groups and I believe among black Americans, brown Americans, yellow Americans, white Americans, everybody will begin to understand this.[576]

Herman Cain
Grow this economy and it's going to help everybody get jobs and to get back in the workforce.[577]

US senator Tim Scott
[T]he best chance we have for a good economy is the private sector. The government cannot create jobs. If the government could create jobs, then Communism would have worked. But it didn't work. So what we have to do is allow the private sector and the entrepreneurial spirit to lead us back to a job-filled recovery.[578]

Success is created in studio apartments and garages, at kitchen tables, and in classrooms across the nation—not in government conference rooms in Washington.[579]

R. Donahue Peebles
Both Sean Combs and Dr. Dre, they're entertainers, that's how they got their start, but they're doing it through business and I think that's a very good thing. Michael Jordan did it through business. Oprah did it through entertainment and business.[580]

African-Americans, unlike other progressive aspects of Democrats, actually admire success and want to emulate it.[581]

It's important that the American people understand that their interest is aligned with business.[582]

My approach is to expand opportunity by increasing the size of the pie, not taking away from others.[583]

Tavis Smiley, referring to Tyler Perry:
What he has done, though, is to create an entertainment empire that has given employment to thousands of blacks and provided entertainment that millions of blacks find satisfying.[584]

Larry Elder
Most people work for the private sector, which cannot exist without profit.[585]

Ben Carson
We have the highest corporate tax rates in the world, which obviously encourage many U.S. companies to conduct business outside of America. We also have high individual taxation rates and high rates for small businesses. None of this is conducive to economic growth, particularly during times that resemble a recession.[586]

Even with the loopholes, the top 10 percent of the populace in terms of income pay 70 percent of the income taxes while earning 46 percent of the taxable income, which means they are indeed paying more than their fair share.[587]

Niger Innis
If you dare want to open up a business, they're going to cripple you with regulations and taxes and they're going to make it easier for you to be a rational human being and just get

government benefits rather than being a liberated individual who can climb that economic ladder.[588]

Larry Elder, speaking to Don Lemon:
And as far as bad fiscal policy is concerned, under Ronald Reagan, the dastardly Ronald Reagan who lowered the top marginal rate from 70 percent to 28 percent, the percentage of blacks, of unemployed blacks fell faster than the percentage of unemployed whites. Black teenage unemployment fell faster than white teenage unemployment. My dad, Don, was a janitor and he worked two full-time jobs as a janitor when I was a kid, he never read (inaudible) but he also said I never got a job from a poor person.[589]

Jason L. Riley
During a 2008 presidential debate, moderator Charlie Gibson of ABC News quizzed Barack Obama over his proposal to raise taxes on investment income, and the candidate's response was instructive. "Bill Clinton in 1997 signed legislation that dropped the capital gains tax to 20%," Mr. Gibson said. "And George Bush has taken it down to 15%. And in each instance, when the rate dropped, revenues from the tax increased. The government took in more money. And in the 1980s, when the tax was increased to 28%, the revenues went down. So why raise it at all, especially given the fact that 100 million people in this country own stock and would be affected?"

Mr. Obama's answer was that raising the capital-gains tax is necessary "to make sure…that our tax system is fair." Like the Democrats who hope to replace him, Mr. Obama's abiding belief is that sticking it to the affluent is the "fair" thing to do, even if it produces no additional revenue. Of course, Mr. Obama ultimately got his desired tax hikes on the rich. He has spent his presidency promoting economic equality over growth—and doing much damage to both. If elected, today's Democratic front-runners can be counted on to do more of the same.[590]

Ben Carson

Wealthy people in the United States have created more charitable organizations and been more philanthropic than any other group in the world.[591]

Geoffrey Canada

People talk about Wall Street greed, but one of the things many people don't understand is that there are a lot of organizations that have been the recipient of largesse from the same Wall Street.[592]

Harry Alford, president of the National Black Chamber of Commerce, on the report "Potential Impact of Proposed EPA Regulations on Low Income Groups and Minorities":

The study finds that the Clean Power Plan will inflict severe and disproportionate economic burdens on poor families, especially minorities.

These communities already suffer from higher unemployment and poverty rates compared to the rest of the country, yet the EPA's regressive energy tax threatens to push minorities and low-income Americans even further into poverty.[593]

Deneen Borelli, in testimony before Congress:

The winners in President Obama's energy policy are the well-connected corporate and social elite while the losers are the hardworking Americans who will have to suffer the economic consequences of higher energy prices, slower economic growth and jobs moving overseas.[594]

Thomas Sowell
Wealth is ultimately the only thing that can reduce poverty. The most dramatic reductions in poverty, in countries around the world, have come from increasing the amount of wealth, rather than from a redistribution of existing wealth.[595]

The key feature of Communist propaganda has been the depiction of people who are more productive as mere exploiters of others.[596]

What effect have recent Democrat economic policies had on African Americans and all Americans?

Tavis Smiley
The data is going to indicate sadly that when the Obama administration is over, black people will have lost ground in every single leading economic indicator category.[597]

Larry Elder
By every key economic measurement, blacks are worse off under Obama. In some cases, far worse off.[598]

Michael Steele
Liberals are ushering in a new America where more people are moving down the ladder of opportunity than are moving up.[599]

Niger Innis
Hope and change liberals have failed the black community.[600]

Walter E. Williams, on Democrats increasing the national debt:
And when economic chaos comes, whom do you think will be more affected by it: rich people or poor people?[601]

African Americans want jobs to be created. They appreciate the rewards of working.

Reverend Jesse L. Jackson
Work is important. Beyond wages, however, character formation, identity, self-esteem, self-fulfillment, and mental stability are all associated with work and achievement.[602]

Oseola McCarty
Hard work gives life meaning. Everyone needs to work hard at something to feel good about themselves. Every job can be done well and every day has its satisfactions.[603]

A. Elizabeth Delany
Nothing brings more satisfaction than doing quality work, than knowing that you've done the very best you can.[604]

George Foreman
The best thing that can ever happen to a human being is a job.[605]

Johnnetta B. Cole
Like many, I found the best therapy in the world is work. Lots of it![606]

Zora Neale Hurston
I don't know any more about the future than you do. I hope that it will be full of work, because I have come to know by experience that work is the nearest thing to happiness that I can find.[607]

Elijah Anderson
As he began working and bringing home a steady income, John was able to purchase an automobile, date young women, and become a popular person in his own peer group.[608]

Leon Dash
I reached a point of being able to tell many things when I walked into anyone's house by the expression on a person's face or a person's body language. If they were happy, I knew they were working. The unemployed and recently laid off were always sullen and hostile, both adults and adolescents.

A lot of the negative behavior I saw and learned about grew out of a person's inability to earn an income.[609]

Man
For a man to be al'right in my book, he got to work, or at least be tryin' to get some work. That's the first thing. Long as he workin' for a living, you know, out there doin' what I'm doin', well I got to respect him. Am I right or wrong? See, 'cause when we was comin' up, my daddy always told us, "Don't be afraid of work. Don't be too proud to shovel shit all day, if you have to." No matter what you have to do, you got to live, you know. When a man is workin' hard all day, 'stead of layin' 'round these here streets, well, he showin' me a good side of hisself.[610]

Father of Bob Teague:
If you want to be somebody, you got to work.[611]

Samuel L. Jackson
There's something right about people who work, and there's something wrong about people who don't. When they look at your resume, and say, "Wow, you have three jobs," they want to hire you too. You know that other cat that ain't worked in a year? Hmmm, "Okay, it's been nice seeing you." Success breeds success.[612]

Louis Armstrong
There isn't anything nicer to know and feel deep down in your heart that you have something—anything—that you've worked and strived for honestly, rather than do a lot of ungodly things to get it. Yes—you appreciate it better.[613]

Devon Greene, former convict, former Doe Fund, Ready, Willing & Able worker, and now a college student:
The harder you work, the more opportunity comes your way.[614]

Charles Barkley
But there is no excuse for anyone—no matter their circumstances—not becoming a hard-working, useful, and productive person in society. No excuse. And that includes racism.[615]

Part III
Obstacles to Progress

Seven

CRIME

Republican View

Republicans value law and order. They don't want people to be beaten, robbed, raped, and murdered. They don't want drug sellers to terrorize neighborhoods. They have sympathy for those who are incarcerated, but they have greater concern for the law-abiding men, women, and children who are oppressed by criminals.

The Obama-Holder-Lynch Justice Department published data showing that African Americans are represented disproportionately among criminals and their victims. The Department collects statistics on the basis of arrests and on testimony from crime victims who described their attackers: both sources give similar results.[616]

Alexia Cooper and **Erica L. Smith**, US Department of Justice, "Homicide Trends in the United States, 1980–2008 Annual Rates for 2009 and 2010":

> Blacks were disproportionately represented as both homicide victims and offenders. The victimization rate for blacks (27.8 per 100,000) was 6 times higher than the rate for whites (4.5 per

100,000). The offending rate for blacks (34.4 per 100,000) was almost 8 times higher than the rate for whites (4.5 per 100,000).

Homicide rates for black children under age 5 have remained substantially higher than rates for white children or children of other races.[617]

Victor Davis Hanson
A small cohort of urban African-American males under fifty—no more than 3-4% of the general population—is responsible for about 50% of many of the violent crimes committed.[618]

The police are deployed to high-crime neighborhoods to protect the people there. From 1990 to 2012 in New York City, active policing and imprisonment lowered the annual number of murder victims from 2,245 to 419. During those years, the police saved approximately 40,000 lives, mostly those of black and Hispanic men.[619]

Fox Butterfield, *New York Times*:
Of course, the huge increase in the number of inmates has helped lower the crime rate by incapacitating more criminals behind bars.[620]

James Comey, FBI Director, 2015:
There are tens of thousands of people who were not murdered or raped or robbed or intimidated because crime dropped in our country.

We heard the voices of real live victims in August in northwest Arkansas, when the FBI and our partners sent hundreds of agents and officers into the predominantly black town of Blytheville to arrest drug dealers who were suffocating the community and overwhelming local police.
As our SWAT teams stood in the street following the arrests of the defendants—70 of them, nearly all of whom were also

black—they were met by applause, hugs, and offers of food from the good people of that besieged community.[621]

Ann Coulter
The reason crime has plummeted around the nation in the last few decades is aggressive policing, increased prison sentences and the expansion of concealed carry permits. (All policies currently being jettisoned by liberals.)[622]

The African American rate of criminal offending accounts for the disproportionate arrests and incarcerations. But it does not explain the difference in police shootings: the police shoot more white people. The *Washington Post* reported that in 2015, American police officers shot 494 whites to death and 258 blacks.[623]

Heather Mac Donald
Standard anti-cop ideology, whether emanating from the ACLU or the academy, holds that law enforcement actions are racist if they don't mirror population data. New York City illustrates why that expectation is so misguided. Blacks make up 23 percent of New York City's population, but they commit 75 percent of all shootings, 70 percent of all robberies, and 66 percent of all violent crime, according to victims and witnesses. Add Hispanic shootings and you account for 98 percent of all illegal gunfire in the city. Whites are 33 percent of the city's population, but they commit fewer than two percent of all shootings, four percent of all robberies, and five percent of all violent crime.

This incidence of crime means that innocent black men have a much higher chance than innocent white men of being stopped by the police because they match the description of a suspect. This is not something the police choose. It is a reality forced on them by the facts of crime.

Shared Values

The geographic disparities are also huge. In Brownsville, Brooklyn, the per capita shooting rate is 81 times higher than in nearby Bay Ridge, Brooklyn—the first neighborhood predominantly black, the second neighborhood predominantly white and Asian. As a result, police presence and use of proactive tactics are much higher in Brownsville than in Bay Ridge. Every time there is a shooting, the police will flood the area looking to make stops in order to avert a retaliatory shooting. They are in Brownsville not because of racism, but because they want to provide protection to its many law-abiding residents who deserve safety.[624]

To be sure, police officers need to treat everyone they encounter with courtesy and respect. Any fatal police shooting of an innocent person is a horrifying tragedy that police training must work incessantly to prevent.[625]

Police shootings account for a much smaller share of homicides in the black community than in other communities: 4 percent of black homicide victims are killed by the police, compared with 12 percent of white and Hispanic homicide victims.[626]

In any case, the strongest predictor of whether a police officer uses force is whether a suspect resists arrest, not the suspect's race.[627]

Police officers, confronted with increased hostility from the media, protestors, and politicians, have become hesitant. Criminals have become more active. After decades of decline, American crime has begun to increase.

Heather Mac Donald, 2016:
The country's political and media elites have relentlessly accused cops of bias when they police inner-city neighborhoods. Pedestrian stops and broken-windows policing (which

targets low-level public-order offenses) are denounced as racist oppression.

In Chicago, where pedestrian stops have fallen nearly 90%, homicides this year are up 60% compared with the same period last year.[628]

Crime in America is often connected to drugs. Republicans are aware of claims that our drug laws are excessively harsh and racist, that the criminal justice system fills prisons with African American marijuana smokers and nonviolent drug dealers. But those assertions don't agree with the data.

Heather Mac Donald
> Fewer than 1% of drug offenders sentenced in federal court in 2014 were convicted of simple drug possession, according to the U.S. Sentencing Commission.
>
> Even on the state level, drug-possession convicts are rare. In 2013 only 3.6% of state prisoners were serving time for drug possession—again, often the result of a plea bargain on more serious charges—compared with 12% of prisoners convicted of trafficking. Virtually all the possession offenders had long prior arrest and conviction records.[629]

Republicans have been exploring the possibility of criminal justice system reforms.

US Attorney Paul Charlton
> The reason we had mandatory minimums, and the reason we put them in place after the all-time high crime rates in the '80s, is because we wanted to reduce crime. We've done that. We need to be careful about how we change course now, and make sure we don't change course too quickly.[630]

Governor Rick Perry
I believe in consequences for criminal behavior. But I also believe in second chances and human redemption, because that is the American story.

Americans who suffer from an addiction need help, not moral condemnation. By treating alcohol and drug abuse as a disease, we have given Texans who have experienced a run-in with the law the help they need. In addition to the real human impact, in 2014, Texas had its lowest crime rate since 1968, and we have been able to close three prisons.

We can reform federal sentencing laws, just as we have done at the state level, to ensure more young people have a shot at a better life. And we can do so while keeping our low-income communities safe from crime, preserving the hard-won policing victories that other states seem hell-bent on rolling back.[631]

Governor Chris Christie speaks passionately for additional drug rehabilitation services here.[632]

US senator Rand Paul, **US senator Rick Santorum**, and others are in favor of giving convicted felons an opportunity to regain their voting rights.[633]

As with education and work, marriage is the key to solving the crime problem.

Patrick F. Fagan, The Heritage Foundation:
There is a widespread belief that race is a major explanatory cause of crime. This belief is anchored in the large disparity in crime rates between whites and blacks. However, a closer look at the data shows that the real variable is not race but family structure and all that it implies in commitment and love between adults.

It is the absence of marriage, and the failure to form and maintain intact families, that explains the incidence of high crime in a neighborhood among whites as well as blacks. High-crime neighborhoods are characterized by high concentrations of families abandoned by fathers.

Even in high-crime inner-city neighborhoods, well over 90 percent of children from safe, stable homes do not become delinquents.

The benefits a child receives from his relationship with his father are notably different from those derived from his relationship with his mother. The father contributes a sense of paternal authority and discipline which is conveyed through his involved presence. The additional benefits of his affection and attachment add to this primary benefit.

In normal families a father gives support to his wife, particularly during the period surrounding birth and in the early childhood years when children make heavy demands on her. In popular parlance, he is her "burn-out" prevention. But a single mother does not have this support, and the added emotional and physical stress may result in fatigue and less parent availability to the child, increasing the risk of a relationship with the child that is emotionally more distant. The single mother generally is less able to attend to all of her child's needs as quickly or as fully as she could if she were well taken care of by a husband. These factors tend to affect the mother's emotional attachment to her child and in turn reduce the child's lifelong capacity for emotional attachment to others and empathy for others. Such empathy helps restrain a person from acting against others' well-being. Violent criminals obviously lack this. At the extreme, and a more common situation in America's inner cities, the distant relationship between a mother and child can become an abusing and neglectful relationship.[634]

Democrat View

Democrats would prefer to have a lower crime rate with fewer people harmed. But they express more concern with protecting criminals from arrest and incarceration than with protecting innocent people from criminals.

They occasionally acknowledge the disproportion in rates of offending.

President Barack Obama, responding to a question from a police officer:
> It is absolutely true that the murder rate in the African-American community is way out of whack compared to the general population. And both the victims and the perpetrators are black, young black men.
>
> The single greatest cause of death for young black men between the ages of 18 and 35 is homicide. And that's crazy. That is crazy.[635]

But Democrats typically say that the incarceration disparity is proof of racism, without mentioning the disparity in criminal offending.

Christopher Hartney and **Linh Vuong**, National Council on Crime and Delinquency:
> African Americans make up 13% of the general US population, yet they constitute 28% of all arrests, 40% of all inmates held in prisons and jails, and 42% of the population on death row.

This overrepresentation of people of color in the nation's criminal justice system, also referred to as disproportionate minority contact (DMC), is a serious issue in our society.[636]

Sophia Kerby, Center for American Progress:
Individuals of color have a disproportionate number of encounters with law enforcement, indicating that racial profiling continues to be a problem.[637]

The Sentencing Project
Racial disparity in the criminal justice system is widespread and its perpetuation threatens to challenge the principle that our criminal justice system is fair, effective and just.[638]

American Civil Liberties Union
Racial bias, both implicit and explicit, keeps more people of color in prisons and on probation than ever before.[639]

Some Democrats take the position that by arresting and jailing criminals, police officers harm society. They see the police as the problem.

Alex S. Vitale wrote an essay in *The Nation* titled:
We Don't Just Need Nicer Cops. We Need Fewer Cops.[640]

Alice Goffman, sociologist, seems to agree. She saw that crime oppressed the African American residents of a Philadelphia neighborhood:
Over the following weeks, young men from 4th Street drove through the 6th Street neighborhood and shot up the block.

Neighbors stopped going outside and instructed children to play indoors.[641]

Shared Values

This is not to say that law-abiding residents of the 6th Street neighborhood are untroubled by the violence and drug selling in which many young men in the neighborhood become engaged. They *are* troubled, and they wish these young men would either leave or change their ways.[642]

But **Goffman** concluded that the police and judges were the problem:
Under these conditions, the role of law enforcement changes from keeping communities safe from a few offenders to bringing an entire neighborhood under suspicion and surveillance.

In this context, the highly punitive approach to crime control winds up being counterproductive, creating entirely new domains of criminality.[643]

Thus, the great paradox of a highly punitive approach to crime control is that it winds up criminalizing so much of daily life as to foster widespread illegality as people work to circumvent it.[644]

So many Black men have been imprisoned and returned home with felony convictions that the prison now plays a central role in the production of unequal groups in US society, setting back the gains in citizenship and socioeconomic position that Black people made during the Civil Rights Movement.[645]

Goffman took that anti-police position, despite seeing that many young men in the neighborhood avoided involvement with the police simply by choosing not to commit crimes:
And yet, the neighborhood also contains many who keep relatively free of the courts and the prisons, who go to school or work every day as the police chase their neighbors through the streets.[646]

Some residents insist that their sons and nephews could get legitimate jobs if they simply tried hard enough to find them.[647]

Despite the data, Democrats suggest that our prisons are populated, to a significant degree, with marijuana smokers and nonviolent drug dealers who present no danger to society.

US senator Bernie Sanders said that the American people see:
...a broken criminal justice system.... They see kids getting arrested for marijuana, getting in prison, getting a criminal record.... So what we have to do is the radical reform of a broken criminal justice system.[648]

President Barack Obama, 2015:
Over the last few decades, we've also locked up more and more nonviolent drug offenders than ever before, for longer than ever before. And that is the real reason our prison population is so high.[649]

Democrats have released 6,000 drug offenders from prison and are considering sending as many as 46,000 back to their home communities.[650]
They also release criminal illegal aliens.

Paul Bedard
The U.S. Immigration and Customs Enforcement agency in 2015 decided not to deport but release 19,723 criminal illegal immigrants, including 208 convicted of murder, over 900 convicted of sex crimes and 12,307 of drunk driving, according to new government numbers.[651]

US senators Chuck Grassley and John Cornyn revealed evidence that the current administration has been placing thousands of

Shared Values

unaccompanied immigrant children in the custody of guardians who have criminal histories of child molestation and human trafficking.[652]

The leniency toward criminals applies to terrorists. Mahmmoud Omar Mohammed Bin Atef promised to cut Americans' throats if he got out of Guantanamo, then he was released and he returned to terrorism.[653] When the United States released **Abu Bakr al-Baghdadi** from detention in Iraq, in September 2009, he said, "I'll see you guys in New York." He's now the leader of the Islamic State.[654]

Some Democrats have not seemed to understand that incarceration prevents crime. **Fox Butterfield**, who had written that imprisonment lowers the crime rate, later referred to "the paradox of a falling crime rate but a rising prison population."[655]

Secretary of State Hillary Clinton
The [incarceration] numbers today are much higher than they were 30, 40 years ago, despite the fact that crime is at historic lows.[656]

African Americans have said that their crime rate is disproportionately high.

Larry Elder
The fact remains that nearly 40 percent of violent crimes—murder, attempted murder, nonnegligent manslaughter, and aggravated assault—are committed by young black men, who account for no more than 3 percent of the nation's population.[657]

Police Chief Willie L. Williams
The black community has a larger proportion of crime within major metropolitan areas than any other community. The majority of that crime is black offender, black victim.[658]

Officer David Lemieux, Chicago:
I work almost exclusively in the Black community. White boys don't come through our community to commit crimes. In six years, I've arrested ten white people. The reality is that the crimes in our community are committed by Black people against Black people.[659]

Michael Steele
And the Left is quick to chastise us with a long, sympathetic description of the life circumstances of convicted criminals, but they rarely detail for us what criminals really do to their victims, or the devastating effect on families that lose someone to crime.[660]

John W. Fountain, on African American criminals in Chicago:
We faced terrorists long before the term became popular. Except the terrorists we knew looked like us and talked like us, even though they seemed to hold so much hatred and disrespect for black folks that they might as well have been honorary members of the Ku Klux Klan.[661]

Robyn Minter Smyers
When the shooting gets bad, children are put to sleep in bathtubs and under beds so they won't be struck by random bullets. Residents must pay tribute to gun-toting teenagers in order to enter their own buildings, get mail, and ride the elevator. Many have become prisoners in their own apartments, afraid to walk hallways strewn with empty crack vials, used condoms, and excrement where the lights have been put out by muggers and drug dealers.[662]

Bob Herbert, after eighty-one-year-old Rosa Parks was robbed and beaten by a black man:

Shared Values

The wars against segregation have been won, but we are lost. With the violence and degradation into which so many of our people have fallen, we have disgraced the legacy of Rosa Parks.

She did not fight so those future generations would be free to ingest endless tons of dope, to populate the nation's streets with armies of all-but-abandoned children, or to engage in a spectacular orgy of killing in which the vast majority of the victims just happen to be other African-Americans, many of them infants and children.[663]

Rosa Parks, after being beaten:
Many gains have been made, but as you can see, at this time we still have a long way to go and so many of our children are going astray.[664]

Debra Dickerson, on the man who shot her nephew:
We rarely wonder about or discuss the brother who shot him because we already know everything about him. When the call came, my first thought was the same one I'd had when I'd heard about Rosa Parks's beating: a brother did it. A non-job-having, middle-of-the-day malt-liquor-drinking, crotch-clutching, loud-talking brother with many neglected children born of many forgotten women. He lives in his mother's basement with furniture rented at an astronomical interest rate, the exact amount of which he does not know. He has a car phone, an $80 monthly cable bill and every possible phone feature but no savings. He steals Social Security numbers from unsuspecting relatives and assumes their identities to acquire large TV sets for which he will never pay. On the slim chance that he is brought to justice, he will have a colorful criminal history and no coherent explanation to offer for this act. His family will raucously defend him and cry cover-up. Some

liberal lawyer just like me will help him plea bargain his way to yet another short stay in a prison pesthouse that will serve only to add another layer to the brother's sociopathology and formless, mindless nihilism. We know him. We've known and feared him all our lives.

He chased all the small entrepreneurs from our neighborhood with his violent thievery, and put bars on our windows. He kept us from sitting on our own front porch after dark and laid the foundation for our periodic bouts of self-hating anger and racial embarrassment. He made our neighborhood a ghetto.[665]

Woman
It's getting to be that black people are more afraid to see a young black man walking behind them than they are to see a white person![666]

Woman, a.k.a. **Firestarter**:
When I walk out my door I'm not looking over my shoulder for a white man to rob, beat, or rape me. No…I'm looking for the person most likely to do it: a black man.[667]

When **Steven A. Holmes** drove a taxi as a college student, an African American man pointed a gun at him and another put a knife to his throat:
I became more choosy about who I let in my cab. I still picked up black women, older men, couples, families and men dressed in suits. But my sense of tolerance and racial solidarity was tested every time a casually dressed young black man, especially one in sneakers, tried to hail my cab. Most times, I drove right by. I sometimes wondered about their reaction, but I kept thinking that if I guessed wrong, I could pay for my mistake with my life.[668]

Shared Values

Elijah Anderson, Philadelphia:
In their conversations with neighbors, both blacks and whites assume that the main offenders are young, black, and male.[669]

Thomas Sowell
The honest consumer pays costs created by vandals, hoodlums, and criminals in his neighborhood, but that is different from saying that his neighborhood as a whole is being "exploited" by the store located there or by other ethnic groups. The steady exit of stores from high-crime neighborhoods suggests that there is no great profit being made there.[670]

Walter E. Williams
Another fact of black existence is a crime rate that is just like a law mandating, "There shall be no economic development in black neighborhoods." A tiny percentage of the black community makes life a living nightmare for its law-abiding majority.[671]

Elaine R. Jones
Not only are we victimized disproportionately by the violence, it's very difficult to have racial progress in the midst of violence. What can you do with the schools? How can you get business to locate? How can you provide meaningful opportunity and jobs?[672]

Bayard Rustin
Riots do not strengthen the power of black people; they weaken it and encourage racist power.[673]

Jason L. Riley, on Watts and Detroit:
Before the riots, both cities had sizable and growing black middle-class populations, where homeownership and employ-

ment exceeded the black national average. After the riots, those populations fled, and economic deprivation set in. Some 50 years later, Watts is still showing "scars" and Detroit remains in the hospital.[674]

Charles Barkley, after the Ferguson, Missouri riots:
Anybody who walks out peacefully, who protests peacefully, that's what this country was built on. But to be burning people's property, burning police cars, looting people's stores, that is 100% ridiculous.[675]

Marian Wright Edelman
Urban employers, remembering Watts and Newark and Detroit, tended not to trust (and therefore not to hire) ghetto blacks.[676]

Walter E. Williams
In the wake of the Charleston murders, some people promote the false narrative that it's white racists who are the interracial murderers. That's nonsense. FBI crime victimization surveys show that blacks commit 80 percent of all interracial violent crime.[677]

Gerald Early
Even though most violent crimes are intra-racial—meaning that whites commit their crimes mainly against other whites, and blacks commit their crimes mainly against other blacks—whites are still twice as likely to be the victim of a violent black perpetrator as my wife or I am to be the victim of a white perpetrator.

…after reviewing these statistics, only a fool would not take some caution around blacks, especially black men, which is a kind of national shame and ought to be a cause of despair.[678]

Shared Values

Thomas Sowell, on an attack by African Americans on a white woman in Milwaukee:
> Variations on such episodes of unprovoked violence by young black gangs against white people on beaches, in shopping malls or in other public places have occurred in Philadelphia, New York, Denver, Chicago, Cleveland, Washington, Los Angeles and other places across the country, often with the attackers voicing anti-white invective and mocking those they left injured or bleeding.[679]

Jason L. Riley
> The reality is that young black men are perceived as likely criminals because a hugely disproportionate number of them commit crimes. And if blacks want to change those perceptions, young black men need to change their behavior.[680]

Reverend Martin Luther King Jr.
> Our crime rate is far too high.[681]

Former criminal
> If Martin Luther King Jr. and Malcolm X were alive they would hang their head in shame at us.[682]

⸻

Drugs have harmed African Americans for centuries.

Frederick Douglass
> But these old slave-holders have their allies, and one is strong drink. Whisky makes the Negro drunk, and drunkenness makes him a criminal as well as a pauper…[683]

Barbara M. Dixon

But it seems as if African Americans have been suffering longer and harder with the results of alcohol and drugs than other groups.[684]

Bob Teague

We further slowed black progress by increasing our consumption of drugs....[685]

Richard Majors and Janet Mancini Billson:

The impact of substance abuse is amplified by its role in premature and low-birth-weight babies, illnesses, premature deaths, inability to hold employment, accidents, rape, and other forms of violence. As a result, more black males are incarcerated than any other group in this country.[686]

Angela Y. Davis

Because of intravenous drug use in the Black community, a disproportionately large number of Black women have been infected with AIDS.[687]

Spike Lee

Entire generations are being wiped out by drugs. If drugs aren't getting them, then the guys shooting over the drugs are.[688]

Marcia Slocum-Greene

Parents seeking the next crack fix have abandoned their young children in the streets and in hospitals. They have sold food stamps and their children's clothes for drug money. A few have sold their children as prostitutes.[689]

Shared Values

Man
> When they first started, they say, "Oh, I can handle it. I can handle it." The next thing I see them in the street. They don't have anything left.[690]

Ta-Nehisi Coates
> When crack hit Baltimore, civilization fell.[691]

Tavis Smiley
> [A]ll across this country there are too many Black folk who are being held hostage in their own neighborhoods because of these thugs—these drug dealers run amok.[692]

John McWhorter
> When it comes to drug policy, there is a significant difference between white teens selling each other drugs to use in their parents' basements and gun-toting hoodlums terrorizing their neighborhoods in drug-trade turf wars.[693]

Woman, describing an addict who "used to be the finest person you would ever want to meet":
> If anybody had told me that he would rob and cut an old lady who had saved his life, I just wouldn't have believed that!
>
> Every time he'd get caught they'd just give him a little time and then just send him back here to worry and rob and cut and shoot us!
>
> If they robbed the mothers and sisters of those judges who keep sending them out here for you and me to deal with, they would never see the street again.[694]

Woman, a.k.a. **Firestarter**:
> The people who sell and distribute drugs bring crime and violence to communities. No matter how you cut it...drugs

Crime

are problematic and should not be written off as "non-violent offenses" when we consider the impact of drugs on communities.[695]

Serena Williams
These days, all you have to do is turn on the TV and you can see people smoking weed or getting drunk in videos and on reality shows. They act like everyone does it and like it's a normal part of growing up. But trust me when I tell you that even though it may seem that way, not everyone gets high. I don't. And Venus doesn't either.[696]

Ta-Nehisi Coates, on claims that our prisons are populated with drug offenders who present no danger to society:
One 2004 study found that the proportion of "unambiguously low-level drug offenders" could be less than 6 percent in state prisons and less than 2 percent in federal ones.[697]

⌒

African Americans have spoken out strongly against crime and in favor of active policing.

Geoffrey Canada wrote that people in poor communities:
[D]esperately need police protection because they are disproportionately the victims of crime in this country....[698]

Police Chief Willie L. Williams
The African-American community wants strong, tough, honest, fair policing. There is no African-American community in America that does not want to see police there.[699]

Steven Craft, former criminal, Harvard graduate, and minister to convicts:

Shared Values

Certainly, it is necessary to incarcerate criminals in order to keep them off the streets, preying on innocent and law-abiding citizens.[700]

Randall Kennedy
[T]he principal injury suffered by African-Americans in relation to criminal matters is not overenforcement but underenforcement of the laws.[701]

Jason L. Riley
But there is no doubt that putting more people in prison for longer periods of time has contributed significantly to lowering crime rates in the United States. There is also no doubt that proactive policing and tough-on-crime policies that the left derides have led to fewer black deaths.[702]

The reality is that locking up lawbreakers has worked better than going easy on them, and has worked best for law-abiding black people.[703]

Sterling Johnson
It's been my experience that the law-abiding citizens who are living on Eighth Avenue and 116th Street want drug pushers to go to jail for the rest of their lives.[704]

Richard Williams
In the depths of my heart, I wished God would rain down brimstone and fire and totally consume every gang member and cast them into the pits of hell. Maybe the police could line them all up and sentence them to death by firing squad. Kill all of the bastards.[705]

John McWhorter
[B]lack legislators were solidly behind the laws penalizing possession of crack more heavily than powder.[706]

Thomas Sowell

Many in the media and among the intelligentsia cherish the romantic tale of an "us" against "them" struggle of beleaguered ghetto blacks defending themselves against the aggression of white policemen. The gullible include both whites who don't know what they are talking about and blacks who don't know what they are talking about either, because they never grew up in a ghetto.[707]

I don't happen to like the idea of "stop and frisk." However, I like even less the idea of armed hoodlums going around shooting people.[708]

Stacey Calhoun, uncle of Jahhad, who was killed by a stray bullet from a playground shootout:
A lot of people would agree with stop-and-frisk if it's for the safety among us. It seems like all these kids have guns these days. We need stop-and-frisk.[709]

Jason L. Riley

I know something about growing up black and male in the inner city and it's not that hard to avoid getting shot by a cop. They pull you over, you answer their questions, you are on your way.

The real difficulty is not getting shot by other black people if you are a young black man in these neighborhoods, and again that is something we need to talk more about. Cops are not the problem.[710]

Walter E. Williams

White liberals in the media and academia, along with many blacks, have been major supporters of the recent marches protesting police conduct. A man from Mars, knowing nothing about homicide facts, would conclude that the major problem black Americans have with murder and brutality results from the behavior of racist policemen. According to the Bureau of Justice Statistics, there are about 200 police arrest–related deaths of blacks each year (between 300 and 400 for whites). That number pales in comparison with the roughly 7,000 annual murders of blacks, 94 percent of which are committed by blacks. The number of blacks being murdered by other blacks is of little concern to liberals.[711]

Minister Louis Farrakhan
Look at the statistics: It is not them killing us from the police side of this thing—it is us killing us.

But if you're not willing to confront the murder and mayhem that's going on in our own community, then you're not serious.[712]

Glenn C. Loury
Of course police behavior is an issue of concern to blacks. But can there be any doubt that the damage done by the criminally violent within their own communities needs to be regarded with greater concern, if only because it occurs on a much larger scale?[713]

Deroy Murdock, on officers in New York City, which has a population of 8.4 million:
The supposedly trigger-happy, bigoted NYPD killed a whopping eight people last year, according to its meticulous, 73-page "2014 Annual Firearms Discharge Report." Of these, four were black. All of them were armed with cutting instruments (scissors, a hatchet, a boxcutter and a knife) and wielded them when they fatally were shot.

But the notion that America's cops simply are gunning down innocent black people is one of today's biggest and deadliest lies.

Thanks to the Ferguson Effect, blistering anti-law-enforcement rhetoric and sometimes fatal attacks on police have made cops timid, if not terrified. The result? A murder explosion that, ironically, is killing the very black people whom Black Lives Matter claims to champion. Year to date, homicides are up 8.3 percent in New York, 19.2 percent in Chicago, 51.5 percent in St. Louis and 52.5 percent in Baltimore.[714]

Lorraine Banks, on the increased caution and inhibition among the police:
They can't do their job no more. Every day they know it could be their last and now they're being demonized just for doing that job.[715]

Sheriff David A. Clarke
I understand there is some lingering racism in the nation, and that some police action is racially motivated. But the serious problems are in the black community. These problems are not being caused by white people anymore. Nor are they being caused by the police. The police, for the most part, are trying to protect law-abiding black people from other African Americans who are committing crimes.[716]

In 2011 and 2012, 386 white people were killed by police officers. One hundred and forty black people were killed by police offers in the same period.[717]

When I hear that "black lives matter," the only people that really believe that statement are American police officers who go into American ghettos every day to keep people from killing each other.[718]

Shared Values

This race and police crisis is a distraction from the real work that must be done of changing the culture in the black community and reducing crime.[719]

Peggy Hubbard criticized protestors for ignoring the violence that blacks inflict on one another, including the shooting of a nine-year-old girl by a black man. Her strong language in this video may offend some listeners.[720]

Pastor Derwood Tate, spoke of off-duty officer Sean Renfro:
Sgt. Renfro was Caucasian and we're African Americans, but he died protecting my kids.[721]

Nada Owusu
Facebook friends, join [me] in expressing my gratitude to God and to Officer [Matt] Okes...a Virginia State Police officer. I took this picture at 2 a.m. in the middle of nowhere. My son had his back tire blown off his car last night on his way home from school. This kind officer approached him, didn't ask if the little Mercedes was stolen but rather got on his knees to replace his tire. When his effort failed, he stayed with my son all night till we arrived at 1 a.m. with Triple A. He provided all the needed protection, especially from those tractor trailers, till we were done by 2 a.m. and drove behind us for a while before exiting. Today I salute Officer Okes! He is our hero and our Good Samaritan.

As far as I was concerned, there was a good person waiting with my son. I didn't care if he was green, blue, yellow. There's a lot of good in America and that needs to be heard. Police need our support.[722]

Officer Crystal Deneen Sheffield, wife and mother, gave her life serving the people of Baltimore. Her video memorial is here.[723]

Judge Joseph B. Williams
The problem is ours, and the solution needs to be ours.[724]

Shaka Senghor rehabilitated himself and was on parole when he went to see his nephew who had just been shot:
When we got to the hospital I was just standing there, standing with him, and all his friends came to visit—young kids from the neighborhood. They were riled up, saying, "We gotta find out who did it," things like that. They were already planning revenge. And I'm looking at all these cats and I see that they've got on "Rest in Peace" T-shirts. It turns out a different young guy in their neighborhood had just been killed not too long ago.

That did it. These cats were mourning one young man, they were at the hospital bed of another young man, and they were already planning revenge on a third young man. I was like, damn, this is a fascinating statement. This is where we're at?[725]

Man
We fight and cut more than anybody on earth, don't we? You can say 'bout Whitey what you want to say about him. I don't love him, now. Never will give a damn 'bout him. But they have a different system than what we have. Whatever it is.[726]

I don't know whether Whitey got to wake up—or we got to wake up. I think we got to wake up—a little bit, anyway.[727]

The police typically respond after crimes have been committed. Families can prevent crime.

W. E. B. Du Bois, Philadelphia, 1899:

Efforts to stop this crime must commence in the Negro homes; they must cease to be, as they often are, breeders of idleness and extravagance and complaint.[728]

Judge Joseph B. Brown Jr.

A typical offender in the system was born to a teenage mother.[729]

Kenneth B. Clark

The child born in the ghetto is more likely to come into a world of broken homes and illegitimacy; and this family and social instability is conducive to delinquency, drug addiction, and criminal violence.[730]

William Raspberry

Black communities are beset by crime and violence but, again, less because of racism than because of lack of discipline in those communities. One key reason for this failure of discipline is the dissolution of black families—not because of discrimination but because black Americans lead the nation in fatherlessness, having allowed marriage to fall to an all-time-low priority.[731]

Kalais Chiron Hunt, prisoner:

Most of us black males growing up in the neighborhood, we don't have fathers. Our fathers have either ran off or they're on drugs or they're here.[732]

Arthur Ashe

We are no more prone to crime, immorality, and other forms of delinquency than any other social group. But I estimate that it would take at least a generation, perhaps more, before African American culture can regain the moral authority it once possessed. Then we would have, as we still did when I was a child, a sense of the integrity of the family, including mother and father....[733]

Judge Veronica S. McBeth
What these kids need is family.[734]

Haki R. Madhubuti
Strong families are key to fighting crime as well as building a strong people.[735]

Jackie Robinson
Sitting down to our holiday meal, I found myself hoping and wishing that there could be more closeness among families—all kinds of families but particularly Negro families. I single out the Negro because we always hear so much about the high rate of crime in Negro communities.

Our leaders talk of the sources of that crime—job discrimination, overcrowding, segregation, neglect.

Usually, this criticism is leveled against white society for keeping the Negro within a walled fence—subtly in the North and openly in the South. While I feel this position is justified, I would like to say it is time for the Negro parent to take a long inward look in an attempt to find out how much he is responsible for.

I have seen so much in the Harlem area—so much that points to the fact that, if our youngsters had the kind of home life they need and deserve, we'd have a lot less of them going around getting themselves into trouble.[736]

Eight

Conformity

A reader could be convinced of the merit of the conservative values espoused in this book but feel pressured to conform to alternative beliefs held by people in his social group. There is strong support in African American literature for rejecting conformity and accepting the freedom of individuality.

Glenn C. Loury
I now understand how this desire to be regarded as genuinely black, to be seen as a "regular brother," has dramatically altered my life. It narrowed the range of my earliest intellectual pursuits, distorted my relationships with other people, censored my political thought and expression, informed the way I dressed and spoke, and shaped my cultural interests.[737]

Debra J. Dickerson
There's a Head Negro anywhere there are African-Americans.[738]

Jason L. Riley
There is a long tradition of policing racial betrayal in the black community, where certain people—sometimes referred to as

"soul patrols"—take it upon themselves to determine black authenticity.[739]

Jo-Issa Rae Diop, a.k.a. **Issa Rae**:
"Black people don't do that." Or so I'm told by a black person.

Who is to say what we do and don't do? What we can and can't do?[740]

John Edgar Wideman, as a college student, home on vacation:
Away from school I worked hard at being the same old home boy everybody remembered, not because I identified with that mask but because I didn't want youall to discover I was a traitor.[741]

Just two choices as far as I could tell: either/or. Rich or poor. White or black. Win or lose.[742]

Signithia Fordham and **John U. Ogbu**:
Among the attitudes and behaviors that black students at Capital High identify as "acting white" and therefore unacceptable are: (1) speaking standard English; (2) listening to white music and white radio stations; (3) going to the opera or ballet; (4) spending a lot of time in the library studying; (5) working hard to get good grades in school; (6) getting good grades in school (those who get good grades are labeled "brainiacs"); (7) going to the Smithsonian; (8) going to a Rolling Stones concert at the Capital Center; (9) doing volunteer work; (10) going camping, hiking, or mountain climbing; (11) having cocktails or a cocktail party; (12) going to a symphony orchestra concert; (13) having a party with no music; (14) listening to classical music; (15) being on time; (16) reading and writing poetry; and (17) putting on "airs," and so forth. This list is not exhaustive, but indicates kinds of

attitudes and behaviors likely to be negatively sanctioned and therefore avoided by a large number of students.[743]

Shelby Steele

This pattern asks us to see ourselves as an embattled minority, and it urges an adversarial stance toward the mainstream and an emphasis on ethnic consciousness over individualism.[744]

And yet this leaves us with an identity that is at war with our own best interests, that magnifies our oppression and diminishes our sense of possibility. I think this identity is a weight on blacks because it is built around our collective insecurity rather than our faith in our human capacity to seize opportunity as individuals.[745]

Stanley Crouch

In order to be "authentic," Negro Americans, so goes the politics of perpetual alienation, aren't supposed to identify with the ideals of the country at large. We are supposed to enlist all of our energies in pretending that we are somehow part of another tradition.[746]

[P]eople are expected to relate to the world only through race and the most stifling conception of group history.[747]

Brent Staples

The most dangerous myth facing African-Americans today is that middle-class life is counterfeit and that only poverty and suffering, and the rage that attends them, are real.

Reginald Hudlin

There is a confusion between Afrocentricity and ghettocentricity, which is very unhealthy for black culture.[748]

Thomas Sowell
The changing social climate of the 1960s and beyond included a celebration of the ghetto culture, essentially an offshoot of the dysfunctional redneck culture of the South, though often regarded as something uniquely black or even African, despite much evidence to the contrary.[749]

Charles Barkley
There's a perception among some black people, if you're not a thug, a hood rat, if you don't wear your pants down about your ass, you're not black enough. And they always holdin us back.[750]

James P. Comer and Alvin F. Poussaint:
This false stereotype is the cause of the absolute terror and psychosocial paralysis we see in some black students from low-income families whose status as students means passage out of this black stereotype. It is a source of great conflict for black teens who would like to maintain friendships with blacks and whites, who enjoy Beethoven as much as Stevie Wonder, who prefer algebra to football, and so on. This confusion reaches its extreme when black students accuse other black students of "acting white" because they work hard and achieve academic success.[751]

We have even seen black teens from supportive, upper-income families become hustlers and drug addicts in a misguided effort to be black or identify with their less-affluent brothers and sisters.[752]

Reverend Jesse Lee Peterson
When group identity replaces individual identity, one must adopt the patterns of opinion mandated by the group, or be excommunicated by the group. That is why we see so much ideological conformity in black America.[753]

Shared Values

Thomas Sowell
> The kind of idealized unity projected by political leaders and intellectuals has seldom existed among any racial or ethnic minority anywhere. Nor has the economic progress of racial or ethnic groups been much correlated with their closeness to, or remoteness from, such unity.[754]

Julius Lester
> For two decades, an honest exchange of ideas in black America has been discouraged in the name of something called unity.[755]

> But American black history had never elevated racial unity above debate, dialogue, difference, or intelligence. In the first part of the 19th century, Negro National conventions were held where black leaders debated and disagreed bitterly and brilliantly with each other over slavery and freedom, abolitionism and separatism. Frederick Douglass, the first national black leader, and Martin Delaney, the first black separatist, were political adversaries and friends.[756]

Stephen L. Carter
> Our community needs dissent, it needs dialogue, it needs all the fresh ideas it can get.[757]

> Free thinking is not treason; on the contrary, it is the greatest service individuals can perform for their communities.[758]

Frederick Douglass, 1889:
> I hold that our union is our weakness.[759]

African Americans have asserted that they are free to explore everything that interests them.

Faith Ringgold
I wanted my daughters to know about art, music and literature; to know about other people's cultures and history as well as their own and to be well traveled. I wanted them to be little "continental colored girls" with a future—if they chose—outside Harlem or, indeed, America. Most of all, I wanted my daughters to have choices.[760]

Stanley Crouch
The world is too big to stay in your little block and fall in love with yourself over and over.[761]

Darold Ferguson Jr., a.k.a. **A$AP Ferg**:
A lot of people don't leave the block. They want to stay—they hug the block so hard they don't get to see other things.[762]

Pharrell Lanscilo Williams, a.k.a. **Pharrell**:
I don't live my life trying to be black. What I do is I nurture my curiosity and music.

The new black is a mentality. You don't do things because you're black, you do things because you're genuinely interested in something.[763]

Grant Hill
I know I'm black. I've been black all my life. I don't have to walk a certain way, dress a certain way. I don't have to do anything to prove my blackness.[764]

W. E. B. Du Bois wrote, in his classic *The Souls of Black Folk*, of "the sovereign human soul":
[T]hat seeks a freedom for expansion and self-development; that will love and hate and labor in its own way....[765]

Shared Values

Shelby Steele
The purpose of freedom is that it enables you to be an individual. It enables you to explore all your talents and pursue dreams that you could not have had when you were oppressed.[766]

The elimination of discrimination will always be largely a collective endeavor, while racial development will always be the effect that results from individuals within the race bettering their own lives.[767]

[T]he individual is the seat of all energy, creativity, motivation, and power.[768]

Ralph Ellison
When we finally achieve the right of full participation in American life, what we make of it will depend upon our sense of cultural values, and our creative use of freedom, not upon our racial identification.[769]

Our task is that of making ourselves individuals.[770]

Zora Neale Hurston
No, we will go where the internal drive carries us like everybody else. It is up to the individual.[771]

All clumps of people turn out to be individuals on close inspection.[772]

James P. Comer and **Alvin F. Poussaint**, advising parents:
Most important, you should help them understand that their own personal development—education, social, and moral—is the most important contribution that they can make to the black cause.[773]

Richard Williams

I believed the greatest civil rights victory I could achieve would be my own success.[774]

Reverend Jesse Lee Peterson

I saw that I was free to decide for myself the kind of person I was going to be, and that I did not have to accept the script of rage written for me by the "black leaders" of the day.[775]

It is time to claim the true freedom dreamed some forty years ago by Dr. King.[776]

Oprah Winfrey

Freedom is about having a choice.[777]

Shelby Steele

We're free. I'm free. You're free. There may be a small degree of racism left in American life but the larger truth is that you are free in this society to make whatever kind of life you want to make for yourself. You can nurture any dreams that you want to nurture in this society. Not only are you going to be free to pursue them but in many cases this society's going to find ways to help you pursue them.[778]

If you are black and you want to be a poet, or a doctor, or a corporate executive, or a movie star, there will surely be barriers to overcome, but white racism will be among the least of them. You will be far more likely to receive racial preferences than to suffer racial discrimination.[779]

Bill T. Jones

Can you choose to live "free at last" as a verb—as an action?[780]

Shared Values

India Arie Simpson, a.k.a. **India Arie**:
> Hey, I am not my hair. I am not this skin. I am a soul that lives within.[781]

Marguerite A. Wright
> Black teens, females and males alike, should learn that there are many different ways to be black. They should not conform to the media-hyped negative image of black youth just because it seems like a "cool" thing to do. They should be allowed the freedom to be themselves.[782]

Jo-Laine, fourteen years old:
> A personality is something all its own; it doesn't have to do with race.[783]

Glenys Rogers, fourteen years old:
> There is no certain way any Black person should have to act to be Black, or a White person to be White.[784]

Myesha, twelve years old:
> I sure hope there is more than one way of being black because if I had to be black like other black people, then I wouldn't be myself.
>
> I think there are a whole lot of ways to be black and to be Myesha is one of them.[785]

Stacey A. Moorehead, fifteen years old:
> To my brothers and sisters: you fought and marched so that one day I'd be able to be equal to White people. That time is now. Even though we haven't reached the finish line, it's a definite improvement. Don't resent my generation because we have White friends, listen to rock music or have non-Black idols or role models. We are only reaping the benefits of your struggle. Wasn't that the whole point of your marches?[786]

Biographical Notes
(persons with three or more quotations)

Charles Barkley (born 1963): professional basketball player, Olympic champion, television commentator

Joseph Biden (born 1942): lawyer, US senator, US vice president

Arthur C. Brooks (born 1964): social scientist, musician, president of the American Enterprise Institute

Geoffrey Canada (born 1952): president of the Harlem Children's Zone, activist

Benjamin S. Carson (born 1951): pediatric neurosurgeon, director of pediatric neurosurgery at Johns Hopkins Medical Center, was awarded the Presidential Medal of Freedom

Farai Chideya (born 1969): novelist, multimedia journalist, radio host, podcast producer

Ron Christie (born 1969): government relations expert, political strategist, professor

David A. Clarke Jr. (born 1956): Sheriff of Milwaukee County, Wisconsin

Hillary Clinton (born 1947): lawyer, presidential candidate, US secretary of state, US senator, First Lady of the United States

Ta-Nehisi Coates (born 1975): journalist, educator, MacArthur genius

Johnnetta B. Cole (born 1936): anthropologist, professor, Director of the Smithsonian National Museum of African Art, chair of the Board of Trustees of United Way of America, president emerita of Spelman and Bennett Colleges

James P. Comer (born 1934): child psychiatrist, professor, founder and chairman of the School Development Program at the Yale University School of Medicine's Child Study Center

Stanley Crouch (born 1945): music critic, columnist, novelist

Debra J. Dickerson (born 1959): attorney, US Air Force officer, blogger, editor

Frederick Douglass (1818–1895): abolitionist, women's rights activist, orator, ordained minister, president of the Freedman's Savings Bank, US Marshal, Recorder of Deeds for the District of Columbia, minister-resident and consul-general to the Republic of Haiti, chargé d'affaires for the Dominican Republic, editor, publisher

W. E. B. Du Bois (1868–1963): sociologist, historian, criminologist, educator, cofounder of the National Association for the Advancement of Colored People, editor, novelist, poet

Marian Wright Edelman (born 1939): lawyer, civil rights activist, director of Harvard's Center for Law and Education, founder and CEO of the Children's Defense Fund

Larry Elder (born 1952): lawyer, radio and television host, business person, columnist

Eric Foner (born 1943): historian

Biographical Notes

Richard Thompson Ford (N/A): law professor

Virginia Walden Ford (N/A): integrated Little Rock high schools, leader of the Black Alliance for Educational Options and the DC Parents for School Choice

Alice Goffman (born 1982): sociologist, urban ethnographer, professor

James Golden, a.k.a. Snerdley (N/A): call screener, producer, and engineer for the Rush Limbaugh talk show, Producer/Executive for Premiere Networks, Senior Partner of Golden Creative Communications, LLC

Bob Herbert (born 1945): reporter, editor, columnist

Zora Neale Hurston (1891–1960): novelist, short story writer, folklorist, anthropologist

Randall Kennedy (born 1954): law professor

Reverend Martin Luther King Jr. (1929–1968): Baptist minister, cofounder and president of the Southern Christian Leadership Conference, civil rights leader, Nobel Peace Prize winner, orator

John Lewis (born 1940): civil rights activist, chairman of the Student Nonviolent Coordinating Committee, US congressman

Glenn C. Loury (born 1948): economist, professor at Brown University, founding director of the Institute on Race and Social Division at Boston University

Heather Mac Donald (born 1956): lawyer, political commentator, journalist, fellow of the Manhattan Institute

Lloyd Marcus (N/A): singer, songwriter, Tea Party activist, chairman of Conservative Campaign Committee PAC

John McWhorter (born 1965): linguist, professor, senior fellow at the Manhattan Institute, columnist

Denisha Merriweather (N/A): student, school voucher winner

Barack Obama (born 1961): community organizer, professor, Illinois state senator, US senator, Nobel Peace Prize winner, US president

Orlando Patterson (born 1940): sociologist, professor at Harvard University, novelist, special advisor to the prime minister of Jamaica

R. Donahue Peebles (born 1960): real estate entrepreneur, political activist

Rick Perry (born 1950): governor of Texas, presidential candidate

Reverend Jesse Lee Peterson (born 1949): minister, radio and television talk show host, founder and president of Brotherhood Organization of A New Destiny

Alvin F. Poussaint (born 1934): psychiatrist, professor, director of the Media Center of the Judge Baker Children's Center in Boston, consultant to The Cosby Show

William Raspberry (1935–2012): Pulitzer Prize–winning columnist, professor

Ronald Reagan (1911–2004): actor, union leader, military veteran, governor of California, US president

Biographical Notes

Condoleezza Rice (born 1954): political scientist, diplomat, secretary of state, professor, college provost, director Stanford University Global Center for Business and the Economy

Jason L. Riley (born 1971): journalist, member of the *The Wall Street Journal* editorial board, senior fellow at the Manhattan Institute

Jackie Robinson (1919–1972): Major League Baseball (MLB) second baseman who became the first African American to play in the major leagues in the modern era, businessman

Bayard Rustin (1910–1987): civil rights activist, strategist, advisor to Dr. King, chief organizer of the 1963 March on Washington, executive director of the A. Phillip Randolph Institute

Bernie Sanders (born 1941): US senator, presidential candidate

Tim Scott (born 1965): entrepreneur, US representative, US senator

Tavis Smiley (born 1964): talk show host, political commentator, entrepreneur, philanthropist

Thomas Sowell (born 1930): economist, professor, columnist, senior fellow at the Hoover Institution at Stanford University

Michael Steele (born 1958): lawyer, MSNBC political analyst, lieutenant governor of Maryland, chair of the Minority Business Enterprise Taskforce, first African-American chairman of the Republican National Committee

Shelby Steele (born 1946): columnist, professor, documentary filmmaker, research fellow at the Hoover Institution at Stanford University

Susan L. Taylor (born 1946): entrepreneur, editorial director of Essence magazine, public speaker

Lynn Toler (born 1958): judge, arbitrator on *Divorce Court*

Elizabeth Warren (born 1949): lawyer, professor, US senator

Booker T. Washington (1856–1915): founder of Tuskegee Institute, national leader of African Americans, advisor to presidents

Richard Williams (born 1942): tennis coach, entrepreneur, father of Serena and Venus Williams

Serena Williams (born 1981): tennis champion, fashion designer, model, actor, entrepreneur, philanthropist

Venus Williams (born 1980): tennis champion, fashion designer, interior designer, entrepreneur, philanthropist

Walter E. Williams (born 1936): economist, commentator, professor, columnist

William Julius Wilson (born 1935): sociologist, professor, president of the American Sociological Association

Oprah Winfrey (born 1954): actor, television talk show host, magazine founder, editorial director, television programming creator, cable network cofounder, satellite radio programmer, book critic, philanthropist

Robert L. Woodson Sr. (born 1937): community development leader, and founder and president of the National Center for Neighborhood Enterprise

Biographical Notes

Malcolm X, born Malcolm Little, a.k.a. El Hajj Malik El-Shabazz (1925–1965): minister and spokesperson for the Nation of Islam, founder of the Organization of Afro-American Unity

Notes

Acknowledgments
1. Eric Holder, "Attorney General Eric Holder at the Department of Justice African American History Month Program," US Department of Justice, Feb. 18, 2009, http://www.justice.gov/ opa/speech/attorney-general-eric-holder-department-justice-african-american-history-month-program; also see Andrew Billingsley: "It is not, of course, our contention that only Negroes can accurately study and make effective recommendations about the Negro experience and the urban condition. We need both Negro and white scholars to undertake these studies;" from *Black Families in White America* (Englewood Cliffs: Prentice Hall, Inc. 1968), p. 162; and Cornel West, "But this tragedy also has to do with the refusal of Black intellectuals to establish and sustain their own institutional mechanisms of criticism and self-criticism, organized in such a way that people of whatever color would be able to contribute to it;" from bell hooks and Cornel West, *Breaking Bread: Insurgent Black Intellectual Life* (Boston: South End Press, 1991), p. 134.

On Senator Obama's Cover Quotation
2. Frederick Douglass, in Philip S. Foner, *Frederick Douglass: A Biography* (New York: Citadel Press, 1964), p. 269.
3. Taylor Branch, "White Privilege and Personal Agency," *WNYC*, Jan. 18, 2016, http://www.wnyc.org/story/white-privilege-personal-agency/ "White Privilege and Personal Agency," at 30:58.
4. US senator Barack Obama, "Remarks of U.S. Senator Barack Obama on the Nomination of Justice Janice Rogers Brown," *obamaspeeches.com*, June 8, 2005, at http://obamaspeeches.com/021-Nomination-of-Justice-Janice-Rogers-Brown-Obama-Speech.htm.
5. Carter G. Woodson, *The Mis-Education of the Negro* (Trenton, N.J.: Africa World Press, Inc., 1933/1990), p. 94; also at http://historyisaweapon.

com/defcon1/misedne.html. This book was one of the inspirations for the album: *The Miseducation of Lauryn Hill.*
6. Rev. Ralph David Abernathy, *And the Walls Came Tumbling Down: An Autobiography* (New York: Harper & Row, 1989), p. 589.
7. Herman Cain, in Todd Beamon, "Obama's Attention to Border Crisis Outrages African-Americans," Newsmax.com, Aug. 17, 2014, http://www.newsmax.com/Draft-Stories/Obama-blacks-illegals-jobs/2014/08/17/id/589249.
8. Stephen A. Smith, in Dylan Stableford, "What I Dream Is That for One Election…Every Black Person in America Vote Republican," March 19, 2015, http://news.yahoo.com/stephen-a-smith-black-americans-should-vote-republican-gop-election-140317220.html
9. Tavis Smiley, *On Air: The Best of Tavis Smiley on the Tom Joyner Morning Show 2002-2003, Volume II* (Carlsbad, California: Smiley Books, 2004), p. 33.
10. Milton Coleman, "Making Black Votes Count," *The Washington Post*, July 7, 1985, https://www.washingtonpost.com/archive/opinions/1985/07/07/making-black-votes-count/5a709f84-77c9-48f0-ae40-53256d4d8aec/
11. Kevin Johnson, "A President for Everyone, Except Black People," *The Philadelphia Tribune*," Apr. 14, 2013, http://www.phillytrib.com/news/a-president-for-everyone-except-black-people/article_164f06d9-abf2-5f29-a531-10ff57edf5f2.html.
12. John Henrik Clarke "The Early Years of Adam Powell" in *Harlem: A community in transition,* ed. John Henrik Clark (New York: The Citadel Press, 1964), p. 230.
13. Robert Woodson, in "Black America Under the Reagan Administration: A Symposium of Black Conservatives," *Policy Review.*
14. Ben Carson, with Candi Carson, *One Nation: What We Can All Do to Save America's Future* (New York: Sentinel, 2014), pp. 32-33.
15. Stanley Crouch, "The Failure of Black Power," *Notes of a Hanging Judge: Essays and Reviews, 1979–1989* (New York: Oxford University Press, 1990), p. 103; originally in *The Village Voice*, November, 1981.

Notes

16. Malcolm X, in David Gallen, *As They Knew Him* (New York: Carroll & Graf Publishers, Inc., 1992), p. 170. From an interview with Claude Lewis in December, 1964.
17. Jackie Robinson, as told to Alfred Duckett, *I Never Had It Made* (New York: G.P. Putnam's Sons, 1972), p. 152.
18. Arthur Ashe with Frank Deford, *Portrait in Motion* (Boston: Houghton Mifflin Company, 1975), p. 173.
19. Elbert Guillory, "Why I Am a Republican," *YouTube*, June 16, 2013, http://www.youtube.com/ watch?v=n_YQ8560E1w.

Introduction

20. Roger Wilkins, in E.J. Dionne Jr., "In Poll, Blacks Defy Political Stereotyping," *The Washington Post*, July 9, 1992, https://www.washingtonpost.com/archive/politics/1992/07/09/in-poll-blacks-defy-political-stereotyping/a6f6377c-2e98-4848-90f6-2a2df54c7179/.
21. Farai Chideya, *Don't Believe the Hype: Fighting Cultural Misinformation About African-Americans* (New York: Plume, 1995), p. 227.
22. US senator Barack Obama, T*he Audacity of Hope: Thoughts on Reclaiming the American Dream* (New York: Crown Publishers, 2006), p. 254.
23. Farai Chideya, "A Matter of Faith: Black Voters and the GOP," *The Root*, March 6, 2012, http://www.theroot.com/articles/politics/2012/03/black_social_conservatives_can_the_gop_win_their_vote.html.
24. Frank Newport, "Blacks as Conservative as Republicans on Some Moral Issues," *Gallup*, Dec. 3, 2008, http://www.gallup.com/poll/112807/blacks-conservative-republicans-some-moral-issues.aspx.
25. ____. "Religion Remains a Strong Marker of Political Identity in U.S.," *Gallup*, July 28, 2014, http://www.gallup.com/poll/174134/religion-remains-strong-marker-political-identity.aspx.
26. Barack Obama, "One Nation…Under God?" *Sojourners*, Nov., 2006, https://sojo.net/magazine/ november-2006/one-nation-under-god#sthash.ZhTvRjFp.dpuf, http://www.sojo.net/ magazine/2006/11/one-nation-under-god.

27. Wayne Allyn Root, "The Party That Booed God," *The Blaze*, Sep. 6, 2012, http://www.theblaze. com/contributions/the-party-that-booed-god/.
28. W. E. B. Du Bois, *W.E.B. Du Bois Speaks: Speeches and Addresses, 1920-1963*, ed. Dr. Philip S. Foner (New York: Pathfinder, 1970), p. 72.
29. Willie W. Herenton, in Henry Louis Gates Jr., *America Behind the Color Line: Dialogues with African Americans* (New York: Warner Books, 2004), p. 176.
30. Marva Collins, in Thomas W. Evans, *Mentors: Making a Difference in Our Public Schools* (Princeton, New Jersey: Peterson's Guides, 1992), p. 108.
31. US representative John Lewis, with Brenda Jones, *Across That Bridge: Life Lessons and a Vision for Change* (New York: Hyperion, 2012), p. 78.
32. Kevin Jackson, "What Happened to Black Pride?" *American Thinker*, April 6, 2012, http://www.americanthinker.com/2012/04/what_happened_to_black_pride.html#ixzz1rIkhpjOx.
33. Reverend Floyd H. Flake and Reverend M. Elaine McCollins Flake, *Practical Virtues: Everyday Values and Devotions for African American Families* (New York: Amistad/HarperCollins Publishers, 2003), p. xii.
34. Susana Martinez, "Susana Martinez RNC Speech," *Politico*, Sept. 4, 2012, http://www.politico.com/story/2012/08/susana-martinez-rnc-speech-text-080421.
35. Juan Williams, *Enough: The Phony Leaders, Dead-End Movements, and Culture of Failure That Are Undermining Black America—and What We Can Do about It* (New York: Crown Publishers, 2006), 215.
36. Ron Haskins, "The Myth of the Disappearing Middle Class," *The Washington Post*, Mar. 29, 2012, https://www.washingtonpost.com/opinions/the-myth-of-the-disappearing-middle-class/2012/ 03/29/gIQAsXlsjS_story.html. Mr. Haskins also writes for NationalAffairs.com.
37. See Linda J. Waite and Maggie Gallagher, *The Case for Marriage: Why Married People Are Happier, Healthier, and Better Off Financially* (New York: Doubleday, 2000).
38. Maya Angelou, in *Mending the World: Stories of Family by Contemporary Black Writers*, ed. Rosemarie Robotham, (New York: BasicCivitas Books, 2003), p. x.

39. George F. Will, "George F. Will: The Left's Half-century of Denial Over Poverty," *The Washington Post*, Mar. 21, 2014, http://www.washingtonpost.com/opinions/george-f-will-the-lefts-half-century-of-denial-over-poverty/2014/03/21/1aeaff4e-b049-11e3-a49e-76adc9210f19_story.html?hpid=z2.
40. Shelby Steele, "On Being Black and Middle Class," *The Content of Our Character: A New Vision of Race in America* (New York: St. Martin's Press, 1990), pp. 95-96.

1. Oppression

41. Barack Obama, "Remarks by the President in Eulogy for the Honorable Reverend Clementa Pinckney," The White House, June 26, 2015, https://www.whitehouse.gov/the-press-office/ 2015/06/26/remarks-president-eulogy-honorable-reverend-clementa-pinckney.
42. ____. "A More Perfect Union," *American Rhetoric*, Mar. 18, 2008, http://www.americanrhetoric.com/speeches/barackobamaperfectunion.htm.
43. Conference, "Legacy of Slavery: Unequal Exchange," UC Santa Barbara, May 2–4, 2002, http://www.research.ucsb.edu/cbs/xsite/lectures/legacy/overview.html.
44. Deborah Foster, "Right Wing Denial and the Legacy of Slavery," *PoliticusUSA*, pmhttp://www.politicususa.com/2012/02/05/right-wing-denial-slavery.html.
45. Robert Oliver, "Should the Democrat Party Apologize for Supporting Slavery?" *Family Security Matters*, http://www.familysecuritymatters.org/publications/detail/should-the-democrat-party-apologize-for-supporting-slavery#ixzz3nzuGMeOZ.
46. Dinesh D'Souza, in Nicholas Ballasy, "D'Souza: Hillary Film Could Earn Me 'Life in Prison,'" *PJMedia*, March 13, 2016, https://pjmedia.com/election/2016/03/13/dsouza-hillary-film-could-earn-me-life-in-prison.
47. Angela McGlowan, *Bamboozled: How Americans Are Being Exploited by the Lies of the Liberal Agenda* (Nashville: Thomas Nelson, 2007), p. 189.

48. Frances Rice, "Does the Democratic Party Owe Blacks an Apology?" *Black Republican Blog*, May 15, 2015, http://blackrepublican.blogspot.com/2015/05/black-republican-frequently-asked.html.
49. Michael Steele, *Right Now: A 12-Step Program for Defeating the Obama Administration* (Washington, DC: Regnery Publishing, Inc., 2009), p. 76.
50. "Trump's Triumph," *The Economist*, May 7, 2016, p. 9.
51. Rick Perry, "Why It's Republicans, Not Democrats, Who Really Offer African-Americans Hope for a Better Life," Fox News, July 2, 2015, http://www.foxnews.com/opinion/2015/07/02/why-it-s-republicans-not-democrats-who-really-offer-african-americans-hope-better-life.html.
52. Elbert Guillory, "Why I Am a Republican," YouTube, http://www.youtube.com/watch?v=n_YQ8560E1w.
53. Michelle Alexander, *The New Jim Crow: Mass Incarceration in the Age of Colorblindness* (New York: The New Press, 2012), p. 43.
54. Eric Foner, "If Lincoln hadn't died...Would the Disastrous Reconstruction Era Have Taken a Different Course?" *American Heritage*, Winter 2009: 47+, http://cr.middlebury.edu/public/amorsman/ Civil%20war%20readings/Week%209%20Recipes%20for%20Reconstruction/Reading%20 1%20If%20Lincoln%20Hadn't%20Died.html.
55. Ibid.
56. David Catron, "Republicans and Race: A Reality Check," *The American Spectator*, Nov. 20, 2015, http://spectator.org/articles/62592/republicans-and-race-reality-check; http://www.vox.com/policy-and-politics/2015/11/20/9766896/woodrow-wilson-racist.
57. Walter E. Williams, "Walter E. Williams: Squandered Resources on College Education," The Tampa Tribune, Dec. 14, 2015, http://www.tbo.com/list/news-opinion-commentary/walter-e-williams-squandered-resources-on-college-education-20151214/#sthash.kH7mygJ2.dpufhttp://www.tbo.com/ list/news-opinion-commentary/walter-e-williams-squandered-resources-on-college-education-20151214/.
58. "Dwight D. Eisenhower," *Wikipedia*, http://en.wikipedia.org/wiki/Eisenhower#Civil_rights; David A. Nichols, "Ike Liked Civil Rights,"

New York Times, Sept. 12, 2007, http://www.nytimes.com/2007/ 09/12/ opinion/12nichols.html?_r=0.
59. Bruce Bartlett, *Wrong on Race: The Democratic Party's Buried Past* (New York: Palgrave Macmillan, 2008), p. 24.
60. Ben Carson, in Stephen Dinan, "Ben Carson Uses Empowerment Message in Bid to Sway Black Voters," *The Washington Times*, Sept. 29, 2015, http://www.washingtontimes.com/news/2015/sep/29/ ben-carson-uses-empowerment-message-in-bid-to-sway/; http://www.cnn.com/2015/01/07/us/klan-numbers/. The Klan dropped from millions to a few thousand members.
61. Eric Foner, *Reconstruction Updated Edition: America's Unfinished Revolution, 1863–1877* (New York: Harper Perennial, 1989, 2014), ebook Loc 8066.
62. Frances Rice, "The Ku Klux Klan Was the Terrorist Arm of the Democrat Party," *Black Republican Blog*, Oct. 2015, http://blackrepublican.blogspot.com/2015/10/the-ku-klux-klan-was-terrorist-arm-of_56.html.
63. Walter E. Williams, *Race and Economics: How Much Can Be Blamed on Discrimination?* (Stanford University, Stanford, California: Hoover Institution Press, 2011), p. 92.
64. Ta-Nehisi Coates, "Ta-Nehisi Coates and Khalil Gibran Muhammad: Live from the New York Public Library," *New York Public Library*, Oct. 13, 2015, http://www.nypl.org/audiovideo/ta-nehisi-coates-khalil-gibran-muhammad; at 10:33; transcript p. 11.
65. Bruce Bartlett, *Wrong on Race: The Democratic Party's Buried Past* (New York: Palgrave Macmillan, 2008), p. 183.
66. Jeffrey Lord, "Will Democrats Apologize for Slavery and Segregation?" *The American Spectator*, http://spectator.org/articles/63244/will-democrats-apologize-slavery-and-segregation.
67. George Wallace, "Segregation Forever," YouTube, https://www.youtube.com/watch?v=hLL Dn7MjbF0.
68. Malcolm X, "The Ballot or the Bullet," *Edchange*, April 12, 1964, http://www.edchange.org/ multicultural/speeches/malcolm_x_ballot.html.

69. Irin Carmon, "For Eugenic Sterilization Victims, Belated Justice," MSNBC, June 27, 2014, http://www.msnbc.com/all/eugenic-sterilization-victims-belated-justice.
70. Thomas Sowell, *Intellectuals and Race* (New York: Basic Books, 2013), p. 27.
71. Bishop E. W. Jackson, "Black Leaders: Remove Planned Parenthood Founder from Taxpayer-Funded Museum," PJ Media, Aug. 28, 2015, http://pjmedia.com/blog/black-leaders-remove-planned-parenthood-founder-from-taxpayer-funded-museum/?singlepage=true.
72. Margaret Sanger, "High Lights in the History of Birth Control," *New York University*, https://www.nyu.edu/projects/sanger/webedition/app/documents/show.php?sangerDoc=306641.xml.
73. Hillary Clinton, in Mona Charen, "Mrs. Clinton Can't Defend Patron Saint of Planned Parenthood," *National Review*, April 24, 2009, http://www.nationalreview.com/article/227369/mrs-clinton-cant-defend-patron-saint-planned-parenthood-mona-charen.
74. Jason L. Riley, "Let's Talk About the Racial Disparity in Abortions," *Wall Street Journal*, Sept 15, 2015, http://www.wsj.com/articles/lets-talk-about-the-racial-disparity-in-abortions-1442356170.
75. Seth Paxton, "Planned Parenthood workers, PACs donated $25M to Dems since 2000," Fox News, Aug. 13, 2015, http://www.foxnews.com/politics/2015/08/13/planned-parenthood-workers-pacs-donated-25m-to-dems-since-2000/?intcmp=hpbt3.
76. "Europe's abortion rules," BBC, Feb. 12, 2007, http://news.bbc.co.uk/2/hi/europe/6235557.stm.
77. Jeremy Bender, "These 22 Charts Reveal Who Serves in America's Military," *Business Insider*, Aug. 14, 2014, http://www.businessinsider.com/us-military-demographics-2014-8?op=1.
78. Melissa Harris-Perry, in Mark Finkelstein, "Melissa Harris-Perry Admits: U.S. Military 'Despised by Many Progressives,'" *MRC NewsBusters*, Jan. 26, 2013, http://www.newsbusters.org/blogs/mark-finkelstein/2013/01/26/melissa-harris-perry-admits-us-military-despised-many-progressives.

79. Michelle Ye Hee Lee, "Vet's Death Highlights Urology Clinic Wait-time Issues," *AZ Central*, May 26, 2014, http://www.azcentral.com/story/news/local/phoenix/2014/05/26/urology-clinic-wait-time-veteran-death/9587959/.
80. Dan Merica and Ashley Killough, "Clinton Campaign Backtracks on VA Claim After Widespread Criticism, CNN, Oct. 28, 2015, http://www.cnn.com/2015/10/27/politics/hillary-clinton-veterans-affairs-gop/index.html.
81. Scott Davis, in Sarah Westwood, "Whistleblower: 34,000 Combat Veterans Still Waiting for VA Benefits," *Washington Examiner*, July 21, 2015, http://www.washingtonexaminer.com/34000-combat-veterans-still-waiting-for-va-benefits/article/2568641.
82. Pete Kasperowicz, "VA Caught Sending Veterans' Mail to the Shredder," *Washington Examiner*, Aug. 18, 2015, http://www.washingtonexaminer.com/va-caught-sending-veterans-mail-to-the-shredder/article/2570354.
83. Roger L. Simon, "The Veterans Scandal: Socialized Medicine on Trial," PJ Media, May 23, 2014, https://pjmedia.com/rogerlsimon/2014/5/23/va-scandal/?singlepage=true.
84. Peggy Noonan, "The VA Scandal Is a Crisis of Leadership," *Wall Street Journal*, May 29, 2014, http://www.wsj.com/articles/noonan-the-va-scandal-is-a-crisis-of-leadership-1401402352.
85. Sarah Palin, in Kyle Blaine, "So, Uh, Here's The Full Text Of Sarah Palin's Bizarre Trump Speech," BuzzFeed News, Jan. 19, 2016, http://www.buzzfeed.com/kyleblaine/so-uh-heres-the-full-text-of-sarah-palins-bizarre-trump-spee#.mqy11qVl8.
86. Garrison Keillor, *Homegrown Democrat: A Few Plain Thoughts from the Heart of America* (New York: Viking, 2004), pp. 20, 137.
87. Paul Krugman, "Keynes Comes to Canada," *New York Times*, Oct. 23, 2015, http://www.nytimes.com/2015/10/23/opinion/keynes-comes-to-canada.html?action=click&pgtype=Homepage&module=opinion-c-col-left-region&region=opinion-c-col-left-region&WT.nav=opinion-c-col-left-region&_r=0.

88. Arthur C. Brooks, "'Be Open-Handed Toward Your Brothers,'—A Conservative Social-Justice Agenda," *Commentary*, Feb. 2014, p. 16.
89. Nicholas D. Kristof, "Bleeding Heart Tightwads," *New York Times*, Dec. 20, 2008, http://www.nytimes.com/2008/12/21/opinion/21kristof.html.
90. Chris Matthews in Geoffrey Dickens, "The Top 20 Worst Chris Matthews Quotes Calling Obama Critics Racist," NewsBusters, Nov. 7, 2013, http://newsbusters.org/blogs/geoffrey-dickens/2013/11/07/top-20-worst-chris-matthews-quotes-calling-obama-critics-racist.
91. Keith Olbermann, *Pitchforks and Torches: The Worst of the Worst, from Beck, Bill, and Bush to Palin and Other Posturing Republicans* (Hoboken, New Jersey: Wiley, 2011), p. 245.
92. Brent Terry, in By Caleb Bonham, "Audio: Professor Rants 'Racist, Misogynist, Money-Grubbing People' Looking to Suppress Liberal Youth Vote, Universities Will Close If GOP Wins," Fox News, April 22, 2014, http://nation.foxnews.com/2014/04/22/audio-professor-rants-'racist-misogynist-money-grubbing-people'-looking-suppress-liberal.
93. Joe Biden, "Biden 'Put You All Back in Chains' Remark Causes Stir," YouTube, Aug 14, 2012, https://www.youtube.com/watch?v=5gII8D-lzbA. The audience was described as "predominantly black" in "Beyond The Soundbite: Biden's 'Chains' Speech," *NPR*, Aug. 16, 2012, http://www.npr.org/ 2012/08/16/158943306/on-the-campaign-trail-biden-chained-to-a-stump-speech.
94. Barack Obama, "Barack Obama's Small Town Guns and Religion Comments," YouTube, April 11, 2008, https://www.youtube.com/watch?v=DTxXUufI3jA.
95. Robert Oliver, "Should the Democrat Party Apologize for Supporting Slavery?" *Family Security Matters*, March 13, 2009, http://www.familysecuritymatters.org/publications/detail/should-the-democrat-party-apologize-for-supporting-slavery#ixzz3uW6yuKqu.
96. Shelby Steele, *Shame: How America's Past Sins Have Polarized Our Country* (New York: Basic Books, 2015), p. 169.

97. David Webb, "Death and Dearth in Black America: Baltimore, a Failure of Leadership," *Breitbart*, May 1, 2015, http://www.breitbart.com/big-government/2015/05/01/death-and-dearth-in-black-america-baltimore-a-failure-of-leadership/.
98. Walter E. Williams, "Fiddling Away the Future," CNS News, July 7, 2015, http://www.cnsnews.com/commentary/walter-e-williams/fiddling-away-future.
99. Robert L. Woodson, "New Approach to the War on Poverty," *Real Clear Radio Hour*, SoundCloud, https://soundcloud.com/realclearradiohour/bob-woodson-podcast.
100. Joseph Watkins, "Chicago Activists Unchained, Destroy Black Leadership," YouTube, Oct. 27, 2014, https://www.youtube.com/watch?v=BUSRZo1BE5o; also see http://www.thegatewaypundit.com/2015/01/chicago-unchained-inner-city-activists-respond-to-obamas-state-of-the-union-2015-video/.
101. Ibid.
102. Ibid.
103. David Clark, "Sheriff Clarke: Obama Has a 'Disdain for the American Police Officer,'" Fox News, April 29, 2015, http://insider.foxnews.com/2015/04/29/sheriff-clarke-obama-has-disdain-american-police-officer.
104. James Golden, in Ginni Thomas, "Rush Limbaugh's Call Screener: 'What Liberalism Has Done to Black Communities Is Horrific,'" *Daily Caller*, Sept. 21, 2014, http://dailycaller.com/2014/09/21/rush-limbaughs-call-screener-what-liberalism-has-done-to-black-communities-is-horrific/; at 8:54.
105. Ibid., at 1:12.
106. Malcolm X, "God's Judgment of White America," *Malcom-X.org*, Dec 4, 1963, http://www.malcolm-x.org/speeches/spc_120463.htm.
107. Man calling in to "In Depth" program (Peter Slen interviewing Shelby Steele), Book TV on C-Span, April 2, 2006, http://www.c-span.org/video/?191760-1/depth-shelby-steele; at 49:44.
108. Patricia L. Dickson, "What White Democrats Really Think About Black Americans," *American Thinker*, May 23, 2014, http://www.

americanthinker.com/articles/2014/05/what_white_democrats_really_think_about_black_americans.html.

2. Progress and Opportunity

109. Condoleezza Rice, in Ben Kamisar, "Rice: Dem Racial Attacks 'Appalling,'" *The Hill*, Nov. 6, 2014, http://thehill.com/blogs/ballot-box/223161-dems-midterm-racial-attacks-appalling-rice-says.
110. Orlando Patterson, "Race, Gender and Liberal Fallacies," *New York Times*, October 20, 1991, E15.
111. US representative John Lewis with Michael D'Orso, *Walking with the Wind: Memoir of the Movement* (New York: Simon & Schuster, 1998), 463.
112. Marian Wright Edelman, *The Measure of Our Success: A Letter to My Children and Yours* (Boston: Beacon Press, 1992), p. 33.
113. Quincy Jones, in Alex Haley, *The Playboy Interviews*, ed. Murray Fisher, (New York: Ballantine Books, 1993), pp. 482-483; originally from *Playboy*, July, 1990.
114. William Julius Wilson, *The Truly Disadvantaged: The Inner City, the Underclass, and Public Policy* (Chicago: University of Chicago Press, 1987), p. 134.
115. ____. *The Declining Significance of Race: Blacks and Changing American Institutions* (Chicago: University of Chicago Press, 1980), p. 2.
116. Walter E. Williams, "Black Progression and Retrogression," CNS News, Dec. 23, 2014, http://cnsnews.com/commentary/walter-e-williams/black-progression-and-retrogression.
117. Thomas Sowell, "Myths About Minorities," *Commentary*, Aug. 1, 1979, https://www.commentarymagazine.com/articles/myths-about-minorities/.
118. ____. *Civil Rights: Rhetoric or Reality?* (New York: William Morrow, 1985), p. 52.
119. ____. *Ethnic America: A History* (New York: Basic Books, Inc., 1981), p. 275.
120. James P. Comer and Alvin F. Poussaint, *Raising Black Children* (New York: Plume, 1992), p. 12.

121. Charles Johnson, in *Best African American Essays, 2010*, eds. Gerald Early and Randall Kennedy (New York: One World, Ballantine Books, 2010), p. 116.
122. Jerald Wolff, in Ibid., p. 206.
123. Colin L. Powell with Joseph E. Persico, *My American Journey* (New York: Random House, 1995), p. 533.
124. Randall Kennedy, *The Persistence of the Color Line: Racial Politics and the Obama Presidency* (New York: Pantheon Books, 2011), p. 233.
125. Ibid., p. 348.
126. Hank Thomas in John A. Tures, "A Black Freedom Rider's Assessment of Whites," *Huffington Post*, May 14, 2015, http://www.huffingtonpost.com/john-a-tures/a-black-freedom-riders-as_b_7280668.html.
127. Bebe Moore Campbell, in Pamela Newkirk, "At Lunch With Expert Unexpectedly," *The New York Times*, Nov. 15, 1995, C8.
128. Lloyd Marcus, "Dad, the Elderly White Woman, and Race Exploiters," *American Thinker*, Jan. 25, 2015, http://www.americanthinker.com/articles/2015/01/dad_the_elderly_white_ woman_ and_ race_ exploiters.html.
129. Tim Scott, "Personal Story from Sen. Tim Scott," *Edgefield Advertiser*, Feb. 1, 2014, http://www.edgefieldadvertiser.com/2014/02/a-personal-story-from-sen-tim-scott/.
130. Maya Angelou, in Tavis Smiley, with David Ritz, *My Journey with Maya* (New York: Little, Brown and Company, 2015), pp. 184-185.
131. Henry Louis Gates Jr., *America Behind the Color Line: Dialogues with African Americans* (New York: Warner Books, 2004), p. 2.
132. Cora Daniels, in Cora Daniels and John L. Jackson Jr., *Impolite Conversations: On Race, Politics, Sex, Money, and Religion* (New York: Atria Books, 2014), p. 148.
133. Randall Kennedy, *The Persistence of the Color Line: Racial Politics and the Obama Presidency* (New York: Pantheon Books, 2011), pp. 12-13.
134. Ta-Nehisi Coates, "Fear of a Black President," *The Atlantic*, Sept. 2012, http://www.theatlantic.com/magazine/archive/2012/09/fear-of-a-black-president/309064/.

135. Harry Belafonte, with Michael Shnayerson, *My Song: A Memoir* (New York: Knopf, 2011), p. 441.
136. Deroy Murdock, "Blacks Lose Ground Under Obama, *National Review,* Apr. 10, 2015, http://www.nationalreview.com/article/416735/blacks-lose-ground-under-obama-deroy-murdock.
137. Tavis Smiley, *On Air: The Best of Tavis Smiley on the Tom Joyner Morning Show 2002-2003, Volume II* (Carlsbad, California: Smiley Books, 2004), pp. 22-23.
138. R. Donahue Peebles, in Susannah Lee, "Future African-American Billionaire on 'Black Lives Matter' Movement," *Yahoo,* Aug. 7, 2015, http://finance.yahoo.com/news/the-next-african-american-billionaire-on-black-lives-matter-movement-115616208.html.
139. Shawn Carter, *Decoded* (New York: Spiegel & Grau, 2010), p. 218.
140. Ben Carson, with Candy Carson, *A More Perfect Union: What We the People Can Do to Reclaim Our Constitutional Liberties* (New York: Sentinel, 2015), p. 1.
141. Julius Erving with Karl Taro Greenfeld, *Dr. J: The Autobiography* (New York. HarperCollins, 2013), p. 167-168.
142. Ibid., p. 124.
143. Lloyd Marcus, "Samuel L. Jackson's America-Bashing: A Huge Disservice,"*American Thinker,*Jan.1,2016,http://www.americanthinker.com/articles/2015/12/12_31_2015_ 16_0. html#ixzz3w0xrjSCW.
144. ____. "Dad, the Elderly White Woman, and Race Exploiters," *American Thinker,* Jan. 25, 2015, http://www.americanthinker.com/articles/2015/01/dad_the_elderly_white_woman_ and_ race_ exploiters.html.
145. Robin Roberts, with Veronica Chambers, *Everybody's Got Something* (New York: Grand Central Publishing, 2014), p. 70.
146. Capt. Norman Alexander McDaniel, in Wallace Terry, *Bloods: An Oral History of the Vietnam War by Black Veterans* (New York: Ballantine Books, 1984), pp. 137-138.
147. Voletta Wallace, with Tremell McKenzie, *Biggie: Voletta Wallace remembers her son, Christopher Wallace, AKA Notorious B.I.G.* (New York: Atria Books, 2005), p. 183.

148. US representative John Lewis with Michael D'Orso, *Walking with the Wind: Memoir of the Movement* (New York: Simon & Schuster, 1998), 461.
149. Eldridge Cleaver, "Brigham Young University Freedom Festival,"1981, https://www.youtube.com/watch?v=-MPxlemtm90; at 9:55.
150. Rosa Parks with Gregory J. Reed, *Dear Mrs. Parks: A Dialogue with Today's Youth* (New York: Lee & Low Books, Inc., 1996), pp. 91-92.
151. Ray Charles, "American the Beautiful," YouTube, Sept. 18, 1972, https://www.youtube.com/ watch?v=TRUjr8EVgBg.
152. W. E. B. Du Bois, *The Philadelphia Negro* (1899), https://archive.org/stream/philadelphianegr 001901mbp/philadelphianegr001901 mbp_djvu.txt.
153. John McWhorter, "Racism in Retreat," *New York Sun*, June 5, 2008, http://www.nysun.com/ opinion/racism-in-retreat/79355/.
154. Lloyd Marcus, "Forget Slavery: Too Uncle Tom Even for Conservatives?" *American Thinker*, Sept. 8, 2014, http://www.americanthinker.com/articles/2014/09/forget_slavery_too_uncle_tom_even_ for_conservatives.html.
155. Lloyd Marcus, "Dad, the Elderly White Woman, and Race Exploiters," *American Thinker*, Jan. 25, 2015, http://www.americanthinker.com/articles/2015/01/dad_the_elderly_white_woman_and_race_exploiters. html.
156. Jason L. Riley, "What Charleston Tells Us About Race Relations," *Wall Street Journal*, June 23, 2015, http://www.wsj.com/articles/SB11670627 175020993366304581066271670992268.
157. Bayard Rustin, "A Word to Black Students," *Down the Line: The Collected Writings of Bayard Rustin* (Chicago: Quadrangle Books, 1971), p. 332.
158. Orlando Patterson, "How Sociologists Made Themselves Irrelevant," *The Chronicle of Higher Education*, Dec. 1, 2014, http://chronicle.com/article/How-Sociologists-Made/150249/.
159. James Golden, in Ginni Thomas, "Rush Limbaugh's Call Screener: 'What Liberalism Has Done to Black Communities Is Horrific,'" *Daily Caller*, Sept. 21, 2014,http://dailycaller.com/ 2014/09/21/

rush-limbaughs-call-screener-what-liberalism-has-done-to-black-communities-is-horrific/.
160. Minister Louis Farrakhan, in John F. Davis, "Farrakhan Speaks," *Village Voice*, May 22, 1984, p. 17.
161. W. E. B. Du Bois, in *Against Racism: Unpublished Essays, Papers, Addresses, 1887-1961*, ed. Herbert Aptheker (Amherst: University of Massachusetts Press, 1985), 205.
162. Robert L. Woodson, ed., *On the Road to Economic Freedom: An Agenda for Black Progress* (Washington, D. C.: Regnery Gateway, 1987), p. x.
163. Jason L. Riley, *Please Stop Helping Us: How Liberals Make It Harder for Blacks to Succeed* (New York: Encounter Books, 2014), p. 33.
164. Walter E. Williams, *Up from the Projects: An Autobiography* (Stanford, California: Hoover Institution Press, 2010), 139.
165. Ibid., p. 346.
166. Ida B. Wells Barnett, in *Black Women in White America: A Documentary History*, ed. Gerda Lerner (New York: Pantheon Books, 1972), p. 539; originally from "Iola's Southern Field," *The New York Age*, Nov. 19, 1892.
167. John Hope Bryant, "Racism and the Silver Rights Movement," *John Hope Bryant Blog*, Feb. 10, 2005, http://johnhopebryant.com/2005/02/_racism_and_the.html.
168. John H. Johnson, in John H. Johnson and Lerone Bennett Jr., *Succeeding Against the Odds: The Autobiography of a Great American Businessman* (New York: Johnson Publishing Company, Inc., 1992), p. 174.
169. Booker T. Washington, in Louis R. Harlan, *Booker T. Washington: The Wizard of Tuskegee, 1901-1915* (New York: Oxford University Press, 1983), p. 117.
170. Rev. Martin Luther King Jr., *Strength to Love* (Cleveland: Collins + World, 1963), p. 83.
171. Itabari Njeri, *Every Good-Bye Ain't Gone: Family Portraits and Personal Escapades* (New York: Random House, 1990), p. 7.
172. Thomas Sowell, "Losing a Generation to the Racial Hustlers," *New York Post*, Apr. 10, 1992, p. 25.

173. ____. *Civil Rights: Rhetoric or Reality* (New York: William Morrow, 1985), p. 118.
174. Louis W. Sullivan, in Larry Elder, *Showdown: Confronting the Bias, Lies, and the Special Interests that Divide America* (New York: St. Martin's Press, 2002), p. 143; original source E.J. Dionne, "Struggling to Find a Way to Teach Values," *Washington Post*, July 9, 1990, p. A-5.
175. Walter E. Williams, "Demoralizing Young Blacks," Walterewilliams.com, Mar. 26, 2001, http://walterewilliams.com/demoralizing-young-blacks/.
176. Malcolm X, with the assistance of Alex Haley, *The Autobiography of Malcolm X* (New York: Grove Press, 1966), p. 344.
177. Jo-Issa Rae Diop, a.k.a Issa Rae, *The Misadventures of Awkward Black Girl* (New York: Atria/37 Ink, 2015), p. 163.
178. Pharrell Lanscilo Williams, in "Oprah Winfrey Interviews Pharrell Williams," YouTube, June 7, 2014, https://m.youtube.com/watch?v=dJ7rZRFNF-o; at 38:23.
179. Randall Kennedy, "Black America's Promised Land: Why I Am Still a Racial Optimist," *American Prospect*, Nov. 10, 2014, http://prospect.org/article/black-americas-promised-land-why-i-am-still-racial-optimist.
180. Robert L. Woodson, *On the Road to Economic Freedom: An Agenda for Black Progress*, ed. Robert L. Woodson (Washington, DC: Regnery Gateway, 1987), p. *xii*. Emphasis deleted.
181. Mary Frances Berry, "Contracting out U.S. security? And will branding tea party 'racist' work?" *Politico*, July 20, 2010, http://www.politico.com/arena/perm/Mary_Frances_Berry_91E3D9D5-C40D-440C-9D48-1C50CBC60C87.html. *The New York Times* corrected its news story claiming that Tea Party members had used a racial slur: www.nytimes.com/2010/07/25/pageoneplus/corrections.html.
182. Tim Scott, in David Brody, "Exclusive Tim Scott Interview: No Racism in Tea Party," CBN News, Sept. 21, 2010, http://blogs.cbn.com/thebrodyfile/archive/2010/09/21/exclusive-tim-scott-interview-no-racism-in-tea-party.aspx?mobile=false.

183. Thomas Sowell, "Random Thoughts," *Townhall*, May 27, 2014, http://townhall.com/columnists/thomassowell/2014/05/27/random-thoughts-n1843545/page/full.
184. Richard Thompson Ford, *The Race Card: How Bluffing About Bias Makes Race Relations Worse* (New York: Farrar, Strauss and Giroux, 2008), p. 19.
185. Ibid., p. 339.
186. Condoleezza Rice, in Ben Kamisar, "Rice: Dem Racial Attacks 'Appalling,'" *The Hill*, Nov. 6, 2014, http://thehill.com/blogs/ballot-box/223161-dems-midterm-racial-attacks-appalling-rice-says.
187. Larry Elder, "Tell the People They're Victims—They'll Act like Victims," WND.com, Apr. 29, 2015, http://www.wnd.com/2015/04/tell-people-theyre-victims-theyll-act-like-victims/.
188. Booker T. Washington, *The Booker T. Washington Papers, Vol. 1*, ed. Louis R. Harlan (Chicago: University of Illinois Press, 1972), p. 430.
189. Shelby Steele, in an interview with Peter Slen on "In Depth," Book TV, C-Span, Apr. 2, 2006, http://www.c-span.org/video/?191760-1/depth-shelby-steele; at 2:40:04.
190. Ron Christie, "Michelle Obama Exemplifies the Progress We've Made on Race—Why Won't She Admit It?" *Daily Beast*, May 13, 2015, http://www.thedailybeast.com/articles/2015/05/13/michelle-obama-exemplifies-the-progress-we-ve-made-on-race-why-won-t-she-admit-it.html.
191. Booker T. Washington, in August Meier, *Negro Thought in America, 1880-1915* (Ann Arbor: Univ. of Michigan Press, 1966), p. 107. Deletions in source.
192. ____. "The Atlanta Exposition Address," *Up from Slavery: An Autobiography* (1901), Etext #2376, at Project Gutenberg, http://www.gutenberg.org/dirs/etext00/slvry10.txt.
193. John H. McWhorter, "Why Blacks Don't Need Leaders," *City Journal*, Summer 2002, http://www.city-journal.org/html/why-blacks-don't-need-leaders-12352.html.

Notes

194. Russell Simmons in Henry Louis Gates Jr., *America Behind the Color Line: Dialogues with African Americans* (New York: Warner Books, 2004), p. 54.
195. Glenn C. Loury, "The Need for *Moral* Leadership in the Black Community," *New Perspectives*, Summer 1984, p. 14.
196. Ron Christie, *Blackwards: How Black Leadership is Returning America to the Days of Separate but Equal* (New York: Thomas Dunne Books, 2012), p. 243.
197. Willie Anthony Jones, in Van Jones, with Ariane Conrad, *Rebuild the Dream* (New York: Nation Books, 2012), p. *xv*.
198. Ibid., p. *xiv*.
199. Van Jones, in *Reach: 40 Black Men Speak on Living, Leading, and Succeeding*, Eds. Ben Jealous and Trabian Shorter (New York: Atria, 2015), p. 97.
200. Michael Steele, *Right Now: A 12-Step Program For Defeating the Obama Administration* (Washington, DC: Regnery Publishing, Inc., 2009), p. 107.
201. John Hope Bryant, in *Reach: 40 Black Men Speak on Living, Leading, and Succeeding*, Eds. Ben Jealous and Trabian Shorter (New York: Atria, 2015), pp. 169-170.
202. Shelby Steele, *The Content of Our Character: A New Vision of Race in America* (New York: St. Martin's Press, 1990), p. 174.
203. Debra J. Dickerson, *The End of Blackness: Returning the Souls of Black Folk to Their Rightful Owners* (New York: Pantheon Books, 2004), p. 123.
204. Rev. Ralph David Abernathy, *And the Walls Came Tumbling Down: An Autobiography* (New York: Harper & Row, 1989), p. 588.
205. Michele Wallace, *Black Macho and the Myth of the Superwoman* (New York: Dial Press, 1979), p. 78.
206. Clarence Thomas, in "Excerpts from Senate's Hearings on the Thomas Nomination," *The New York Times*, Sept. 11, 1991, p. A22.

Shared Values

3. Self-Reliance

207. Barack Obama, "Transcript: Barack Obama's Speech on Race," NPR, Mar. 18, 2008, http://www.npr.org/templates/story/story.php?storyId=88478467.
208. Hillary Clinton, "It Takes a Village: And Other Lessons Our Children Teach Us," *Booknotes*, C-Span, Mar. 3, 1996, http://www.booknotes.org/Watch/70144-1/Hillary+Rodham+Clinton.aspx.
209. Chuck Schumer, in Sarah Mimms, "Schumer Says Democrats Should 'Embrace Government,' Focus on Middle Class," *The Atlantic*, Nov. 25, 2014, http://www.theatlantic.com/politics/archive/2014/11/schumer-says-democrats-should-embrace-government-focus-on-middle-class/449697/.
210. Harry Reid, with Mark Warren, *The Good Fight: Hard Lessons from Searchlight to Washington* (New York: G. P. Putnam's Sons, 2008), p. 67.
211. Vice President Joseph Biden, in Michelle Malkin, *Who Built That: Awe-inspiring Stories of American Tinkerpreneurs* (New York: Threshold Editions/Mercury Ink, 2015), p. 3.
212. Louis D. Brandeis, "Olmstead v. United States: The Constitutional Challenges of Prohibition Enforcement," *Federal Judicial Center*, 1928, http://www.fjc.gov/history/ home.nsf/ page/ tu_olmstead_doc_15.html.
213. Democrats no longer make this ad available on the Internet, but commentary and replicas are available, for example: "The Real Life of Julia," YouTube, May 3, 2012, https://www.youtube.com/watch?v=Ir6gEvmwQtc.
214. Mary Kate Cary, "What's Hidden in Obama's 'Julia' Campaign," *U.S. News & World Report*, May 4, 2012, http://www.usnews.com/opinion/blogs/mary-kate-cary/2012/05/04/whats-hidden-in-obamas-julia-campaign.
215. Jessica Gavora, "Obama's 'Julia' Ad and the New Hubby State," *Washington Post*, May 11, 2012, https://www.washingtonpost.com/opinions/obamas-julia-ad-and-the-new-hubby-state/2012/05/11/gIQAcRdoIU_story.html.

216. Jerry Brown, "Jerry Brown Flashback: 'We Need More Welfare and Fewer Jobs,'" *Fox News*, Oct.14, 2010, http://nation.foxnews.com/jerry-brown/2010/10/14/jerry-brown-flashback-we-need-more-welfare-and-fewer-jobs.
217. Ronald Reagan, "Inaugural Address," *convio.net*, Jan. 5, 1967, http://reagan.convio.net/site/DocServer/ReaganMomentsFeb_-_4_-_Inaugural_Address_1967_-_Governor.pdf?docID=584.
218. ____. "The Nine Most Terrifying Words," YouTube, https://www.youtube.com/watch?v=xhYJS80MgYA.
219. ____. *A Time for Choosing*, October 27, *Reagan Library*, 1964, http://www.reagan.utexas.edu/archives/reference/timechoosing.html.
220. Paul Ryan, "Rep. Paul Ryan Responds: Our Day of Reckoning Is Around the Corner," *Real Clear Politics*, Jan. 25, 2011, http://www.realclearpolitics.com/video/2011/01/25/rep_paul_responds_our_day_of_reckoning_is_around_the_corner.html.
221. Barbara Bush, "Mrs. Bush's Commencement Address to the Wellesley College Class of 1990, *Wellesley College*, 1990, http://www.wellesley.edu/events/commencement/archives/1990commencement/commencementaddress.
222. Frederick Douglass, *Narrative of the Life of Frederick Douglass, an American Slave* (New York: Signet, New American Library, 1845/1968), p. 107.
223. W. E. B. Du Bois, *John Brown* (1909), at https://ia600206.us.archive.org/6/items/johnbrown00dubo/johnbrown00dubo.pdf, p. 390.
224. Carter G. Woodson, *The Mis-Education of the Negro* (Trenton, N.J.: Africa World Press, Inc., 1933/1990); also at http://historyisaweapon.com/defcon1/misedne.html.
225. Zora Neale Hurston, in Damon Root, "The Black Conservative Tradition," *Reason.com*, Oct. 27, 2009, http://reason.com/blog/2009/10/27/the-black-conservative-tradition; originally from the *Saturday Evening Post*, 1951.
226. Elbert Guillory, "Why I Am a Republican," YouTube, June 16, 2013, http://www.youtube.com/watch?v=n_YQ8560Elw.

Shared Values

227. Mia Love, in J. Arthur Bloom, "Rep. Mia Love Decries New 'Slavery' Of 'Being Dependent On People in Power' at RNC Black Outreach Event," *Daily Caller*, Feb. 11, 2015, http://dailycaller.com/2015/02/11/rep-mia-love-decries-new-slavery-of-being-dependent-on-people-in-power-at-rnc-black-outreach-event/.
228. E. W. Jackson, "E. W. Jackson on the Tenth Amendment," *The Political Guide*, Jan. 1, 2012, http://www.thepolitical-guide.com/Profiles/Senate/Virginia/E.W._Jackson/Views/The_Tenth_Amendment/.
229. Jason L. Riley, "The Next Welfare Reform: Food Stamps," *Wall Street Journal*, Mar. 24, 2015, http://www.wsj.com/articles/jason-l-riley-the-next-welfare-reform-food-stamps-1427238766.
230. Alfonzo Rachel, *Weapon of A.S.S. Destruction* (Powder Springs, Georgia: White Hall Press, 2012), p. 105. Mr. Rachel blogs at http://alfonzorachel.com.
231. Michael Steele, *Right Now: A 12-Step Program for Defeating the Obama Administration* (Washington, DC: Regnery Publishing, Inc., 2009), p. 109.
232. Thomas Sowell, "Two Different Worlds," *Creators.com*, Sept. 1, 2011, http://www.creators.com/ conservative/thomas-sowell/two-different-worlds.html.
233. Shelby Steele, interviewed by Peter Slen on "In Depth," *Book TV*, C-Span, Apr. 2, 2006, http://www.c-span.org/video/?191760-1/depth-shelby-steele; at 51:40.
234. Patricia L. Dickson, "What White Democrats Really Think About Black Americans," *American Thinker*, May, 2014, http://www.americanthinker.com/articles/2014/05/what_white_democrats_really_think_about_black_americans.html.
235. Tom Joyner, in Felicia R. Lee, "Building a Conversation, One Radio Show at a Time," *New York Times*, Feb. 13, 2007, http://www.nytimes.com/2007/02/13/arts/13joyn.html?pagewanted=all&_r=0.
236. Shawn Carter, *Decoded* (New York: Spiegel & Grau, 2010), p. 221.

237. Marian Wright Edelman, *Families in Peril: An Agenda for Social Change* (Cambridge: Harvard University Press, 1987), pp. 18-19.
238. Frances Ellen Watkins Harper, "An Address Delivered at the Centennial Anniversary of the Pennsylvania Society for Promoting the Abolition of Slavery," *Freedom on My Mind: The Columbia Documentary History of the African American Experience*, ed. Manning Marable (New York: Columbia University Press, 2003), p. 325.
239. Frederick Douglass, "From the Address at the Odd Fellows Festival, in Minerva Hall, Rochester, New York, January 1854," *The Life and Writings of Frederick Douglass, Vol. 5*, ed. Philip S. Foner (New York: International Publishers, 1975), p. 305; originally in *Frederick Douglass's Paper*, Jan. 6, 1851.
240. ____. "The Nation's Problem," in *Negro Social and Political Thought, 1850-1920, Representative Texts*, ed. Howard Brotz, (New York: Basic Books, 1966), p. 316; originally from a speech delivered before the Bethel Literary and Historical Society in Washington, DC, Apr. 16, 1889; originally published as a pamphlet (Washington, DC, 1889).
241. ____. In Lerone Bennett Jr., "A Living History: Voices of the Past Speak to the Present," *Ebony*, Feb. 1985, p. 28; original source not listed.
242. W. E. B. Du Bois, *The Philadelphia Negro* (1899), at https://archive.org/stream/philadelphianegr001901mbp/philadelphianegr001901mbp_djvu.txt.
243. James Brown with Bruce Tucker, *The Godfather of Soul* (New York: Thunder's Mouth Press, 1990), p. 206. Brown refers to a record from James Brown Productions, King record label.
244. Ibid., p. 197.
245. Malcolm X, with the assistance of Alex Haley, *The Autobiography of Malcolm X* (New York: Grove Press, 1966), pp. 275-276.
246. Spike Lee, in Jack Kroll, "Spiking a Fever," *Newsweek*, June 10, 1991, p. 165.
247. Robert Woodson in *And Still We Rise: Interviews with 50 Black Role Models*, ed. Barbara Reynolds (Washington DC: USA Today Books, 1988), p 212.

248. Susan L. Taylor, *In the Spirit: The Inspirational Writings of Susan L. Taylor* (New York: Amistad, 1993), pp. 96-97.
249. Glenn C. Loury, "The Need for Moral Leadership in the Black Community," *New Perspectives*, Summer 1984, p. 14.
250. Jason L. Riley "'Soul Mates' Goes Where Politicians Fear to Tread," *Wall Street Journal*, Jan. 12, 2016, http://www.wsj.com/articles/soul-mates-goes-where-politicians-fear-to-tread-1452642910.
251. Sarah L. Delany, with A. Elizabeth Delany and Amy Hill Hearth, in *The Delany Sisters' Book of Everyday Wisdom* (New York: Kodansha International, 1994), p. 41.
252. Orlando Patterson, "The Moral Crisis of the Black American," *The Public Interest*, No. 32, Summer 1973, p. 52.
253. Jelani Cobb, in Julia Ioffe, "No One Treats African-Americans Worse Than We Treat Each Other," *New Republic*, Aug. 19, 2014, http://www.newrepublic.com/article/119148/ferguson-renews-debate-among-blacks-politics-respectability.
254. James Todd Smith with David "Scooter" Honig, *LL Cool J's Platinum 360 Diet and Lifestyle: A Full Circle Guide to Developing Your Mind, Body, and Soul* (New York, Rodale, 2010), pp. 9-10.
255. Shelby Steele, *A Bound Man: Why We Are Excited About Obama and Why He Can't Win* (New York: Free Press, 2008), 112.
256. ____. *White Guilt: How Blacks and Whites Together Destroyed the Promise of the Civil Rights Era* (New York: HarperCollins Publishers, 2006), p. 63.
257. ____. Interviewed by Peter Slen on "In Depth," Book TV on C-Span, Apr. 2, 2006, http://www.c-span.org/video/?191760-1/depth-shelby-steele; at 2:36:29.
258. Ibid., at 1:23:15.
259. Sojourner Truth, in *Black Women in White America: A Documentary History*, ed. Gerda Lerner, (New York: Pantheon Books, 1972), p. 570; originally 1867.
260. Martin Luther King Jr., "I See the Promised Land," *A Testament of Hope: Essential Writings and Speeches of Martin Luther King Jr.*, ed. James Melvin Washington (San Francisco: Harper and Row, 1986), p. 282;

originally Dr. King's last sermon, given in Memphis, Tennessee on Apr. 3, 1968.

261. C. Eric Lincoln and Lawrence H. Mamiya, *The Black Church in the African American Experience* (Durham, North Carolina: Duke University Press, 1990), p. 241.

262. Alice Walker, *In Search of Our Mothers' Gardens* (San Diego: Harcourt Brace Jovanovich, 1983), p. 90.

263. Dennis Kimbro and Napoleon Hill, *Think and Grow Rich: A Black Choice* (New York: Fawcett, 1991), p. 223.

264. Susan Taylor, in Terrie Williams with Joe Cooney, *The Personal Touch: What You Really Need to Succeed in Today's Fast-paced Business World* (New York: Warner Books, Inc., 1994), p. 161.

265. George Clinton, with Ben Greenman, *Brothers Be, Yo Like George, Ain't that Funkin' Kind of Hard on You?* (New York: Atria Books, 2014), p. 53.

266. Bernie Mac in Henry Louis Gates, Jr., *America Behind the Color Line: Dialogues with African Americans* (New York: Warner Books, 2004), p. 323.

267. Oprah Winfrey, "Oprah Winfrey," *Entrepreneur.com*, Oct. 9, 2008, http://www.entrepreneur.com/article/197558.

268. Frederick J. Eikerenkoetter II, a.k.a. Reverend Ike, in Jill Nelson, *Volunteer Slavery: My Authentic Negro Experience* (Chicago: Noble Press, Inc., 1993), p. 30.

269. Deval Patrick, *Reason to Believe: Lessons from an Improbable Life*, (New York: Broadway, 2011), pp. 52-53.

270. Serena Williams, with Hilary Beard, in *Venus and Serena: Serving from the Hip: 10 Rules for Living, Loving, and Winning* (Boston: Houghton Mifflin Company, 2005), p. 104.

4. Marriage

271. Linda J. Waite and Maggie Gallagher, *The Case for Marriage: Why Married People are Happier, Healthier, and Better Off Financially* (New York: Doubleday, 2000); Kay S. Hymowitz, *Marriage and Caste in America: Separate and Unequal Families in a Post-marital Age* (Chicago: Ivan R.

Dee, 2006); Amy Roberts, "Single vs. Married: A Valentine's Day Showdown," CNN, Feb. 13, 2016, http://www.cnn.com/2016/02/12/living/single-married-valentines-day-showdown/index.html.

272. Linda J. Waite and Maggie Gallagher, *The Case for Marriage*, Chapter 6; Linda Bloom and Charlie Bloom, "6 Reasons Why Married People Should Have Better Sex Lives," *Psychology Today*, Sept. 26, 2015, https://www.psychologytoday.com/blog/stronger-the-broken-places/201509/6-reasons-why-married-people-should-have-better-sex-lives; Amy Roberts, "Single vs. Married: A Valentine's Day Showdown, CNN, Feb. 13, 2016, http://www.cnn.com/2016/02/12/living/single-married-valentines-day-showdown/.

273. David Blankenhorn, *Fatherless America: Confronting Our Most Urgent Social Problem* (New York: BasicBooks, 1996); Sara McLanahan and Gary Sandefur, *Growing Up with a Single Parent: What Hurts, What Helps* (Cambridge, Massachusetts: Harvard University Press, 1994); David Popenoe, *Life Without Father: Compelling New Evidence that Fatherhood and Marriage are Indispensable for the Good of Children and Society* (New York: The Free Press, 1996); Barbara Dafoe Whitehead, "Dan Quayle Was Right," *The Atlantic*, April 1993, 47, http://www.theatlantic.com/magazine/archive/ 1993/04/dan-quayle-was-right/307015/; and James Q. Wilson, *The Marriage Problem: How Our Culture Has Weakened Families* (New York: HarperCollins Publishers, 2002).

274. David Popenoe, *Families Without Fathers: Fathers, Marriage and Children in American Society* (New Brunswick, New Jersey: Transaction Publishers, 2009), pp. 3-4.

275. Jim DeMint, *Falling in Love with America Again* (New York: Center Street, 2014), p. 120.

276. Bill O'Reilly, "Helping the Kids," BillOReilly.com, Aug. 1, 2013, http://www.billoreilly.com/ newslettercolumn?pid=41127.

277. Robert Rector, "Marriage: America's Greatest Weapon Against Child Poverty," *Heritage Foundation*, Sept. 2010, http://www.heritage.org/research/reports/2010/09/marriage-america-s-greatest-weapon-against-child-poverty.

278. William A. Galston, "The Poverty Cure: Get Married," *Wall Street Journal*, Oct. 27, 2015, http://www.wsj.com/articles/the-poverty-cure-get-married-1445986205.
279. Barbara Dafoe Whitehead, "Dan Quayle Was Right," *The Atlantic*, April 1993; http://www.theatlantic.com/magazine/archive/1993/04/dan-quayle-was-right/307015/.
280. David Popenoe, *Families Without Fathers: Fathers, Marriage and Children in American Society* (New Brunswick, New Jersey: Transaction Publishers, 2009), p. 2.
281. Ellen Sauerbrey, "The Dreadful Truth of Moynihan's Prophecy," *Washington Times*, June 3, 2015, http://www.washingtontimes.com/news/2015/jun/3/ellen-sauerbrey-baltimore-broken-families-breed-br/.
282. Paul Winfree, "How Welfare Spending Hurts the People It's Supposed to Help," *Daily Signal*, Aug. 1, 2015, http://dailysignal.com/2015/08/01/how-welfare-spending-hurts-the-people-its-supposed-to-help/.
283. Elizabeth Gilbert, *Committed: A Love Story* (New York: Penguin Books, 2010), pp. 166-167.
284. Kay S. Hymowitz, *Marriage and Caste in America: Separate and Unequal Families in a Post-marital Age*, (Chicago: Ivan R. Dee, 2006), p. 3.
285. Isabel Sawhill, "20 Years Later, it Turns out Dan Quayle Was Right About Murphy Brown and Unmarried Moms," *Washington Post*, May 25, 2012, http://www.washingtonpost.com/opinions/20-years-later-it-turns-out-dan-quayle-was-right-about-murphy-brown-and-unmarried-moms/2012/05/25/ gJQAsNCJqU_story.html.
286. George Gilder, *Wealth and Poverty: A New Edition for the Twenty-first Century* (Washington, DC: Regnery Publishing, Inc., 2012), p. 104.
287. Paul Taylor, "Republicans: Still Happy Campers," Pew Research Center, Oct. 23, 2008, http://www.pewsocialtrends.org/2008/10/23/republicans-still-happy-campers/#fn-718-6; Note 6.
288. Bernardine Dohrn, Bill Ayers, Jeff Jones, and Celia Sojourn, *Prairie Fire*, Communications Co., 1974, http://site2.littlegreenfootballs.com/pdf/Prairie-fire.pdf; p. 126.

Shared Values

289. Gloria Steinem, in "Irina Dunn," *Wikipedia*, https://en.wikipedia.org/wiki/Irina_Dunn. The Yahoo Best Answer about the meaning of this statement is, "a woman can live a complete and happy life without requiring to be in a relationship with a man!!!" https://in.answers.yahoo.com/question/ index?qid=20100720142956AAcwSGo.
290. Robin Morgan, "Robin Morgan Quotes," *About Education*, 1970, http://womenshistory.about. com/od/quotes/a/robin_morgan.htm.
291. Elizabeth Warren, "Elizabeth Warren: Republicans Are 'Trying To Deny Women Access To Birth Control,'" *Truth Revolt*, July 16, 2014, http://www.truthrevolt.org/news/elizabeth-warren-republicans-are-trying-deny-women-access-birth-control.
292. S. E. Cupp, "S.E. Cupp: Democrats' Spiteful Objection to Over-the-counter Birth Control," *Dallas News*, May, 31, 2015, http://www.dallasnews.com/opinion/latest-columns/20150531-s.e.-cupp-democrats-spiteful-objection-to-over-the-counter-birth-control.ece; also see Willis L. Krumholz, "Democrats Birth Control Deception," *Federalist*, July 1, 2015, http://thefederalist.com/ 2015/07/01/democrats-birth-control-deception/.
293. Kelly Ayotte, "Ayotte, Gardner Introduce Bill Aimed at Increasing Availability of Safe and Effective Over-the-Counter Contraceptives," Ayotte.Senate.gov, May 21, 2015, http://www.ayotte. senate.gov/?p=press_release&id=1962.
294. Hillary Rodham Clinton, *It Takes a Village* (New York: Simon & Schuster, 1996), 2006, p. 110.
295. Ibid., p. 136.
296. Ibid., p. 5.
297. Greg Allen, "Florida's Dozier School for Boys: A True Horror Story," *National Public Radio*," Oct. 15, 2012, http://www.npr.org/2012/10/15/162941770/floridas-dozier-school-for-boys-a-true-horror-story.
298. Jim Lynch, "EPA Stayed Silent on Flint's Tainted Water," *Detroit News*, Jan. 12, 2016, http://www.detroitnews.com/story/news/politics/2016/01/12/epa-stayed-silent-flints-tainted-water/78719620/.

299. Alex Haley, *The Playboy Interviews*, ed. Murray Fisher (New York: Ballantine Books, 1993), p. 433; originally from *Playboy*, Jan. 1977.
300. Barack Obama, *Change We Can Believe In: Barack Obama's Plan to Renew America's Promise* (New York: Broadway Books, 2008), p. 234.
301. William Raspberry, "Poor Marriages, Poor Health," *Washington Post*, Oct. 24, 2005, http://www.washingtonpost.com/wp-dyn/content/article/2005/10/23/AR2005102300770.html.
302. William Raspberry, "The Trouble with Fatherless Households," *Washington Post*, Sept. 22, 1993, https://news.google.com/newspapers?nid=1755&dat=19931001&id=EXAeAAAAIBAJ&sjid=oXsEAAAAIBAJ&pg=5315,124020&hl=en; also see Robert Rector, Patrick F. Fagan, and Kirk A. Johnson, "Marriage: Still the Safest Place For Women and Children," *Heritage Foundation*, Mar. 2004, http://www.heritage.org/research/reports/2004/03/marriage-still-the-safest-place-for-women-and-children.
303. Thomas Sowell, "Is the Family Becoming Extinct," *The Thomas Sowell Reader* (New York: Basic Books, 2011), p. 15. Sowell cites Linda Waite and Maggie Gallagher, *The Case for Marriage*.
304. Thomas Sowell, *Wealth, Poverty, and Politics: An International Perspective* (New York: Basic Books, 2015), p. 117.
305. Jesse Lee Peterson with Brad Stetson, *From Rage to Responsibility: Black Conservative Jesse Lee Peterson and America Today* (St. Paul, MN: Paragon House, 2000), 100.
306. Ibid., p. 40.
307. Ibid., pp. 43-44.
308. Geoffrey Canada, *Reaching Up for Manhood: Transforming the Lives of Boys in America* (Boston: Beacon Press, 1998), p. 33.
309. William Raspberry, "The Trouble with Fatherless Households," *Washington Post*, Sept. 22, 1993, https://news.google.com/newspapers?nid=1755&dat=19931001&id=EXAeAAAAIBAJ&sjid=oXsEAAAAIBAJ&pg=5315,124020&hl=en.
310. Serena Williams, in Melissa Harris Perry, "Serena Williams Is Unstoppable: 'Am I the Greatest? I Don't Know. I'm the Greatest That

I Can Be,'" *Glamour,* June 7, 2016, http://www.glamour.com/story/serena-williams-the-worlds-greatest-athlete.
311. Lynn Toler, *Making Marriage Work: New Rules for an Old Institution* (Evanston, Illinois: Agate Publishing, 2012), p. 16.
312. Ibid., p. 15.
313. Don Lemon, "Problems the Black Community Faces; Don Lemon's Suggestions," CNN, July 27, 2013, http://edition.cnn.com/TRANSCRIPTS/1307/27/cnr.06.html.
314. Earvin "Magic" Johnson Jr., with Roy S. Johnson, *Magic's Touch* (Reading, Massachusetts: Addison-Wesley Publishing Company, 1989), p. 18.
315. Byron Hurt, in April R. Silver, ed., B*e a Father to Your Child: Real Talk from Black Men on Family, Love, and Fatherhood* (Berkeley, California: Soft Skull Press, 2008), pp. 170-172.
316. "Turning the Corner on Father Absence in Black America," *Morehouse Conference on African American Fathers,* Nov. 4-6, 1998, http://americanvalues.org/catalog/pdfs/turningthecorner.pdf, p. 16.
317. Richard Williams, with Bart Davis, *Black and White: The Way I See It* (New York: Atria Books, 2014), p. 209.
318. Ibid., pp. 261-262
319. Ibid., p. 212.
320. Ibid., p. 229.
321. Ibid., p. 24.
322. Ibid., p. 213.
323. Ibid., p. 276.
324. Ibid., p. 210.
325. Oseola McCarty, *Oseola McCarty's Simple Wisdom for Rich Living* (Atlanta, Georgia: Longstreet Press, 1996), p. 50.
326. Ossie Davis, Ossie Davis and Ruby Dee, *With Ossie and Ruby: In This Life Together* (New York: William Morrow and Company, Inc., 1998), p. 28.
327. Eleanor Holmes Norton, "Restoring the Traditional Black Family," *New York Times Magazine,* June 2, 1985, p. 93.

328. James P. Comer and Alvin F. Poussaint, *Raising Black Children* (New York: Plume, 1992), p. 418.
329. Bob Teague, *The Flip Side of Soul: Letters to My Son* (New York: William Morrow and Company, Inc., 1989), p. 164.
330. Bob Herbert, "Tiger's Best Shot," *New York Times*, Apr. 18, 1997, p. A33.
331. Dr. Emiel Hamberlin in Henry Louis Gates, Jr., *America Behind the Color Line: Dialogues with African Americans* (New York: Warner Books, 2004), p. 424.
332. Sylvia Ann Hewlett and Cornel West, *The War Against Parents: What We Can Do for America's Beleaguered Moms and Dads* (New York: Mariner Books, 1999), p. 166.
333. US senator Barack Obama, *The Audacity of Hope: Thoughts on Reclaiming the American Dream* (New York: Crown Publishers, 2006), pp. 333-334.
334. Elijah Anderson, *Code of the Street: Decency, Violence, and the Moral Life of the Inner City* (New York: W.W. Norton & Company, 1999), p. 204.
335. Bob Herbert, "Tiger's Best Shot," *New York Times*, Apr. 18, 1997, p. A33.
336. Jackie Robinson, as told to Alfred Duckett, *I Never Had It Made* (New York: G. P. Putnam's Sons, 1972), p. 16.
337. John W. Fountain, "Reflections on Fatherhood with John W. Fountain," YouTube, https://www.youtube.com/watch?v=GWpGEmuJ-7U.
338. Alvin Ailey with A. Peter Bailey, *Revelations: The Autobiography of Alvin Ailey* (New York: Birch Lane Press, 1995), p. 26.
339. Kevin Powell, *Keepin' It Real: Post-MTV Reflections on Race, Sex, and Politics* (New York: One World Ballantine Books, 1997), p. 82.
340. Kevin Powell, in April R. Silver, ed., *Be a Father to Your Child: Real Talk from Black Men on Family, Love, and Fatherhood* (Berkeley, California: Soft Skull Press, 2008), p. 34.
341. Patrice Gaines, *Laughing in the Dark: From Colored Girl to Woman of Color—A Journey from Prison to Power* (New York: Crown Publishers, Inc., 1994), p. 59.

342. Stephanie Gadlin, in John W. Fountain, *Dear Dad: Reflections on Fatherhood* (Chicago: Westside Press, 2011), p. 18.
343. Lolly Bowean, in Ibid., p. 90.
344. John McWhorter, *Winning the Race: Beyond the Crisis in Black America* (New York: Gotham Books, 2006, pp. 117-118.
345. Ibid., pp. 125-126.
346. Ibid., pp. 127-128.
347. Ibid., p. 128.
348. In John Langston Gwaltney, *Drylongso: A Self-Portrait of Black America* (New York: Random House, 1981), pp. 284-285.
349. Jason L. Riley, "Still Right on the Black Family After All These Years," *Wall Street Journal*, Feb. 10, 2015, http://www.wsj.com/articles/jason-l-riley-still-right-on-the-black-family-after-all-these-years-1423613625.
350. Don Lemon, "Problems the Black Community Faces; Don Lemon's Suggestions," CNN, July 27, 2013, http://edition.cnn.com/TRANSCRIPTS/1307/27/cnr.06.html
351. Sylvia Ann Hewlett and Cornel West, *The War Against Parents: What We Can Do for America's Beleaguered Moms and Dads* (New York: Mariner Books, 1999), p. 177.
352. Marian Wright Edelman, *Families in Peril: An Agenda for Social Change* (Cambridge: Harvard University Press, 1987), p. 72.
353. Dorothy Height, *Ebony*, Mar. 1985, p. 78; my source is https://books.google.com/books ?id=x3ULccwPBrcC&pg=PA78&lpg=PA78&dq=eleanor+holmes+norton+%22a+threat+to+the+future+of+black+people+without+equal.
354. Cecil Blye, in Penny Starr, "Pastor: 'Government As Parent Has Destroyed the Black Family,' Made 'Black Fatherhood Irrelevant,'" CNS News, Dec. 9, 2015, http://www.cnsnews.com/news/ article/penny-starr/pastor-government-parent-has-destroyed-black-family-america-made-black.

355. Star Parker, *Uncle Sam's Plantation: How Big Government Enslaves America's Poor and What We Can Do About It, Revised and Updated Edition* (Nashville, Tennessee: Thomas Nelson, 2010), p. 22
356. Tammie Cathery, in Henry Louis Gates Jr., *America Behind the Color Line: Dialogues with African Americans* (New York: Warner Books, 2004), p. 386.
357. Thomas Sowell, *The Thomas Sowell Reader* (New York: Basic Books, 2011), p. 214.
358. Shelby Steele, interviewed by Peter Slen on "In Depth," *Book TV* on C-Span, Apr. 2, 2006, http://www.c-span.org/video/?191760-1/depth-shelby-steele; at 2:55:50.
359. Ibid., at 2:56:20.
360. Lerone Bennett Jr., "The 10 Biggest Myths About the Black Family," *Ebony*, Nov. 1990, p. 168.
361. Farai Chideya, *Don't Believe the Hype: Fighting Cultural Misinformation About African-Americans* (New York: Plume, 1995), pp. 25-26.
362. Andrew Young, in Walter C. Jones, "Andrew Young's Blunt Talk at Atlanta's Carter Center," *Florida Times-Union*, Nov. 3, 2010, http://jacksonville.com/news/georgia/2010-11-03/story/andrew-youngs-blunt-talk-atlantas-carter-center#.
363. Thomas Sowell, *Intellectuals and Race* (New York: Basic Books, 2013), p. 120.
364. Thomas Sowell, "Political Translations," *Townhall*, Nov.5, 2015, http://townhall.com/columnists/thomassowell/2015/11/25/political-translations-n2084502/page/full.
365. Walter E. Williams, "Black Progression and Retrogression," CNS News, Dec. 23, 2014, http://cnsnews.com/commentary/walter-e-williams/black-progression-and-retrogression.
366. Earl Ofari Hutchinson, *Black Fatherhood: The Guide to Male Parenting* (Los Angeles, California: Middle Passage Press, 1994), p. 71.

367. Malcolm X, *Malcolm X on Afro-American History* (New York: Pathfinder, 1967), pp. 12-13.
368. Colin L. Powell with Joseph E. Persico, *My American Journey* (New York: Random House, 1995), pp. 611-612.
369. Ossie Davis, in *A Wealth of Wisdom: Legendary African American Elders Speak*, eds. Camille O. Cosby and Renee Poussaint (New York: Washington Square Press, 2004), p. 87.
370. Johnnetta B. Cole, *Conversations: Straight Talk with America's Sister President* (New York: Doubleday, 1993), 152.
371. Joan Morgan, *When Chickenheads Come Home to Roost: My Life as a Hip-hop Feminist* (New York: Simon & Schuster, 1999), 166.
372. Charles Drew, in Pamela Newkirk, *A Love No Less: Two Centuries of African American Love Letters* (New York: Random House, 2003), pp. 139 and 141.
373. Daphne Reid, in Ibid., p. 207.
374. Jerald Wolff, in Henry Louis Gates Jr., *America Behind the Color Line: Dialogues with African Americans* (New York: Warner Books, 2004), p. 205.
375. Jackie Robinson, in Michael G. Long, ed., *Beyond Home Plate: Jackie Robinson on Life After Baseball* (Syracuse, New York: Syracuse University Press, 2013), p. 53.
376. Ibid., pp. 53-54.
377. Terry English, in *Souls of My Brothers: Black Men Break Their Silence, Tell Their Truths, and Heal Our Spirits*, edited and written by Dawn Marie Daniels and Candace Sandy (New York: Plume, 2003), p. 43.
378. Lynn Toler, *Making Marriage Work: New Rules for an Old Institution* (Evanston, Illinois: Agate Publishing, 2012), p. 15.
379. Charley Pride, with Jim Henderson, *Pride: The Charley Pride Story* (New York: William Morrow and Company, Inc., 1994), p. 7.
380. Beth Martin, in *Live Your Best Life: A Treasury of Wisdom, Wit, Advice, Interviews, and Inspiration from O, The Oprah Magazine*, eds. of O, (Birmingham, Alabama: Oxmoor House, 2005), p. 163.
381. Candy Carson, *A Doctor in the House: My Life with Ben Carson* (New York: Sentinel, 2016), p. 3.

382. Mayor David Dinkins, in *A Wealth of Wisdom: Legendary African American Elders Speak*, Camille O. Cosby and Renee Poussaint, eds. (New York: Washington Square Press, 2004), p. 113.
383. L. Taylor, *All About Love* (West Babylon, New York: Urban Books, 2008), p. 130.
384. Ruby Dee, in Susan L. Taylor, *All About Love* (West Babylon, New York: Urban Books, 2008), pp. 232-237.
385. Kierna Mayo, "Mother Has Lived!" *Ebony*, May 2015, p. 95.
386. Pride, with Jim Henderson, *Pride: The Charley Pride Story* (New York: William Morrow and Company, Inc., 1994), p. 89.
387. Ruby Dee, in Ossie Davis and Ruby Dee, *With Ossie and Ruby: In This Life Together* (New York: William Morrow and Company, Inc., 1998), p. 185.

5. Education

388. Chris Christie, in *Remembering Who We Are: A Treasury of Conservative Commencement Addresses*, ed. Zev Chafets (New York: Sentinel, 2015), p. 56.
389. Martin R. West, "Schools of Choice," *Education Next*, Spring 2016, Vol. 16, NO. 2, http://educationnext.org/schools-of-choice-expanding-opportunity-urban-minority-students/.
390. Mitchell D. Chester, "Student Achievement in Massachusetts' Charter Schools," *Center for Education Policy Research, Harvard University*, Jan. 2011, http://scholar.harvard.edu/files/ cohodes/files/student_achievement_in_ma_charter_schools_2011.pdf.
391. John Gabrieli, "The Promise of the Harlem Children's Zone," *Harvard Political Review*, June 11, 2014, http://harvardpolitics.com/united-states/promise-harlem-children-zone/.
392. Success Academies, "2015 Results," *Successacademies.org*, http://www.successacademies.org/results/.
393. KIPP, "College Completion Report," Kipp.org, http://kipp.org/results/college-completion-report.

394. Stephen Ford, "Fighting Congress for a Capital Education," *Wall Street Journal*, Feb. 12, 2016, http://www.wsj.com/articles/fighting-congress-for-a-capital-education-1455318874.
395. Rick Cohen, "National School Choice Week: Know the Players and the Funders," *Nonprofit Quarterly*, Jan. 28, 2014, https://nonprofitquarterly.org/policysocial-context/23590-national-school-choice-week-know-the-players-and-the-funders.html; "Funders," *National Alliance for Public Charter Schools*, http://www.publiccharters.org/get-the-facts/about-us/funders/.
396. William McGurn, "Brooklyn's Other Jackie Robinson," *Wall Street Journal*, Apr. 18, 2016, http://www.wsj.com/articles/brooklyns-other-jackie-robinson-1461021744; Selim Algar, "Charter School Blasts Mayor de Blasio as Saboteur," *New York Post*, June 1, 2016, http://nypost.com/2016/06/01/charter-school-blasts-mayor-de-blasio-as-saboteur/.
397. Carly Fiorina, in Nicholas Ballasy, "Fiorina: Now Is the Time to Have a National Conversation About Women in the U.S.," PJ Media, June 20, 2015, http://pjmedia.com/blog/fiorina-national-conversation/; also see Editorial Board, "The Justice Department Bids to Trap Poor, Black Children in Ineffective Schools," *Washington Post*, Sept. 9, 2013, http://www.washingtonpost.com/opinions/the-justice-department-bids-to-trap-poor-black-children-in-ineffective-schools/2013/09/01/2173e5a6-0f77-11e3-85b6-d27422650fd5_story.html.
398. John Steele Gordon, "Helping the Poor and Downtrodden," *Commentary Magazine*, May 3, 2015, https://www.commentarymagazine.com/politics-ideas/liberals-democrats/helping-the-poor-and-downtrodden-nicholas-kristof/.
399. Eric A. Hanushek, "Why Quality Matters in Education," *Stanford University*, June 2005, http://hanushek.stanford.edu/sites/default/files/publications/Hanushek.FinDev.june05.pdf; p. 18.
400. Naomi Schaefer Riley, *Opportunity and Hope: Transforming Children's Lives Through Scholarships* (Lanham, Maryland: Rowman & Littlefield, 2014), p. 104.

401. CBS News, "U.S. Education Spending Tops Global List, Study Shows," CBS News, June 25, 2013, http://www.cbsnews.com/news/us-education-spending-tops-global-list-study-shows/.
402. Editorial Board, "Why Chicago Bonds Are Junk," *Wall Street Journal*, May 13, 2015, http://www.wsj.com/articles/why-chicagos-bonds-are-junk-1431559103.
403. US Census Bureau, "Public Education Finances: 2013," G13-ASPEF, US Government Printing Office, Washington, DC, 2015, Table 11, States Ranked According to Per Pupil Public Elementary-Secondary School System Finance Amounts: Fiscal Year 2013, http://www2.census. gov/govs/school/ 13f33pub.pdf. Also see Josh Gelernter, "Republicans Need to Stop Conceding Defeat in Black and Hispanic Neighborhoods," *National Review*, Oct. 30, 2015, http://www.nationalreview. com/article/426378/take-cities-back-democrats-josh-gelernter.
404. Jason Russell, "No, Baltimore Schools Are Not Under-funded," *Washington Examiner*, May 5, 2015, http://www.washingtonexaminer.com/no-baltimore-schools-are-not-under-funded/article/2564013.
405. Linda Chavez, "Let Us By All Means Have an Honest Conversation About Race," *Commentary Magazine*, June 2008, http://www.commentarymagazine.com/article/let-us-by-all-means-have-an-honest-conversation-about-race/.
406. Naomi Schaefer Riley, *Opportunity and Hope: Transforming Children's Lives Through Scholarships* (Lanham, Maryland: Rowman & Littlefield, 2014), p. 105.
407. Dan Lips, "Head Start: A $150 Billion Failure," Daily Signal, Jan. 15, 2010, http://dailysignal. com/2010/01/15/head-start-a-150-billion-failure/; "Third Grade Follow-up to the Head Start Impact Study, Final Report," OPRE Report, 2012-45, October 2012, http://www.acf.hhs.gov/sites/ default/files/opre/ head_start_report.pdf.
408. David J. Armor and Sonia Sousa, "The Dubious Promise of Universal Preschool," *National Affairs*, Issue 18, Winter 2014,

http://www.nationalaffairs.com/publications/detail/the-dubious-promise-of-universal-preschool.
409. Joe Klein, "Time to Ax Public Programs That Don't Yield Results," *Time*, July 7, 2011, http://content.time.com/time/nation/article/0,8599,2081778,00.html.
410. Jeb Bush, "Education Reform: A Choice Between Teachers Unions and Kids," *Townhall*, Aug. 19, 2015, http://townhall.com/columnists/jebbush/2015/08/19/education-reform-a-choice-between-teachers-unions-and-kids-n2040906?utm_source=thdaily&utm_medium=email&utm_ campaign=nl&newsletterad=.
411. William J. Bennett, *Our Country and Our Children: Improving America's Schools and Affirming the Common Culture* (New York: Simon and Schuster, 1988), p. 2.
412. Cassie Spodak, "Major Teachers Union Endorses Hillary Clinton," CNN, July 11, 2015, http://www.cnn.com/2015/07/11/politics/hillary-clinton-american-federation-of-teachers/.
413. Kimberly Hefling, "The National Education Association Endorsement Comes Amid Grumbling from Some Members that It's Too Soon," *Politico*, Oct. 3, 2015, http://www.politico.com/story/ 2015/10/clinton-nea-teachers-union-endorsement-214402.
414. Sam Ford, "D.C. School Voucher Funding Left Out of 2013 Federal Budget," *WJLA*, Feb. 14, 2012, http://wjla.com/news/local/d-c-school-voucher-funding-left-out-of-2013-federal-budget-72594.
415. Barack Obama, in Valerie Strauss, "Obama Smacks Bill O'Reilly on School Vouchers," *Washington Post*, Feb. 5, 2014, https://www.washingtonpost.com/news/answer-sheet/wp/2014/ 02/05/obama-smacks-bill-oreilly-on-school-vouchers/.
416. Bernie Sanders, with Huck Gutman, *Outsider in the White House* (New York: Verso, 1997, 2015), p. 300.
417. Bernie Sanders, in Jason Russell, "Bernie Sanders 'Not in Favor' of Charter Schools," *Washington Examiner*, Jan. 7, 2016, http://www.washingtonexaminer.com/bernie-sanders-not-in-favor-of-charter-schools/article/2579869.

418. "Clinton Turns Against Charters," *Wall Street Journal*, Nov. 11, 2015, http://www.wsj.com/ articles/clinton-turns-against-charters-1447287564.
419. Hillary Clinton, in Phyllis Schlafly, "The NEA Lists its Goals and the Democratic Party Agrees," *Free Republic*, Aug. 20, 2007, http://www.freerepublic.com/focus/news/1883843/posts? page=54.
420. Hillary Clinton, "Hillary on the Defensive," *New York Sun*, Feb. 23, 2006, http://www.nysun.com/editorials/hillary-on-the-defensive/28068/.
421. John Bel Edwards, in Julia O'Donoghue, "John Bel Edwards Says He's Sticking by Teachers—and Their Unions," NOLA.com, Feb 3, 2016, http://www.nola.com/politics/index.ssf/ 2016/02/ john_bel_edwards_teachers.html.
422. Ibid.
423. Diane Ravitch, "The Myth of Charter Schools," *New York Review of Books*, Nov. 11, 2010, http://www.nybooks.com/articles/2010/11/11/myth-charter-schools/.
424. Joy Resmovits, "Charter School Performance Study Finds Small Gains," *Huffington Post*, June 25, 2013, http://www.huffingtonpost.com/2013/06/25/charter-school-performance-study_n_ 3493023.html.
425. Barack Obama, "Remarks by the President in Conversation on Poverty at Georgetown University," The White House, May 12, 2015, https://www.whitehouse.gov/the-press-office/ 2015/05/12/remarks-president-conversation-poverty-georgetown-university.
426. Frederick Douglass, "Speech Delivered at the Mass Free Democratic Convention at Ithaca, New York, October 14th, 1852," *The Life and Writings of Frederick Douglass, Vol. 5*, ed. Philip S. Foner (New York: International Publishers, 1975), p. 246; originally published in Frederick Douglass's Paper, Oct. 22, 1852.
427. Carl T. Rowan, *Just Between Us Blacks* (New York: Random House, 1974) p. 60; emphasis deleted.
428. Pam Grier, with Andrea Cagan, *Foxy: My Life in Three Acts* (New York: Grand Central Publishing, 2010), pp.92-93.

429. Rev. Claude C. Brown, in J. L. Chestnut Jr., and Julia Cass, *Black in Selma: The Uncommon Life of J. L. Chestnut Jr.* (New York: Farrar, Straus and Giroux, 1990), p. 159.
430. Booker T. Washington, *Black Diamonds: The Wisdom of Booker T. Washington*, Selected and Arranged by Victoria Earle Mathews (Deerfield Beach, Florida: Health Communications, Inc., 1995), p. 7.
431. Joycelyn Elders, "Educating on Behalf of Black Public Health," *Black Genius: African American Solutions to African American Problems*, eds. Walter Mosley, Manthia Diawara, and Clyde Taylor (New York: W. W. Norton & Company, Inc., 1999), p. 190.
432. Barbara M. Dixon, with Josleen Wilson, *Good Health for African-American Kids* (New York: Crown Trade Paperbacks, 1996), p. 220.
433. Glenn C. Loury, "The Need for Moral Leadership in the Black Community," *New Perspectives*, Summer 1984, p. 19.
434. Ron Christie, *Blackwards: How Black Leadership is Returning America to the Days of Separate but Equal* (New York: Thomas Dunne Books, 2012), p. 243.
435. Tavis Smiley, *Keeping the Faith: Stories of Love, Courage, Healing, and Hope from Black America* (New York: Doubleday, 2002), p. 210.
436. Malcolm X, *By Any Means Necessary: Speeches, Interviews and a Letter by Malcolm X*, ed. George Breitman (New York: Pathfinder Press, 1970), p. 178.
437. Rosemary L. Bray, "So How Did I Get Here?" *New York Times Magazine*, Nov. 8, 1992, p. 39.
438. Former Representative Shirley Chisholm, *Unbought and Unbossed* (Boston: Houghton Mifflin, 1979), p. 27.
439. J. L. Chestnut Jr., and Julia Cass, *Black in Selma: The Uncommon Life of J. L. Chestnut Jr.* (New York: Farrar, Straus and Giroux, 1990), pp. 25-26.
440. Muhammad Ali with Hana Yasmeen Ali, *The Soul of a Butterfly: Reflections on Life's Journey* (NY: Simon & Schuster, 2004), p. 4.
441. Judge Greg Mathis with Blair S. Walker, *Judge Greg Mathis: Inner City Miracle, A Memoir* (New York: Ballantine Books, 2002), p. 93.

442. Eugene Rivers, "Reverend Eugene Rivers, Extended Interview," *Public Broadcasting Service*, Nov. 11, 2005, http://www.pbs.org/wnet/religionandethics/2005/11/11/november-11-2005-rev-eugene-rivers-extended-interview/11523/.
443. Thomas Sowell, "American Education: More Funding is NOT the Answer," *Examiner.com*, June 6, 2012, http://www.examiner.com/article/american-education-1; at 00:38.
444. Walter E. Williams, "Education Insanity," *Jewish World Review*, Jan. 27, 2016, http://jewish worldreview.com/cols/williams012716.php3.
445. Venus Williams, with Hilary Beard, in *Venus and Serena: Serving from the Hip: 10 Rules for Living, Loving, and Winning* (Boston: Houghton Mifflin Company, 2005), p. 20.
446. Ibid., pp. 20-21.
447. Serena Williams, in Ibid., p. 19.
448. Venus Williams, in Ibid., p. 23.
449. Earvin "Magic" Johnson with William Novak, *My Life* (New York: Random House, 1992), p. 328.
450. Frances Jackson Coppin, in *Black Women in Nineteenth Century American Life: Their Words, Their Thoughts, Their Feelings*, eds. Bert James Loewenberg and Ruth Bogin, (University Park: Pennsylvania State University Press, 1985), p. 316; originally from Fanny Jackson Coppin, Reminiscences of School Life, and Hints on Teaching, 1913.
451. Neil DeGrasse Tyson, *The Sky Is Not the Limit: Adventures of an Urban Astrophysicist* (Amherst, NY: Prometheus Books, 2004), p. 141.
452. Ibid., p. 179.
453. Oprah Winfrey, in Alan Ebert, "Oprah Winfrey Talks Openly about Oprah," *Good Housekeeping*, Sept. 1991, p. 64.
454. Richard Wright, *Black Boy* (New York: New American Library, 1951), pp. 48-9.
455. Ibid., p. 283.
456. Langston Hughes, *The Langston Hughes Reader* (New York: George Braziller Inc., 1958), p. 337; originally from *The Big Sea*, 1940.

457. Johnnetta Cole, "Johnnetta Cole Interview," *Academy of Achievement*, June 28, 1996, http://www.achievement.org/autodoc/page/col0int-1.
458. Pearl Bailey, *Between You and Me* (New York: Doubleday, 1989), p. 31. My deletion.
459. Venus Williams, with Hilary Beard, *Venus and Serena: Serving from the Hip: 10 Rules for Living, Loving, and Winning* (Boston: Houghton Mifflin Company, 2005), p. 18.
460. In Robert D. Putnam, *Our Kids: The American Dream in Crisis* (New York: Simon & Schuster, 2015), p. 87.
461. Talib Kweli, in April R. Silver, ed., *Be a Father to Your Child: Real Talk from Black Men on Family, Love, and Fatherhood* (Berkeley, California: Soft Skull Press, 2008), p. 101.
462. Woody Strode and Sam Young, *Goal Dust: An Autobiography* (Lanham, Maryland: Madison Books, 1990), p. 37.
463. Condoleezza Rice, "Condi Rice: Today's True Racists Are Liberals Who Defend Teachers' Unions," *Breitbart*, Nov. 10, 2014, http://www.breitbart.com/video/2014/11/10/condoleezza-todays-true-racists-are-liberal-who-defend-teachers-unions/. Rice referred to a California judicial ruling that teacher tenure laws violated students' civil rights: Jennifer Medina, "California Teacher Tenure Laws Ruled Unconstitutional," *New York Times*, June 11, 2014, http://www.nytimes.com/2014/06/11/us/california-teacher-tenure-laws-ruled-unconstitutional.html. However, an appeals court ruled in favor of tenure: Howard Blume, Joy Resmovits, and Sonali Kohli, "In a Win for Unions, Appeals Court Reverses Ruling that Threw Out Teacher Tenure in California," *Los Angeles Times*, Apr. 14, 2016, http://www.latimes.com/local/lanow/la-me-ln-court-rejects-bid-to-end-teacher-tenure-in-california-marking-huge-win-for-unions-20160414-story.html. The legal activities continue.
464. Geoffrey Canada, in Jacob Osterhout, "'Waiting for Superman's' Geoffrey Canada, President of Harlem's Children Zone, Talks Education," *New York Daily News*, Sept. 22, 2010, http://www.nydailynews.com/entertainment/tv-movies/waiting-superman-geoffrey-canada-president-harlem-children-zone-talks-education-article-1.440349#ixzz2iZ1zk6Lr.

Notes

465. Thomas Sowell, "The Left Versus Minorities," *Real Clear Politics*, Mar. 11, 2014, http://www.realclearpolitics.com/articles/2014/03/11/the_left_versus_minorities_121875.html.
466. Ibid.
467. Thomas Sowell, "Random Thoughts," *Townhall*, Jan. 27, 2015, http://townhall.com/columnists/thomassowell/2015/01/27/random-thoughts-n1948441.
468. Anthony Sanchez, "A Union Charter Flunks Out," *Wall Street Journal*, Mar. 6, 2015, http://www.wsj.com/articles/a-union-charter-flunks-out-1425685352.
469. Jason L. Riley, "Obama's Education Fibs," *Wall Street Journal*, Feb. 4, 2014, http://www. wsj.com/articles/SB10001424052702303442704579363140003847878.
470. Shawnee Jackson, in Stephen Ford, "Fighting Congress for a Capital Education, *Wall Street Journal*, Feb. 12, 2016, at http://www.wsj.com/articles/fighting-congress-for-a-capital-education-1455318874; also see "Testimony of Sheila D. Jackson," *House Committee on Oversight and Government Reform Subcommittee on Health Care, District of Columbia, Census and the National Archives*, Mar. 1, 2011, https://oversight.house.gov/wp-content/uploads/2012/01/Jackson_Full.pdf.
471. Denisha Merriweather, "How I Learned Not to Hate School," *Wall Street Journal*, Oct. 22, 2014, http://online.wsj.com/articles/denisha-merriweather-how-i-learned-not-to-hate-school-1414019224.
472. ____. "Denisha Merriweather Introduces Governor Bush: College Grad Gives Thanks for a Life-Changing Scholarship," ExelinEd, Nov. 20, 2014, http://www.excelined.org/ news/ denisha-merriweather-introduces-governor-bush-college-grad-gives-thanks-life-changing-scholarship/.
473. ____. YouTube, https://www.youtube.com/watch?v=k4YjkeVNH9o.
474. Joseph Kelly, in Stephen Moore, "President Obama, Are You Listening?" *Wall Street Journal*, May 1, 2015, http://www.wsj.com/articles/president-obama-are-you-listening-1430522350.
475. Matthew M. Chingos and Paul E. Peterson, "A Generation of School-Voucher Success," *Wall Street Journal*, Aug. 23, 2012, http://www.wsj.com/articles/SB10000872396390444184704577585582150808386.

476. Naomi Schaefer Riley, *Opportunity and Hope: Transforming Children's Lives Through Scholarships* (Lanham, Maryland: Rowman & Littlefield, 2014), p. 50.
477. Virginia Walden-Ford, and ed. Karen Risch, *Voices, Choices, and Second Chances: How to Win the Battle to Bring Opportunity Scholarships to Your State* (Washington, DC: DC Parents for School Choice, 2005), p. 79.
478. Virginia Walden-Ford, "School Choice: An Enduring Legacy of Little Rock and the Civil Rights Struggle," *My Heritage*, 2011, http://www.myheritage.org/events/school-choice-an-enduring-legacy-of-little-rock-and-the-civil-rights-struggle/.
479. Virginia Walden-Ford, in Jim Stergios, "Civil Disobedience Protest in DC for School Choice," *Pioneer Institute*, Sept. 8, 2009, http://pioneerinstitute.org/news/civil-disobedience-protest-indc-for-school-choice/.
480. Naomi Schaefer Riley, *Opportunity and Hope: Transforming Children's Lives Through Scholarships* (Lanham, Maryland: Rowman & Littlefield, 2014), p. 100.
481. Kevin P. Chavous, "The Key to Winning Back Voters," *US News and World Report*, May 15, 2015, http://www.usnews.com/news/the-report/articles/2015/05/15/hillary-clinton-should-campaign-on-school-choice.
482. Jonathan Capehart, "Mayor's Race May Be Stirred by Vouchers," *New York Daily News*, Mar. 27, 2000, http://www.nydailynews.com/archives/opinions/mayor-race-stirred-vouchers-article-1.859324.
483. The Five, "Al Jazeera English Bans Employees from Using Words Like 'Terrorist,' 'Jihad' and 'Islamist,'" Fox News, Jan. 28, 2015, http://www.foxnews.com/on-air/the-five/transcript/2015/01/28/al-jazeera-english-bans-employees-using-words-terrorist-jihad-and-islamist.

6. Work

484. Stephen Moore, *Who's the Fairest of Them All: The Truth About Opportunity, Taxes, and Wealth in America* (New York: Encounter Books, 2012), p. 36.

Notes

485. Karen Frazier, "Charities of Oprah Winfrey," *LoveToKnow.com*, http://charity.lovetoknow.com/ Charities_of_Oprah_Winfrey.
486. Joseph P. Williams, "Beyond the Boogeyman," *US News and World Report*, June 26, 2015, http://www.usnews.com/news/the-report/articles/2015/06/26/the-koch-brothers-gifts-to-society.
487. Arthur C. Brooks, *The Conservative Heart: How to Build a Fairer, Happier, and More Prosperous America*, (New York: Broadside Books, 2015), p. 128.
488. Ibid., pp. 18-19.
489. Andy Puzder, "Killing the Working Class at Wal-Mart," *Wall Street Journal*, Feb. 4, 2016, http://www.wsj.com/articles/killing-the-working-class-at-wal-mart-1454633345.
490. John Mackey, in Joel Griffith, "Whole Foods CEO: 'Business Has Been Hated by the Intellectuals and Elites for All Time,'" Breitbart, Feb. 18, 2013, http://www.breitbart.com/big-government/2013/02/18/whole-foods-ceo-business-has-been-hated-by-the-intellectuals-and-elites-for-all-time/.
491. Rick Perry, "Why It's Republicans, Not Democrats, Who Really Offer African-Americans Hope for a Better Life," Fox News, July 2, 2015, http://www.foxnews.com/opinion/2015/07/02/why-it-s-republicans-not-democrats-who-really-offer-african-americans-hope-better-life.html; also see Kurt Badenhausen, "Texas Leads Best States For Future Job Growth," *Forbes*, Nov. 12, 2014, http://www.forbes.com/sites/kurtbadenhausen/2014/11/12/texas-leads-best-states-for-future-job-growth/#43d2cbf73ad5; James Taylor, *Forbes*, "Yes, Rick Perry Deserves Credit For The Texas Economy," Aug. 24, 2011, http://www.forbes.com/sites/jamestaylor/2011/08/24/yes-rick-perry-deserves-credit-for-the-texas-economy/.
492. Ted Cruz, *A Time for Truth: Reigniting the Promise of America* (New York: Broadside Books, 2015), p. 325.
493. Carly Fiorina, *Rising to the Challenge: My Leadership Journey* (New York: Sentinel, 2015), p. 16.
494. Milton Friedman, "Notable & Quotable: Milton Friedman," *Wall Street Journal*, June 14, 2015, http://www.wsj.com/articles/notable-quotable-milton-friedman-1434318595.

495. Nitin Nohria, "Imagine an Economy Without Wall Street," *Wall Street Journal*, June 1, 2016, http://www.wsj.com/articles/imagine-an-economy-without-wall-street-1464821303.
496. Bret Stephens, "Bernie's Wall Street Slander," *Wall Street Journal*, Feb. 8, 2016, http://www.wsj.com/articles/bernies-wall-street-slander-1454976868.
497. Alan Cole, "Fixing the Corporate Income Tax," *Tax Foundation*, Feb. 4, 2016, http://taxfoundation.org/article/fixing-corporate-income-tax.
498. Stephen Moore, *Who's the Fairest of Them All: The Truth About Opportunity, Taxes, and Wealth in America* (New York: Encounter Books, 2012).
499. James Pierson, "The Redistribution Fallacy," *Commentary Magazine*, Sept. 1, 2015, https://www.commentarymagazine.com/articles/redistribution-fallacy/.
500. Grover Norquist, in Angie Drobnic Holan, "Grover Norquist Said the Economy Has Grown or Been Damaged by Capital Gains Tax Changes," *Politifact*, July 19, 2011, http://www.politifact.com/truth-o-meter/statements/2011/jul/19/grover-norquist/grover-norquist-said-economy-has-grown-or-been-dam/.
501. Ira Stoll, "The Trump Recession: Markets Start to React To the Rise of the Donald," *New York Sun*, Aug. 24, 2015, http://www.nysun.com/national/the-trump-recession-markets-start-to-react-to/89263/.
502. John F. Kennedy, "Address to the Economic Club of New York," *American Rhetoric*, Dec. 14, 1962, http://www.americanrhetoric.com/speeches/jfkeconomicclubaddress.html.
503. John F. Kennedy, in Stephen Moore, "The U.S. Tax System: Who Really Pays?" Manhattan Institute, http://www.manhattan-institute.org/pdf/ir_22.pdf.
504. Edwin J. Feulner Jr., in Mallory Factor and Elizabeth Factor, *Big Tent: The Story of the Conservative Revolution—As Told by the Thinkers and Doers Who Made It Happen* (New York: Broadside Books, 2014), p. xxiv.
505. Haley Barbour, in Ibid., p. 368.
506. Clyde Wayne Crews, "Ten Thousand Commandments 2015: An Annual Snapshot of the Federal Regulatory State," *Competitive*

Enterprise Institute, May 8, 2015, https://cei.org/10kc2015; the full report is at https://cei.org/sites/default/files/10%2C000%20 Commandments%202015%20-%2005-12-2015.pdf.

507. Walter Russell Mead, "Black and Blue 2: Blacks Flee Blue States in Droves," *American Interest,* Mar. 27, 2011, http://blogs.the-american-interest.com/wrm/2011/03/27/black-and-blue-2-blacks-flee-blue-states-in-droves/.

508. Donald J. Trump, *Crippled America: How to Make America Great Again* (New York: Threshold Editions, 2015), p. 155.

509. "Not Always with Us," *Economist,* June 1, 2013, http://www.economist.com/news/briefing/21578643-world-has-astonishing-chance-take-billion-people-out-extreme-poverty-2030-not. My emphasis.

510. Dinesh D'Souza, *America: Imagine a World Without Her* (Washington, DC: Regnery Publishing, 2014), p. 194.

511. John Mackey and Raj Sisodia, *Conscious Capitalism: Liberating the Heroic Spirit of Business* (Boston: Harvard Business Review Press, 2013), p. 20.

512. Ibid., pp. 11-12.

513. Larry Kudlow, "Larry Kudlow Signs Off of CNBC with Salute to Freedom and Faith," *Real Clear Politics,* Mar. 29, 2014, http://www.realclearpolitics.com/video/2014/03/29/larry_kudlow_ signs_off_of_cnbc_with_salute_to_freedom_and_faith.html.

514. Arthur C. Brooks, *The Conservative Heart: How to Build a Fairer, Happier, and More Prosperous America* (New York: Broadside Books, 2015), p. 10.

515. Paul Krugman, "A Permanent Slump?" *New York Times,* Nov. 17, 2013, http://www. nytimes.com/2013/11/18/opinion/krugman-a-permanent-slump.html?ref=opinion.

516. Rush Limbaugh, "Liberals and the Violence Card," *Wall Street Journal,* Apr. 23, 2010, http://www.wsj.com/articles/SB10001424052748703876404575199743566950622.

517. Hillary Rodham Clinton, *It Takes a Village* (New York: Simon & Schuster, 1996, 2006), p. 267.

518. Amy Goodman, "Vermont's Bernie Sanders Becomes First Socialist Elected to U.S. Senate," *Democracy Now,* Nov. 08, 2006, http://

www.democracynow.org/2006/11/8/vermonts_bernie_sanders_becomes_first_socialist; Andrew Kaczynski, "The 19 Most Revealing Documents From Bill De Blasio's Socialist Past," *Buzzfeed*, Sept. 24, 2013, http://www.buzzfeed.com/andrewkaczynski/the-19-most-revealing-documents-from-documents-from-bill-de#.ob155wqOQ; "Discover The Networks Guide to the Political Left," *Discover The Networks*, May 30, 2016, http://www.discoverthenetworks.org/individual Profile.asp?indid=2592.

519. Brian Lamb, "Booknotes: A People's History of the United States," *Booknotes*, Mar. 12, 2000, http://www.booknotes.org/Watch/155006-1/Howard+Zinn.aspx.

520. Garrison Keillor, *Homegrown Democrat: A Few Plain Thoughts from the Heart of America* (New York: Viking, 2004), p. 192.

521. Jeff Jacoby, "No, Bernie Sanders, Scandinavia Is Not a Socialist Utopia," *Boston Globe*, Oct. 10, 2015, https://www.bostonglobe.com/opinion/2015/10/15/bernie-sanders-scandinavia-not-socialist-utopia/1Uk9N7dZotJRbvn8PosoIN/story.html; also see Nima Sanandaji, *Scandinavian Unexceptionalism: Culture, Markets and the Failure of Third-Way Socialism*.

522. Robert Conquest, *The Great Terror: A Reassessment 40th Anniversary Edition*.

523. Yang Jisheng, *Tombstone: The Great Chinese Famine, 1958-1962*.

524. Chapter 2, "Adolph Hitler: Man of the Left," in Jonah Goldberg, *Liberal Fascism: The Secret History of the American Left, From Mussolini to the Politics of Change*.

525. Henry Louis Gates Jr., "What Happens When Cubans Speak About Racism in Their Country," *The Root*, July 19, 2015, http://www.theroot.com/articles/history/2015/07/what_happens_when_cubans_speak_about_racism_in_their_country.html; Human Rights Watch, "World Report 2015: Cuba, Events of 2014," *Human Rights Watch*, https://www.hrw.org/world-report/2015/country-chapters/cuba; http://www.theroot.com/articles/culture/2010/07/racism_is_alive_and_well_in_cuba.html.

526. Marian Tupy, "5 Ways Capitalist Chile is Much Better Than Socialist Venezuela," Reason.com, May 24, 2016, http://reason.com/archives/2016/05/24/5-ways-capitalist-chile-is-much-better-t; Tyler Durden, "Scenes From The Venezuela Apocalypse: 'Countless Wounded' After 5,000 Loot Supermarket Looking For Food," ZeroHedge.com, May 15, 2016, http://www.zerohedge.com/news/2016-05-13/scenes-venezuela-apocalypse-countless-wounded-after-5000-loot-supermarket-looking-fo.
527. Winston Churchill, in John Hawkins, "5 Reasons Socialism Is Inferior to Capitalism," *Townhall*, March 20, 2012, http://townhall.com/columnists/johnhawkins/2012/03/20/5_reasons_socialism_is_inferior_to_capitalism/page/full.
528. Alan Charles Kors, "Can There be an 'After Socialism?'" Atlas Society, Sept. 27, 2003, http://atlassociety.org/objectivism/atlas-university/deeper-dive-blog/3962-can-there-be-an-after-socialism.
529. Bernie Sanders, "Senator Bernie Sanders on Occupy Wall Street #whyoccupy," YouTube, Oct. 21, 2011, https://www.youtube.com/watch?v=9HSaZOSWfrU.
530. Bernie Sanders, "United Against the War on Women," Sanders.senate, Apr. 28, 2012, http://www.sanders.senate.gov/newsroom/press-releases/united-against-the-war-on-women.
531. Hillary Clinton, "The Brooklyn Democratic Debate Transcript, Annotated," *Washington Post*, Apr. 14, 2014, https://www.washingtonpost.com/news/the-fix/wp/2016/04/14/the-brooklyn-democratic-debate-transcript-annotated/.
532. Elizabeth Warren, in Samuel P. Jacobs, "Warren Takes Credit for Occupy Wall Street," *Daily Beast*, Oct. 24, 2011, http://www.thedailybeast.com/articles/2011/10/24/elizabeth-warren-i-created-occupy-wall-street.html.
533. Michelle Obama, in Bryon York, "Michelle Obama: 'Don't Go into Corporate America,'" *National Review*, Feb. 29, 2008, http://www.nationalreview.com/corner/159678/michelle-obama-dont-go-corporate-america-byron-york.

534. Naomi Klein, "Naomi Klein Says Climate Activists Need to Get Comfortable Attacking Capitalism," *Grist*, Oct. 9, 2014, http://grist.org/climate-energy/naomi-klein-says-climate-activists-need-to-get-comfortable-attacking-capitalism/; at 0:50 and 2:10.
535. Michael Moore, in Cahir O'Doherty, "Michael Moore Talks 'Capitalism' and How Irish Background Shapes His Views," *Irish Central*, Sept. 30, 2009, http://www.irishcentral.com/culture/entertainment/michael-moore-talks-capitalism-and-how-irish-background-shapes-his-views-62868527-237662321.html.
536. Michael Moore, "Discussing 'Capitalism' with Michael Moore," *Washington Post*, Sept. 28, 2009, http://www.washingtonpost.com/wp-dyn/content/discussion/2009/09/28/DI2009092802121.html.
537. Caren Bohan, Emily Flitter, and Amanda Becker, "Hillary Clinton Surprises with Early Attack on CEO Pay," *Reuters*, Apr. 13, 2015, http://www.reuters.com/article/us-usa-election-clinton-inequality-idUSKBN0N421620150413.
538. Paul Bedard, "Wage Gap: One Hillary Clinton Speech More Than Average CEO Salary," *Washington Examiner*, Feb. 21, 2016, http://www.washingtonexaminer.com/wage-gap-one-hillary-clinton-speech-more-than-average-ceo-salary/article/2583804; "Occupational Employment Statistics, Occupational Employment and Wages, May 2015 11-1011 Chief Executives," *Bureau of Labor Statistics*, May, 2015, http://www.bls.gov/oes/current/oes111011.htm#(5); Daniel Halper, "Bernie Earned Less in Year than Hillary Made in Single Speech," *Weekly Standard*, Apr. 15, 2016, http://www.weeklystandard.com/article/2001999.
539. Carl Levin, in John Tammy, "'Obscene' Profit Hypocrisy," *National Review*, Sept. 26, 2006, http://www.nationalreview.com/article/218823/obscene-profit-hypocrisy-john-tamny.
540. Justin McCarthy, "Little Change in Percentage of Americans Who Own Stocks," *Gallup*, Apr. 22, 2015, http://www.gallup.com/poll/182816/little-change-percentage-americans-invested-market.aspx.
541. Ira Stoll, "New York City Council Wages War on Walmart," Reason.com, Mar. 11, 2013, https://reason.com/archives/2013/03/11/

wal-mart-and-ny; http://www.npr.org/2011/02/04/ 133483848/ new-york-city-officials-to-walmart-keep-out.

542. Doug Altner, "Why Do 1.4 Million Americans Work At Walmart, With Many More Trying To?" *Forbes*, Nov. 27, 2013, http://www.forbes.com/sites/realspin/2013/11/27/why-do-1-4-million-americans-work-at-walmart-with-many-more-trying-to/#b8c86454285b; Mark J. Perry, "Wal-Mart Saves Consumers Two Ways," American Enterprise Institute, Nov. 30, 2006, https://www.aei.org/publication/wal-mart-saves-consumers-two-ways/; https://www.mackinac.org/archives/2006/walmart.pdf.

543. Charles Barron, in Robert Smith, "New York City Officials to Walmart: Keep Out," NPR, Feb. 4, 2011, http://www.npr.org/2011/02/04/133483848/new-york-city-officials-to-walmart-keep-out.

544. Hillary Clinton, "Full Rush Transcript Hillary Clinton Part//CNN TV One Democratic Presidential Town Hall," CNN, Mar. 13, 2016, http://cnnpressroom.blogs.cnn.com/2016/03/13/full-rush-transcript-hillary-clinton-partcnn-tv-one-democratic-presidential-town-hall/.

545. Editorial Board, "Middle-Class Backers Shocked Obama Raised Their Taxes," *Investor's Business Daily*, Jan. 7, 2013, http://news.investors.com/ibd-editorials/010713-639637-reelected-obama-immediately-raises-middle-class-taxes.htm?p=2; John Kartch, "Comprehensive List of Obama Tax Increases," *Americans for Tax Reform*, Sept. 27, 2012, https://www.atr.org/full-list-ACA-tax-hikes-a6996; Diana Furchtgott-Roth, "How Obama's Tax Hikes Actually Hurt the Middle Class," *Fiscal Times*, Jan. 20, 2015, http://www.thefiscaltimes.com/2015/01/20/How-Obama-s-Tax-Hikes-Actually-Hurt-Middle-Class.

546. Joe Biden, in Charlie Spiering, "Joe Biden Denounces the Rich: 'I'm Hot…I'm Mad, I'm Angry,'" *Breitbart*, Sept. 7, 2015, http://www.breitbart.com/big-government/2015/09/07/joe-biden-denounces-the-rich-im-hot-im-mad-im-angry/.

547. Howard Dean, in Matthew J. Belvedere, "Going Off 'Cliff' Would Help Wall Street: Gov. Dean," CNBC, Dec. 4, 2012, http://www.cnbc.com/id/100275871.

548. Al Gore, in David Roberts, "A Chat with Al Gore on Carbon Taxes, Natural Gas, and the 'Morally Wrong' Keystone Pipeline," *Grist*, Nov. 20, 2012, http://grist.org/climate-energy/a-chat-with-al-gore-on-carbon-taxes-natural-gas-and-the-morally-wrong-keystone-pipeline/.

549. Hillary Clinton, in Alexander Hendrie, "Hillary Confirms Trillion Dollar Tax Hike Plan," *Americans for Tax Reform*, Apr. 12, 2016, http://www.atr.org/hillary-confirms-trillion-dollar-tax-hike-plan#ixzz4ABkKJvdX;Hillary Clinton, "Hillary: We'll Take Your Money for 'Common good,'" WND, June 29, 2004, http://www.wnd.com/2004/06/25332/#R5QVZProJS81PXDd.99http://www.wnd.com/2004/06/25332/.

550. Bernie Sanders, "Bernie Sanders, The Bum Who Wants Your Money," *Investor's Business Daily*, Jan. 26, 2016, http://www.investors.com/politics/editorials/bernie-sanders-the-bum-who-wants-your-money/.

551. Laura Meckler, "Price Tag of Bernie Sanders's Proposals: $18 Trillion," *Wall Street Journal*, Sept. 14, 2015, http://www.wsj.com/articles/price-tag-of-bernie-sanders-proposals-18-trillion-1442271511.

552. Alan Cole and Scott Greenberg, "Details and Analysis of Senator Bernie Sanders's Tax Plan," Tax Foundation, Jan. 28, 2016, http://taxfoundation.org/article/details-and-analysis-senator-bernie-sanders-s-tax-plan.

553. Elizabeth Warren, in Reihan Salam, "Elizabeth Warren's Quote," *National Review*, Sept. 22, 2011, http://www.nationalreview.com/agenda/278106/elizabeth-warrens-quote-reihan-salam.

554. Barack Obama, in Aaron Blake, "Obama's 'You Didn't Build That' Problem," *Washington Post*, July 18, 2012, http://www.washingtonpost.com/blogs/the-fix/post/obamas-you-didnt-build-that-problem/2012/07/18/gJQAJxyotW_blog.html.

555. Hillary Clinton, in Linda Feldman, "Hillary Clinton Says Businesses Don't Create Jobs. Uh-oh. (+video)," *Christian Science Monitor*, Oct. 27,

2014, http://www.csmonitor.com/USA/Politics/Decoder/2014/1027/Hillary-Clinton-says-businesses-don-t-create-jobs.-Uh-oh.-video.

556. Alana Marie Burke, "Barack Obama Solyndra Scandal: 8 Facts About Green Energy Company Controversy," *Newsmax*, Jan. 29, 2015, http://www.newsmax.com/FastFeatures/Barack-Obama-Solyndra-Scandal-Green-Energy/2015/01/29/id/621537/; Joe Stephens and Carol D. Leonnig, "Solyndra: Politics Infused Obama Energy Programs," *Washington Post*, Dec. 25, 2011, https://www.washington post.com/solyndra-politics-infused-obama-energy-programs/2011/12/14/gIQA4HllHP_story.html.

557. Joe Biden, in Penny Starr, "Joe Biden: 'We Have to Go Spend Money to Keep from Going Bankrupt,'" CNS News, July 16, 2009, http://cnsnews.com/news/article/joe-biden-we-have-go-spend-money-keep-going-bankrupt; https://www.youtube.com/watch?v=-wPO1xVAO_Y.

558. Liz Kreutz, "Hillary Clinton Calls for Additional $275 Billion to Modernize Infrastructure Nationwide," ABC News, Nov. 29, 2015, http://abcnews.go.com/Politics/hillary-clinton-calls-additional-275-billion-modernize-infrastructure/story?id=35477628.

559. Glenn Kessler, "Bernie Sanders's Claims About His $1 Trillion Infrastructure Plan," *Washington Post*, Nov. 16, 2015, https://www.washingtonpost.com/news/fact-checker/wp/2015/11/16/bernie-sanderss-claims-about-his-1-trillion-infrastructure-plan/.

560. Debbie Wasserman Schultz, "We Own the Economy," *New York Post*, June 18, 2011, http://nypost.com/2011/06/18/we-own-the-economy/; http://www.politico.com/story/2011/06/dnc-chair-we-own-the-economy-057025.

561. Jim Clifton, in Jim Hoft, "Gallup CEO: Number of Full-Time Jobs as Percent of Population Is Lowest It's Ever Been (Video)," *Gateway Pundit*, Feb. 5th, 2015, http://www.thegatewaypundit.com/2015/02/gallup-ceo-number-of-full-time-jobs-as-percent-of-population-is-lowest-its-ever-been-video/.

562. Jim Clifton, in Deroy Murdock, "Obama's Lackluster Economy Still Lacks Luster," *National Review*, Mar. 11, 2016,

http://www.nationalreview.com/article/432688/president-obama-economy-slow-recovery.

563. Phil Gramm, "What's Wrong with the Golden Goose?" *Wall Street Journal*, Apr. 20, 2015, http://www.wsj.com/articles/whats-wrong-with-the-golden-goose-1429575426.

564. Mitt Romney, in Jonathan Martinjan, "Romney Signals Interest in 2016 Run for President," *New York Times*, Jan. 17, 2015, http://www.nytimes.com/2015/01/17/us/politics/romney-signals-interest-in-2016-run-for-president.html?_r=1.

565. Katie Kieffer, *Let Me Be Clear: Barack Obama's War on Millennials, and One Woman's Case for Hope* (New York: Crown Forum, 2014), p. *ix*.

566. Adriana Cohen "'Hope and Change' Hard for Women to Find under Dems," *Boston Herald*, June 12, 2016, http://www.bostonherald.com/news/columnists/adriana_cohen/2016/06/adriana_cohen_hope_and_change_hard_for_women_to_find_under.

567. Paul Krugman, "A Permanent Slump?" *New York Times*, Nov. 17, 2013, http://www.nytimes. com/2013/11/18/opinion/krugman-a-permanent-slump.html?ref=opinion.

568. Gretchen Morgenson and Joshua Rosner, *Reckless Endangerment: How Outsized Ambition, Greed, and Corruption Created the Worst Financial Crisis of Our Time* (New York: Times Books, 2011); also see Thomas Sowell, *The Housing Boom and Bust* (New York: Basic Books, 2009); Thomas Sowell, *Basic Economics: A Common Sense Guide to the Economy* (New York: Basic Books, 2015), p. 391.

569. William Greider, "Hillary Clinton Is Whitewashing the Financial Catastrophe," *The Nation*, Dec. 11, 2015, http://www.thenation.com/article/hillary-clinton-is-whitewashing-the-financial-catastrophe/.

570. Mark Levin, *Liberty and Tyranny: A Conservative Manifesto* (New York: Threshold Editions, 2009), p. 70.

571. Barney Frank, in Larry Kudlow, "In Praise (!) of Barney Frank," CNBC, Aug. 20, 2010, http://www.cnbc.com/id/38791383.

572. Booker T. Washington, in Joseph A. Pierce, "The Evolution of Negro Business," in Ronald W. Bailey, *Black Business Enterprise* (New York: Basic Books, 1971), p. 38; originally from Booker T. Washington, *The Negro in Business*, 1907, pp. 19-20.
573. Bayard Rustin, *Strategies for Freedom: The Changing Patterns of Black Protest* (New York: Columbia University Press, 1976), p. 77.
574. William Julius Wilson, *The Declining Significance of Race: Blacks and Changing American Institutions, Second Edition* (Chicago: University of Chicago Press, 1980), p. 161.
575. William Julius Wilson, *The Truly Disadvantaged: The Inner City, the Underclass, and Public Policy* (Chicago: University of Chicago Press, 1987), p. 122.
576. Ben Carson, on the Brian Lehrer show, "Dr. Carson's Prescription for Liberty," WNYC, Oct. 9, 2015, http://www.wnyc.org/story/dr-carsons-prescription-liberty/; at 17:29.
577. Herman Cain, in Josh Feldman, "I Don't Believe Racism...Holds Anybody Back in A Big Way Today," *Mediaite*, Oct. 9, 2011, http://www.mediaite.com/tv/herman-cain-on-cnn-i-dont-believe-racism-holds-anybody-back-in-a-big-way-today/.
578. Tim Scott, Tim Scott Quotes, Brainyquote, http://www.brainyquote.com/quotes/quotes/t/timscott413311.html.
579. Tim Scott, "A Personal Story from Sen. Tim Scott," *Edgefield Advertiser*, Feb. 1, 2014, http://www.edgefieldadvertiser.com/2014/02/a-personal-story-from-sen-tim-scott/.
580. R. Donahue Peebles, interviewed by Susannah Lee, "Future African-American Billionaire on 'Black Lives Matter' Movement," Yahoo, Aug. 7, 2015, http://finance.yahoo.com/news/the-next-african-american-billionaire-on--blacklivesmatter-movement-115616208.html, on video at 1:09.
581. R. Donahue Peebles, interviewed by Chuck Ross, "Black CEO Says African-Americans Want to 'Emulate' Donald Trump [VIDEO]," Daily Caller, Aug. 21, 2015, http://dailycaller.com/2015/08/21/black-ceo-peebles-says-african-americans-want-to-emulate-trump-video/.

Shared Values

582. R. Donahue Peebles, "Peebles' Perspective," *Leadership Magazine*, Oct. 4, 2010, http://www.leadersmag.com/issues/2010.4_Oct/ROB/LEADERS-R.-Donahue-Peebles-The-Peebles-Corporation.html.
583. R. Donahue Peebles, in Carl Campanile, "Top de Blasio Backer Mulling Run Against 'Anti-business, Anti-cop Socialist,'" *New York Post*, Aug. 19, 2015, http://nypost.com/2015/08/19/top-de-blasio-backer-considers-2017-run-against-anti-business-anti-cop-socialist/.
584. Tavis Smiley, with David Ritz, *My Journey with Maya* (New York: Little, Brown and Company, 2015), pp. 184-185.
585. Larry Elder, "Hey, Occupy Wall Street: Wealth Isn't a Civil Right," *Townhall*, Nov. 25, 2011, http://townhall.com/columnists/larryelder/2011/11/24/hey,_occupy_wall_street_wealth_isnt_a_civil_right.
586. Ben Carson, with Candy Carson, *One Nation: What We Can All Do to Save America's Future*, (New York: Sentinel, 2014), p. 75.
587. Ibid., pp. 120-121.
588. Alveda King, in Matthew Boyle, "Martin Luther King Jr. Niece: 'Moral Bankruptcy' Ruling Washington D.C. Under Obama," Breitbart, Oct. 18, 2014, http://www.breitbart.com/big-government/2014/10/18/martin-luther-king-jr-niece-moral-bankruptcy-ruling-washington-dc-under-obama/.
589. Larry Elder, in Don Lemon, "Problems the Black Community Faces; Don Lemon's Suggestions," CNN, July 27, 2013, http://edition.cnn.com/TRANSCRIPTS/1307/27/cnr.06.html.
590. Jason L. Riley, "Bernie Sanders and the Soak-the-Rich Myth," *Wall Street Journal*, Oct. 20, 2015, http://www.wsj.com/articles/bernie-sanders-and-the-soak-the-rich-myth-1445379556.
591. Ben Carson, with Candi Carson, *One Nation: What We Can All Do to Save America's Future* (New York: Sentinel, 2014), p. 106.
592. Geoffrey Canada, in Timothy Williams, "Wall Street's Tremors Leave Harlem Shaken," *New York Times*, Oct. 8, 2008, http://www.nytimes.com/2008/10/08/nyregion/08harlem.html?pagewanted=print.

593. Harry Alford, in Ali Meyer, "Black Chamber of Commerce: EPA Clean Air Plan Will Increase Black Poverty 23%, Strip 7,000,000 Black Jobs," CNS News, June 24, 2015, http://www.cnsnews.com/news/article/ali-meyer/black-chamber-commerce-epa-clean-air-plan-will-increase-black-poverty-23; also see Oren Cass, "Who Pays the Bill for the 2016 Obama Climate Agenda?" *Manhattan Institute*, https://www.manhattan-institute.org/html/issues-2016-who-pays-bill-obama-climate-agenda-8802.html.

594. Deneen Borelli, *Blacklash: How Obama and the Left Are Driving Americans to the Government Plantation* (New York: Threshold Editions, 2012), p. 251.

595. Thomas Sowell, in David Harsanyi, "Do No Harm: An Interview with Thomas Sowell," *Federalist*, Jan. 13, 2015, http://thefederalist.com/2015/01/13/do-no-harm-an-interview-with-thomas-sowell/.

596. Thomas Sowell, *Compassion Versus Guilt and Other Essays* (New York: William Morrow and Company, Inc., 1987), p. 240.

597. Tavis Smiley, in Noel Sheppard, "Tavis Smiley: 'Black People Will Have Lost Ground in Every Single Economic Indicator' Under Obama," *Newsbusters*, Oct. 11, 2013, http://newsbusters.org/blogs/noel-sheppard/2013/10/11/tavis-smiley-black-people-will-have-lost-ground-every-single-economic#ixzz2hQqlEq3z.

598. Larry Elder, "Under Obama, Blacks Are Worse Off—Far Worse," *Townhall*, July 23, 2015, http://townhall.com/columnists/larryelder/2015/07/23/under-obama-blacks-are-worse-off--far-worse-n2028985/page/full.

599. Michael Steele, *Right Now: A 12-Step Program for Defeating the Obama Administration* (Washington, DC: Regnery Publishing, Inc., 2009), p. 188.

600. Niger Innis, in Jcappucc, "Dr. Alveda King and Niger Innis Announce 'Restore the Dream 2014,'" *Restore the Dream*, Oct. 21, 2014, http://restorethedream2015.com/2014/10/21/welcome-to-restore-the-dream-2014/.

601. Walter E. Williams, "The Rich Don't Pay Enough?" *Townhall*, Aug. 29, 2012, http://townhall.com/columnists/walterewilliams/2012/08/29/the_rich_dont_pay_enough/page/full.
602. Rev. Jesse L. Jackson, "Religious Liberty," *Straight from the Heart*, eds. Roger D. Hatch and Frank E. Watkins (Philadelphia: Fortress Press, 1987), p. 152.
603. Oseola McCarty, *Oseola McCarty's Simple Wisdom for Rich Living* (Atlanta, Georgia: Longstreet Press, 1996), p. 5.
604. A. Elizabeth Delany, with Sarah Louise Delany and Amy Hill Hearth, *The Delany Sisters' Book of Everyday Wisdom* (New York: Kodansha International, 1994), p. 39.
605. George Foreman, in Daniel Roberts, "Pro Files: George Foreman," *Sports Illustrated*, Mar. 10, 2015, http://www.si.com/more-sports/2015/03/10/profiles-george-foreman-business.
606. Johnnetta B. Cole, *Conversations: Straight Talk with America's Sister President* (New York: Doubleday, 1993), p. 33.
607. Zora Neale Hurston, *Dust Tracks on a Road* (New York: Harper Collins, 1991) p. 208; originally published in 1942.
608. Elijah Anderson, *Code of the Street: Decency, Violence, and the Moral Life of the Inner City* (New York: W. W. Norton & Company, 1999), pp. 242-243.
609. Leon Dash, *When Children Want Children: The Urban Crisis of Teenage Childbearing* (New York: William Morrow and Co., Inc., 1989), p. 263.
610. In Elijah Anderson, *A Place on the Corner, Second Edition* (Chicago: University of Chicago Press, 2003), p. 61.
611. Father of Bob Teague, *The Flip Side of Soul: Letters to My Son* (New York: William Morrow, 1989), p. 53.
612. Samuel Jackson, in Charles Barkley, *Who's Afraid of a Large Black Man?* ed. Michael Wilbon (New York: The Penguin Press, 2005), pp. 58-59.
613. Louis Armstrong, *Louis Armstrong, in His Own Words: Selected Writings* (New York: Oxford University Press, 1999), p. 10. Emphasis deleted.
614. Devon Greene, in Arthur C. Brooks, *The Conservative Heart: How to Build a Fairer, Happier, and More Prosperous America* (New York: Broadside Books, 2015), p. 93.

615. Charles Barkley and Roy S. Johnson, *Outrageous: The Fine Life and Flagrant Good Times of Basketball's Irresistible Force* (New York: Simon & Schuster, 1992), p. 76.

7. Crime

616. Uniform Crime Report, "Crime in the United States, 2013," Overview Table 43, US Department of Justice—Federal Bureau of Investigation, Released Fall 2014, Arrests, by Race, 2013, https://www.fbi.gov/about-us/cjis/ucr/crime-in-the-u.s/2013/crime-in-the-u.s.-2013/tables/table-43; http://www.bjs.gov/content/pub/pdf/cvl4.pdf; Criminal Victimization in the United States, 2008, Statistical Tables, National Crime Victimization Survey, March 2010, US Department of Justice Bureau of Justice Statistics, Tables 42, 48, http://www.bjs.gov/content/pub/pdf/cvus08.pdf; for 2012-2013 data, see Heather Mac Donald, "The Shameful Liberal Exploitation of the Charleston Massacre," *National Review*, July 1, 2015, http://www.nationalreview.com/article/420565/charleston-shooting-obama-race-crime.
617. Alexia Cooper and Erica L. Smith, US Department of Justice, Office of Justice Programs, Bureau of Justice Statistics, "Homicide Trends in the United States, 1980-2008, Annual Rates for 2009 and 2010," Nov. 2011, Statisticians, http://www.bjs.gov/content/pub/pdf/htus8008.pdf.
618. Victor Davis Hanson, "The Tragic and Complete Collapse of Racial Relations," PJ Media, Aug. 16, 2015, http://pjmedia.com/victordavishanson/racial-relations-tragic-collapse/?singlepage=true.
619. James Freeman, "The Political War on the NYPD," *Wall Street Journal*, Apr. 5, 2013, http://www.wsj.com/articles/SB10001424127887323501004578388311774675612.
620. Fox Butterfield, in James Taranto, "Dr. Butterfield, I Presume," *Wall Street Journal*, Jan. 7, 2013, http://www.wsj.com/articles/SB10001424127887323482504578227664228137272.

621. James B. Comey, "Speeches: Law Enforcement and the Communities We Serve: Bending the Lines Toward Safety and Justice," Federal Bureau of Investigation, Oct. 23, 2015, https://www.fbi.gov/news/speeches/law-enforcement-and-the-communities-we-serve-bending-the-lines-toward-safety-and-justice.
622. Ann Coulter, "Every Pro-immigration Claim Is a Lie," AnnCoulter.com, July 15, 2015, http://www.anncoulter.com/columns/2015-07-15.html.
623. *Washington Post*, "990 People Shot Dead by Police in 2015," *Washington Post*, Dec. 2015, https://www.washingtonpost.com/graphics/national/police-shootings/; also see Tom Jackman, "This Study Found Race Matters in Police Shootings, but the Results May Surprise You," *Washington Post*, April 27, 2016, https://www.washingtonpost.com/news/true-crime/wp/2016/04/27/this-study-found-race-matters-in-police-shootings-but-the-results-may-surprise-you; Valerie Richardson, "The Real Racial Bias: Cops More Willing to Shoot Whites than Blacks, Research Finds," *Washington Times*, Jan. 5, 2015, http://www.washingtontimes.com/news/2015/jan/5/police-officers-more-hesitant-to-shoot-black-suspe/; Lois James, Bryan Vila, and Kenn Daratha, "Results from Experimental Trials Testing Participant Responses to White, Hispanic and Black Suspects in High-fidelity Deadly Force Judgement and Decision-making Simulations," *Journal of Experimental Criminology*, Oct. 23, 2012, http://link.springer.com/article/10.1007/s11292-012-9163-y#page-2. This study was funded by the U.S. Government including the Justice Department.
624. Heather Mac Donald, "The Danger of the 'Black Lives Matter' Movement," *Imprimis*, April 2016, Volume 45, Number 4, https://imprimis.hillsdale.edu/the-danger-of-the-black-lives-matter-movement/.
625. Heather Mac Donald, "The New Nationwide Crime Wave," *Wall Street Journal*, May 29, 2015, http://www.wsj.com/articles/the-new-nationwide-crime-wave-1432938425.

626. ____. "Violent Criminals, Not the Police, Pose the Real Threat to African-Americans," Manhattan Institute, 2016, http://www.manhattan-institute.org/sites/default/files/IB-HM-0116.pdf; https://www.washingtonpost.com/graphics/national/police-shootings/
627. ____. "The New Nationwide Crime Wave," *Wall Street Journal*, May 29, 2015, http://www.wsj.com/articles/the-new-nationwide-crime-wave-1432938425.
628. ____. "The Nationwide Crime Wave Is Building," *Wall Street Journal*, May 23, 2016, http://www.wsj.com/articles/the-nationwide-crime-wave-is-building-1464045462.
629. ____. "Obama's Tragic Let 'em Out Fantasy," *Wall Street Journal*, Oct. 23, 2015, http://www.wsj.com/articles/obamas-tragic-let-em-out-fantasy-1445639113.
630. Paul Charlton, in Claudia Cowan, "Federal Prosecutors Balk at Holder Push to Reduce Drug Sentences," Fox News, Mar. 21, 2014, http://www.foxnews.com/politics/2014/03/21/federal-prosecutors-balk-at-holder-push-to-reduce-drug-sentences/.
631. Rick Perry, "Why it's Republicans, Not Democrats, Who Really Offer African-Americans Hope for a Better Life," Fox News, July 2, 2015, http://www.foxnews.com/opinion/2015/07/02/why-it-s-republicans-not-democrats-who-really-offer-african-americans-hope-better-life.html.
632. Chris Christie, "'It Can Happen to Anyone': Christie's Impassioned Plea on Addiction Goes Viral," Fox News, Nov. 5, 2015, http://insider.foxnews.com/2015/11/05/it-can-happen-anyone-christie-goes-viral-impassioned-plea-addiction.
633. Emma Roller, "Something Rand Paul, Rick Santorum, and Eric Holder Can All Agree On," *Slate*, Feb. 19, 2014, http://www.motherjones.com/mojo/2012/01/rick-santorum-voting-rights-activist; Stephen Dinan, "Santorum Defends Support for Restoring Felons' Voting Rights," *Washington Times*, Jan. 16, 2012, http://www.washingtontimes.com/news/2012/jan/16/santorum-defends-support-restoring-felons-voting-r/.

634. Patrick F. Fagan, "The Real Root Causes of Violent Crime: The Breakdown of Marriage, Family, and Community," Heritage Foundation, Mar. 17, 1995, http://www.heritage.org/research/reports/1995/03/bg1026nbsp-the-real-root-causes-of-violent-crime.
635. President Barack Obama, in Jordyn Phelps, "Obama: Murder Rate in African-American Community 'Way out of Whack,'" *Yahoo!News*, July 15, 2016, https://www.yahoo.com/gma/obama-murder-rate-african-american-community-way-whack-004719323--abc-news-topstories.html.
636. Christopher Hartney and Linh Vuong, "Created Equal: Racial and Ethnic Disparities in the US Criminal Justice System," National Council on Crime and Delinquency, March 2009, http://www.nccdglobal.org/sites/default/files/publication_pdf/created-equal.pdf.
637. Sophia Kerby, "The Top 10 Most Startling Facts About People of Color and Criminal Justice in the United States," Center for American Progress, Mar. 13, 2012, https://www.americanprogress. org/issues/race/news/2012/03/13/11351/the-top-10-most-startling-facts-about-people-of-color-and-criminal-justice-in-the-united-states/.
638. The Sentencing Project, "Reducing Racial Disparity in the Criminal Justice," The Sentencing Project, 2008, http://www.sentencingproject.org/wp-content/uploads/2016/01/Reducing-Racial-Disparity-in-the-Criminal-Justice-System-A-Manual-for-Practitioners-and-Policymakers.pdf.
639. ACLU, "Racial Disparities in Criminal Justice," ACLU, https://www.aclu.org/issues/mass-incarceration/racial-disparities-criminal-justice.
640. Alex S. Vitale, "We Don't Just Need Nicer Cops. We Need Fewer Cops," *The Nation*, Dec. 4, 2014, http://www.thenation.com/article/we-dont-just-need-nicer-cops-we-need-fewer-cops/.
641. Alice Goffman in *On the Run: Fugitive Life in an American City* (Chicago: The University of Chicago Press, 2014), p. 250.
642. Ibid., p. 200.

643. Ibid., pp. 201-202.
644. Ibid., p. 202.
645. Ibid., p. 3.
646. Ibid., p. 165.
647. Ibid., p. 202.
648. Bernie Sanders, "Transcript: The Democratic Debate in Milwaukee, Annotated," *Washington Post*, Feb. 11, 2016, https://www.washingtonpost.com/news/the-fix/wp/2016/02/11/transcript-the-democratic-debate-in-milwaukee-annotated/.
649. Barack Obama, "Remarks by the President at the NAACP Conference," *Whitehouse.gov*, July 14, 2015, https://www.whitehouse.gov/the-press-office/2015/07/14/remarks-president-naacp-conference.
650. Sari Horwitz, "Justice Department Set to Free 6,000 Prisoners, Largest One-time Release," *Washington Post*, Oct. 6, 2015, https://www.washingtonpost.com/world/national-security/justice-department-about-to-free-6000-prisoners-largest-one-time-release/2015/10/06/961f4c9a-6ba2-11e5-aa5b-f78a98956699_story.html.
651. Paul Bedard, "ICE releases 19,723 Criminal Illegals, 208 Convicted of Murder, 900 of Sex Crimes," *Washington Examiner*, Apr. 8, 2016, http://www.washingtonexaminer.com/ice-releases-19723-criminal-illegals-208-convicted-of-murder-900-of-sex-crimes/article/2589785; also see Maria Sacchetti, "Criminal Immigrants Reoffend at Higher Rates Than ICE Has Suggested," *Boston Globe*, June 4, 2016, https://www.bostonglobe.com/metro/2016/06/04/criminal-immigrants-reoffend-higher-rates-than-ice-has-suggested/l0OpCWfTdCuTNLIAfxApAO/story.html.
652. Paul Bedard, "Whistleblower: Immigrant Youths Placed with Child Molesters, Slave Lords, Murderers," *Washington Examiner*, Nov. 25, 2015, http://www.washingtonexaminer.com/grassley-administration-placing-illegal-children-with-child-molesters-slave-lords-murderers/article/2577107; John Cornyn, "Cornyn: The Administration Must Prevent Criminals from Taking Custody of Unaccompanied Immigrant Children," Cornyn.Senate.gov, Dec. 2, 2015, https://www.

Shared Values

cornyn.senate.gov/content/cornyn-administration-must-prevent-criminals-taking-custody-unaccompanied-immigrant-children.

653. Stephen F. Hayes and Thomas Joscelyn, "The Terrorists Freed by Obama," *Wall Street Journal*, Jan. 15, 2016, http://www.wsj.com/articles/the-terrorists-freed-by-obama-1452901430; Fox News, "Freed Gitmo Detainee, Ex-bin Laden Aide Cements Place as Top Jihadist in Videos," Fox News, Feb. 17, 2016, http://www.foxnews.com/world/2016/02/17/freed-gitmo-detainee-ex-bin-laden-aide-cements-place-as-top-jihadist-in-videos.html?intcmp=hpbt1.

654. Michael Daly, "ISIS Leader: 'See You in New York,'" *Daily Beast*, June 14, 2014, http://www.thedailybeast.com/articles/2014/06/14/isis-leader-see-you-in-new-york.html; Democracy Now, "US Closes Camp Bucca Prison," *Democracy Now*, Sept. 17, 2009, http://www.democracynow.org/ 2009/9/17/headlines.

655. James Taranto, "Dr. Butterfield, I Presume," *Wall Street Journal*, Jan. 7, 2013, http://www. wsj.com/articles/SB10001424127887323482504578 227664228137272.

656. Hillary Clinton, in James Taranto, "Mrs. Clinton Takes a Risk: But Does She Know it?" *Wall Street Journal*, Apr. 30, 2015, http://www.wsj.com/articles/mrs-clinton-takes-a-risk-1430414627; my insertion.

657. Larry Elder, *The Ten Things You Can't Say in America* (New York: St. Martin's Press, 2000), p. 43. Law Professor Katheryn Russell-Brown agrees that black males, between the ages of 15 and 40, make up approximately 3 percent of the American population. It is likely that most felons are within those ages. See *The Color of Crime: Racial Hoaxes, White Fear, Black Protectionism, Police Harassment, and other Macroaggressions, Second Edition* (New York: NYU Press; 2008), p. 68.

658. Willie L. Williams, in Daniel S. Levy, "Interview: New Top Cop Takes Command," *Time*, May 11, 1992, Volume 139, No. 19, p. 37.

659. David Lemieux, in Haki R. Madhubuti, *Black Men, Obsolete, Single, Dangerous?: The Afrikan American Family in Transition* (Chicago: Third World Press, 1990), p. 37.

660. Michael Steele, *Right Now: A 12-Step Program for Defeating the Obama Administration* (Washington, DC: Regnery Publishing, Inc., 2009), p. 120.
661. John W. Fountain, *True Vine: A Young Black Man's Journey of Faith, Hope, and Clarity* (New York: PublicAffairs, 2003), p. 232.
662. Robyn Minter Smyers, "High Noon in Public Housing: The Showdown Between Due Process Rights and Good Management Practices in the War on Drugs and Crime," *The Urban Lawyer*, Vol. 30, No. 3 (Summer 1998), pp. 573-615, http://www.jstor.org/stable/27895130?seq=1#page_scan_tab_contents; also in Thomas Sowell, *Wealth, Poverty and Politics: An International Perspective* (New York: Basic Books, 2015), p. 162.
663. Bob Herbert, "Mrs. Parks's Bequest," *New York Times*, Sept. 4, 1994, p. E 11. http://www.nytimes.com/1994/09/04/opinion/in-america-mrs-parks-s-bequest.html.
664. Rosa Parks, in James Bennet, "Sadness and Anger After a Legend Is Mugged," *New York Times*, Sept. 1, 1994, p. A16.
665. Debra Dickerson, "Who Shot Johnny, A Day in the Life of Black America," *AfricanAmerican.org*, Jan. 1, 1998, http://www.africanamerica.org/topic/who-shot-johnnyh-an-essay-by-debra-dickerson.
666. In John Langston Gwaltney, *Drylongso: A Self-Portrait of Black America* (New York: Random House, 1981), p. 197.
667. Firestarter, "Black Women Need to Stop Making Excuses for Black Male Failure," *Amazon Customer Review*, Jan. 16, 2012, http://www.amazon.com/review/R8L3X23BNNAGB.
668. Steven A. Holmes, "Correspondence/Black and Middle Class; Both a Victim of Racial Profiling—And a Practitioner," *New York Times*, Apr. 25, 1999, http://www.nytimes.com/1999/04/25/weekinreview/correspondence-black-middle-class-both-victim-racial-profiling-practitioner.html?ref=stevenaholmes.
669. Elijah Anderson, *Streetwise: Race, Class and Change in an Urban Community* (Chicago: University of Chicago Press, 1990), pp. 4-5.

Shared Values

670. Thomas Sowell, *Ethnic America: A History* (New York: Basic Books, Inc., 1981), p. 292.
671. Walter E. Williams, *All It Takes Is Guts: A Minority View* (Washington, DC: Regnery Books, 1987), pp. 27-28.
672. Elaine R. Jones, in Karen De Witt, "In a Color-Conscious Society, She Challenges the 'Color-Blind,'" *New York Times*, July 18, 1993, http://www.nytimes.com/1993/07/18/weekinreview/ conversations-elaine-r-jones-color-conscious-society-she-challenges-color-blind.html.
673. Bayard Rustin, *Down the Line: The Collected Writings of Bayard Rustin* (Chicago: Quadrangle Books, 1971), p. 184.
674. Jason L. Riley, "The Lawbreakers of Baltimore—and Ferguson," *Wall Street Journal*, Apr. 28, 2015, http://www.wsj.com/articles/the-lawbreakers-of-baltimoreand-ferguson-1430263032.
675. Charles Barkley, in Steve Almasy, "Charles Barkley: We Never Talk About Race Until Something Bad Happens," CNN, Dec. 8, 2014, http://www.cnn.com/2014/12/02/us/charles-barkley-on-race/index.html?hpt=hp_t1.
676. Marian Wright Edelman, "The Black Family in America," *Families in Peril: An Agenda for Social Change* (*The W. E. B. Du Bois Lectures*), Revised Edition (Cambridge, Massachusetts: Harvard University Press; 1989) p. 15.
677. Walter E. Williams, "Fiddling Away the Future," CNS News, July 7, 2015, http://www. cnsnews.com/commentary/walter-e-williams/fiddling-away-future.
678. Gerald Early, *Best African American Essays, 2010*, Gerald Early, Series Editor, Randall Kennedy, Guest Editor (New York: One World, Ballantine Books, 2010), pp. 244-245.
679. Thomas Sowell, *Intellectuals and Race* (New York: Basic Books, 2013), pp. 113-114; my deletion; Fox News, "Decorated Marine Vet Attacked, Robbed at Washington DC McDonald's, Police Say," Fox News, Feb. 17, 2016, http://www.foxnews.com/us/2016/02/17/decorated-marine-vet-attacked-robbed-at-washington-dc-mcdonalds-police-say.html?intcmp=hpbt4; also search the Internet and YouTube for "knockout game" and "flash mob violence."

680. Jason L. Riley, "Quoting King," *Wall Street Journal*, July 18, 2013, http://www.wsj.com/ articles/SB10001424127887323309404578613941506544024.
681. Rev. Martin Luther King Jr., *Stride Toward Freedom: The Montgomery Story* (New York: Harper and Row, 1964), p. 199; originally published in 1958.
682. In Earl Ofari Hutchinson, *Black Fatherhood: The Guide to Male Parenting* (Los Angeles: IMPACT! Publications, 1992), p. 35.
683. Frederick Douglass, "The Nation's Problem," in *Negro Social and Political Thought, 1850-1920, Representative Texts*, ed. Howard Brotz, (New York: Basic Books, 1966), pp. 323-324; originally from a speech delivered before the Bethel Literary and Historical Society in Washington, DC, on Apr. 16, 1889. My deletion.
684. Barbara M. Dixon, with Josleen Wilson, *Good Health for African Americans* (New York: Crown Publishers, Inc., 1994), p. 52.
685. Bob Teague, *The Flip Side of Soul: Letters to My Son* (New York: William Morrow, 1989), p. 32.
686. Richard Majors and Janet Mancini Billson, *Cool Pose: The Dilemmas of Black Manhood in America* (New York, Lexington/Macmillan, Inc., 1992), p. 22.
687. Angela Y. Davis, "Sick and Tired of Being Sick and Tired: The Politics of Black Women's Health," *The Black Woman's Health Book: Speaking for Ourselves*, ed. Evelyn C. White, (Seattle: The Seal Press, 1990), p. 22.
688. Spike Lee with Lisa Jones, *Do the Right Thing: A Spike Lee Joint* (New York: Simon & Schuster Inc./Fireside, 1989), p. 68.
689. Marcia Slocum-Greene, in LaSalle D. Lefall Jr., "Health Status of Black Americans," in Janet Dewart, *The State of Black America* (Piscataway, New Jersey: Transaction Publishers, 1990), p. 134; originally in the *Washington Post*.
690. In Elijah Anderson, *Streetwise: Race, Class and Change in an Urban Community* (Chicago: University of Chicago Press, 1990), p. 99.
691. Ta-Nehisi Coates, *The Beautiful Struggle: A Father, Two Sons, and an Unlikely Road to Manhood* (New York: Spiegel & Grau, 2008), p. 29.

692. Tavis Smiley, *On Air: The Best of Tavis Smiley on the Tom Joyner Morning Show 2002-2003, Volume II* (Carlsbad, California, Smiley Books, 2004), p. 114.
693. John McWhorter, in J. L. A. Garcia, John McWhorter, and Glenn C. Loury, "Race & Inequality: An Exchange," *First Things* (May 2002): 22-40, http://www.firstthings.com/article/2002/05/race-amp-inequality-an-exchange.
694. In John Langston Gwaltney, *Drylongso: A Self-Portrait of Black America* (New York: Random House, 1981), p. 199.
695. Firestarter, "Black Women Need to Stop Making Excuses for Black Male Failure," *Amazon Customer Review*, Jan. 16, 2012, http://www.amazon.com/review/R8L3X23BNNAGB.
696. Serena Williams, with Hilary Beard, in *Venus and Serena: Serving from the Hip: 10 Rules for Living, Loving, and Winning* (Boston: Houghton Mifflin Company, 2005), p. 46.
697. Ta-Nehisi Coates, "The Black Family in the Age of Mass Incarceration," *The Atlantic*, Oct. 2015, http://www.theatlantic.com/magazine/archive/2015/10/the-black-family-in-the-age-of-mass-incarceration/403246/.
698. Geoffrey Canada, *Fist Stick Knife Gun: A Personal History of Violence in America* (Boston: Beacon Press, 1995), p. 129.
699. Willie L. Williams, in Daniel S. Levy, "Interview: New Top Cop Takes Command," *Time*, May 11, 1992, Volume 139, No. 19, p. 37.
700. Steven Craft, "The Setback Is a Setup for a Comeback," in *Black and Right: The Bold New Voice of Black Conservatives in America*, eds. Stan Faryna, Brad Stetson, and Joseph G. Conti, (Westport, Connecticut: Praeger, 1997), p. 104.
701. Randall Kennedy, *Race, Crime, and the Law* (New York: Vintage, 1998), p. 19.
702. Ibid., p. 80.
703. Jason L. Riley, *Please Stop Helping Us: How Liberals Make It Harder for Blacks to Succeed* (New York: Encounter Books, 2014), p. 78.

704. Sterling Johnson in *Black Perspectives on Crime and the Criminal Justice System: A Symposium*, National Urban League, ed. Robert L. Woodson (Boston: G. K. Hall, 1977), p. 161.
705. Richard Williams, with Bart Davis, *Black and White: The Way I See It* (New York: Atria Books, 2014), p. 193.
706. John McWhorter, "Racism in Retreat," *The New York Sun*, June 5, 2008, http://www.nysun.com/opinion/racism-in-retreat/79355/.
707. Thomas Sowell, "The Race Card's Steep Cost," *National Review*, Dec. 23, 2014. Read more at: http://www.nationalreview.com/article/395255/race-cards-steep-cost-thomas-sowell.
708. Thomas Sowell, "Random Thoughts," *Townhall*, Feb. 11, 2014, http://townhall.com/columnists/thomassowell/2014/02/11/random-thoughts-n1792776/page/full.
709. Stacey Calhoun, in Aaron Feis, Jennifer Bain, Aaron Short, and Laura Italiano, "Shooting Victim's Family Begs de Blasio: 'We Need Stop-and-Frisk,'" *New York Post*, May 31, 2015, http://nypost.com/2015/05/31/new-yorkers-plead-for-stop-and-frisk-amid-murder-surge/.
710. Jason L. Riley, "WSJ's Jason Riley: Black Men Are Afraid of Being Shot by Other Black Men, Not by Cops," *Real Clear Politics*, Aug. 8, 2018, http://www.realclearpolitics.com/video/2014/08/18/wsjs_jason_riley_black_men_are_afraid_of_being_shot_by_other_black_men_not_by_cops.html.
711. Walter E. Williams, "Liberals' Use of Black People," *Creators Syndicate*, Dec. 31, 2014, http://www.creators.com/conservative/walter-williams/liberals-use-of-black-people.html.
712. Louis Farrakhan, "Justifiable Homicide: Black Youth in Peril, 'An Executive Decision'—Part 2 Continued," *Final Call*, Sep. 30, 2014, http://www.finalcall.com/artman/publish/Minister_Louis_Farrakhan_9/article_101804.shtml.
713. Glenn C. Loury, "Who Speaks for Black America?" in *Commentary*, Jan. 1987, Vol. 83, Number 1, p. 36.

714. Deroy Murdock, "Black Lives Matter's Numbers Are Bogus," *New York Post*, Nov. 6, 2015, http://nypost.com/2015/11/06/black-lives-matters-numbers-are-bogus/.
715. Lorraine Banks, in Toby Harnden, "Black America Rages as Murder Rate Soars," *Real Clear Politics*, June 9, 2015, http://www.realclearpolitics.com/articles/2015/06/09/black_america_ rages_ as_murder_rate_soars_126911.html.
716. David Clarke, in Keith Koffler, "Milwaukee Sheriff Practically Blames Obama for Shootings," *White House Dossier*, May 15, 2015, http://www.whitehousedossier.com/2015/03/12/milwaukee-police-chief-practically-blames-obama-shootings/.
717. David Clarke, interviewed by Poppy Harlow, "Clarke Clobber Caper," *Powerline*, Dec. 30, 2014, http://www.powerlineblog.com/archives/2014/12/clarke-clobber-caper.php; at 5:30.
718. Ibid.; at 6:18.
719. David Clarke, in Keith Koffler, "Milwaukee Sheriff Practically Blames Obama for Shootings," *White House Dossier*, May 15, 2015, http://www.whitehousedossier.com/2015/03/12/milwaukee-police-chief-practically-blames-obama-shootings/.
720. Peggy Hubbard, "Peggy Hubbard Talks About Ferguson and Protests," YouTube, Aug. 20, 2015, https://www.youtube.com/watch?v=dG7mZQvaQDk.
721. Derwood Tate, in Valerie Richardson, "Black Family Calls White Officer 'Guardian Angel' After He Died Helping Them," *Washington Times*, Jan. 7, 2015, http://www.washingtontimes.com/news/2015/jan/7/black-family-calls-white-officer-sean-renfro-guard/?page=all.
722. Nada Owusu, in Rachel Bertsche, "Mom's Facebook Photo of 'Hero' Cop Strikes a Chord," *Yahoo*, May 20, 2015, https://www.yahoo.com/parenting/moms-facebook-photo-of-hero-cop-strikes-a-chord-119449508142.html.
723. "In Memory of Crystal D. Sheffield," YouTube, Aug. 22, 2012, https://www.youtube.com/watch?v=n9Y-frbjTOM&app=desktop.
724. Bruce Lambert, "Joseph B. Williams, Retired Judge and Lindsay Aide, Is Dead at 70," *New York Times*, Apr. 19, 1992, p. L30.

725. Shaka Senghor, in *Reach: 40 Black Men Speak on Living, Leading, and Succeeding*, Ben Jealous and Trabian Shorter, eds. (New York: Atria, 2015), pp. 35-36.
726. Elijah Anderson, *A Place on the Corner, Second Edition* (Chicago: University of Chicago Press, 2003), p. 74.
727. Ibid., p. 75.
728. W. E. B. Du Bois, *The Philadelphia Negro* (1899), https://archive.org/stream/philadelphia negr001901mbp/philadelphianegr001901mbp_djvu.txt.
729. Joseph B. Brown Jr., in Linn Washington, *Black Judges on Justice: Perspectives from the Bench* (New York: The New Press, 1994), 52.
730. Kenneth B. Clark, *Dark Ghetto: Dilemmas of Social Power* (New York: Harper Torchbooks, 1965), p. 81.
731. William Raspberry, "A Path Beyond Grievance," *Washington Post*, Nov. 11, 2008, http://www.washingtonpost.com/wp-dyn/content/article/2008/11/10/AR2008111001544.html.
732. Kalais Chiron Hunt, in Henry Louis Gates Jr., *America Behind the Color Line: Dialogues with African Americans* (New York: Warner Books, 2004), p. 409.
733. Arthur Ashe and Arnold Rampersad, *Days of Grace* (New York: Knopf, 1993), p. 143.
734. Veronica S. McBeth, in *Linn Washington, Black Judges on Justice: Perspectives from the Bench* (New York: The New Press, 1994), 44.
735. Haki R. Madhubuti, *Black Men: Obsolete, Single, Dangerous? The Afrikan American Family in Transition: Essays in Discovery, Solution, and Hope* (Chicago: Third World Press, 1990), p. 14.
736. Jackie Robinson, ed. Michael G. Long, *Beyond Home Plate: Jackie Robinson on Life After Baseball* Syracuse (New York: University Press, 2013), p. 56.

8. Conformity

737. Glenn C. Loury, "Free at Last?" *Commentary*, Oct. 1992, p. 32; https://www.commentarymagazine.com/articles/free-at-last/

Shared Values

738. Debra J. Dickerson, *An American Story* (New York: Pantheon Books/Random House, 2000), p. 110.
739. Jason L. Riley, "Jim Brown's Soul Patrol," *Wall Street Journal*, Dec. 16, 2013, http://online. wsj.com/news/articles/SB10001424052702303949504579262533228226604?mod=Opinion_newsreel_3.
740. Jo-Issa Rae Diop, a.k.a. Issa Rae, *The Misadventures of Awkward Black Girl* (New York: Atria/37 Ink, 2015), pp. 162-163.
741. John Edgar Wideman, *Brothers and Keepers* (New York: Penguin, 1985), p. 33.
742. Ibid., p. 27.
743. Signithia Fordham and John U. Ogbu, "Black Students' School Success: Coping with the 'Burden of Acting White,'" *The Urban Review: Issues and Ideas in Public Education*, Volume 18, Number 3, 1986, p. 186. Capital High is in Washington DC.
744. Shelby Steele, *The Content of Our Character: A New Vision of Race in America* (New York: St. Martin's Press, 1990), pp. 95-96. Originally from *Commentary*, Jan. 1988.
745. Shelby Steele, Ibid., pp. 170-171.
746. Stanley Crouch, *The All-American Skin Game, or, The Decoy of Race: The Long and Short of It, 1990-1994* (New York: Pantheon Books, Random House, Inc., 1995), p. xiv.
747. Stanley Crouch, "The Rage of Race," *Notes of a Hanging Judge: Essays and Reviews, 1979-1989* (New York: Oxford University Press, 1990), p. 232; my deletion.
748. Reginald Hudlin, in Henry Louis Gates Jr., *America Behind the Color Line: Dialogues with African Americans* (New York: Warner Books, 2004), p. 277.
749. Thomas Sowell, *Wealth, Poverty, and Politics: An International Perspective* (New York: Basic Books, 2015), pp. 114-115.
750. Charles Barkley, in Husna Haq, "Why Charles Barkley Supports the Ferguson Grand Jury Decision (+video)," *Christian Science Monitor*, Dec. 1, 2014, http://www.csmonitor.com/USA/Society/2014/1201/Why-Charles-Barkley-supports-the-Ferguson-grand-jury-decision-video.

751. James P. Comer and Alvin F. Poussaint, *Raising Black Children* (New York: Plume, 1992), pp. 302-303.
752. Ibid., pp. 299-300.
753. Rev. Jesse Lee Peterson, with Brad Stetson, *From Rage to Responsibility: Black Conservative Jesse Lee Peterson and America Today* (St. Paul, MN: Paragon House, 2000), pp. 20-21.
754. Ibid., p. 147.
755. Julius Lester, "What Price Unity?" *Village Voice*, Sept. 17, 1991, p. 39.
756. Ibid., p. 39.
757. Stephen L. Carter, *Reflections of an Affirmative Action Baby* (New York: Basic Books, 1991), p. 115.
758. Ibid., p. 114.
759. Frederick Douglass, in *Negro Social and Political Thought, 1850-1920, Representative Texts*, ed. Howard Brotz, (New York: Basic Books, 1966), pp. 318-319; originally 1889.
760. Faith Ringgold, in *Rise Up Singing: Black Women Writers on Motherhood*, ed. Cecelie S. Berry (New York: Doubleday/Random House, 2004), pp. 39-40.
761. Stanley Crouch, "The Photographer," *Village Voice*, June 28, 1983, p. 34.
762. Darold Ferguson Jr., in Ali Shaheed Muhammad, "ASAP Ferg: I Want This Moment to Last Forever," NPR, Mar. 18, 2015, http://www.npr.org/blogs/microphonecheck/2015/ 03/18/ 392132375/asap-ferg-i-want-this-moment-to-last-forever?
763. Pharrell Lanscilo Williams, in Stereo Williams, "Dr. Neil DeGrasse Tyson Should Educate 'New Black' Pharrell," *RollingOut*, Apr. 21, 2014, http://rollingout.com/2014/04/21/dr-neil-degrasse-tyson-educate-new-black-pharrell/; originally at https://m.youtube.com/watch?v=dJ7rZRFNF-o; at 40:40.
764. Grant Hill, in Tom Junod, "The Savior," *Gentlemen's Quarterly*, Apr. 1995, p. 239.
765. W. E. B. Du Bois, *The Souls of Black Folk* (1903), http://www.gutenberg.org/files/408/408-h/408-h.htm; my deletion.

766. Shelby Steele, interviewed by Peter Slen on "In Depth," Book TV, C-Span, Apr. 2, 2006, http://www.c-span.org/video/?191760-1/depth-shelby-steele; at 24:11.
767. Shelby Steele, *The Content of Our Character: A New Vision of Race in America* (New York: St. Martin's Press, 1990) pp. 158-159.
768. Ibid., p. 29. My deletion.
769. Ralph Ellison, *Shadow and Act* (New York: Vintage/Random House, 1972), p. 271; originally from "Some Questions and Some Answers" in *Preuves*, May 1958.
770. Ralph Ellison, *Invisible Man*, https://drive.google.com/file/d/0Bz1OS3L3UdX1TE 5kTmwySXFQZUE/view?pli=1
771. Zora Neale Hurston, *Dust Tracks on a Road* (New York: HarperCollins, 1991), p. 172; originally published in 1942.
772. Ibid., p. 238.
773. James P. Comer and Alvin F. Poussaint, *Raising Black Children* (New York: Plume, 1992), p. 184.
774. Richard Williams, with Bart Davis, *Black and White: The Way I See It* (New York: Atria Books, 2014), p. 129.
775. Rev. Jesse Lee Peterson, with Brad Stetson, *From Rage to Responsibility: Black Conservative Jesse Lee Peterson and America Today* (St. Paul, MN: Paragon House, 2000), p. 12.
776. Rev. Jesse Lee Peterson, *SCAM: How the Black Leadership Exploits Black America* (Nashville: WND Books, 2003), p. 203.
777. Oprah Winfrey, *What I Know for Sure* (New York: Flatiron Books, 2014), p. 194.
778. Shelby Steele, interviewed by Peter Slen on "In Depth," Book TV, C-Span, Apr. 2, 2006, http://www.c-span.org/video/?191760-1/depth-shelby-steele; at 37:20.
779. Shelby Steele, *Shame: How America's Past Sins Have Polarized Our Country* (New York: Basic Books, 2015), p. 17.
780. Bill T. Jones, in *Reach: 40 Black Men Speak on Living, Leading, and Succeeding*, Ben Jealous and Trabian Shorter, eds. (New York: Atria, 2015), p. 201.

781. India Arie, in Robin Roberts, with Veronica Chambers, *Everybody's Got Something* (New York: Grand Central Publishing, 2014), p. 52.
782. Marguerite A. Wright, *I'm Chocolate, You're Vanilla: Raising Healthy Black and Biracial Children in a Race-Conscious World* (San Francisco: Jossey-Bass Publishers, 1998), p. 234.
783. Jo-Laine, in Rebecca Carroll, *Sugar in the Raw: Voices of Young Black Girls in America* (New York: Clarkson Potter, 1997), p. 38.
784. Glenys Rogers, *Ebony*, Nov. 1985, p. 18.
785. Myesha, in Rebecca Carroll, *Sugar in the Raw: Voices of Young Black Girls* (New York: Crown, 2011), p. 109.
786. Stacey A. Moorehead, *Ebony*, Nov. 1985, p. 16.

Made in the USA
Middletown, DE
16 October 2016